Living Existentialism

Living Existentialism

Essays in Honor of Thomas W. Busch

EDITED BY
Gregory Hoskins
AND
J. C. Berendzen

◆PICKWICK *Publications* · Eugene, Oregon

LIVING EXISTENTIALISM
Essays in Honor of Thomas W. Busch

Copyright © 2017 Wipf and Stock Publishers. All rights reserved. Except for brief quotations in critical publications or reviews, no part of this book may be reproduced in any manner without prior written permission from the publisher. Write: Permissions, Wipf and Stock Publishers, 199 W. 8th Ave., Suite 3, Eugene, OR 97401.

Pickwick Publications
An Imprint of Wipf and Stock Publishers
199 W. 8th Ave., Suite 3
Eugene, OR 97401

www.wipfandstock.com

PAPERBACK ISBN: 978-1-4982-9851-3
HARDCOVER ISBN: 978-1-4982-4984-3
EBOOK ISBN: 978-1-4982-9852-0

Cataloguing-in-Publication data:

Names: Hoskins, Gregory, editor | Berendzen, J. C., editor.

Title: Living existentialism : essays in honor of Thomas W. Busch / edited by Gregory Hoskins and J. C. Berendzen.

Description: Eugene, OR: Pickwick Publications, 2017 | Includes bibliographical references.

Identifiers: ISBN 978-1-4982-9851-3 (paperback) | ISBN 978-1-4982-4984-3 (hardcover) | ISBN 978-1-4982-9852-0 (ebook).

Subjects: LCSH: Existentialism | Busch, Thomas W., 1937– | Marcel, Gabriel 1889–1973 | Merleau-Ponty, Maurice, 1908–1961 | Sartre, Jean Paul, 1905–1980 | Beauvoir, Simone, 1908–1986 | Kierkegaard, Søren, 1813–1855 | Stein, Edith, 1891–1942.

Classification: B819 L51 2017 (print) | B819 (ebook).

Manufactured in the U.S.A.   03/22/17

Contents

List of Contributors | vii

Preface | xi
—Gregory Hoskins and J. C. Berendzen

Acknowledgments | xix

Part One: Gabriel Marcel in Contemporary Context

1. Marcel and Derrida: Christian Existentialism and the Genesis of Deconstruction | 3
   —John Caputo

2. Reading Marcel's Philosophy of Dialogical Inter-subjectivity in a Contemporary Light | 24
   —Sally Fischer

3. Reflections on Gabriel Marcel's Belief in the Afterlife | 45
   —Geoffrey Karabin

Part Two: Living French Existentialism: Beauvoir, Merleau-Ponty, Sartre

4. Picking Out the "Right" Color: Perceptual Normativity in Merleau-Ponty | 61
   —J. C. Berendzen

5. Misadventures of the Dialectic: Merleau-Ponty and Sartre | 78
   —*Thomas Flynn*

6. The End of the Gaze | 99
   —*Shaun Gallagher*

7. Sartre in Dialogue with Husserl and Beauvoir: The Evolution of Existential Freedom | 111
   —*Shannon M. Mussett*

8. "Bad Faith" in *Being and Nothingness*: Unambiguously Epistemological as well as Ontological | 128
   —*Ronald E. Santoni*

9. Beauvoir on Communication and Incorporation in *The Mandarins*: Building on Insights from Thomas Busch | 135
   —*Sally Scholz*

10. The Devil and the Good Lord: Demystifying Feudalism, God, and the Devil | 152
    —*Adrian van den Hoven*

Part Three: Beyond French Existentialism

11. Kierkegaard on the Positive Role of Reason in Leading to Christian Faith | 177
    —*Thomas Anderson*

12. Farewell to Postmodernism? | 189
    —*William McBride*

13. Edith Stein's Experiential Critique of Heidegger | 197
    —*Robert Wood*

14. Living Existentialism: An Interview with Thomas W. Busch | 214
    —*Thomas Busch and Gregory Hoskins*

Contributors

Thomas Anderson, Professor Emeritus of Philosophy at Marquette University. His noted publications on existentialism include *The Foundation and Structure of Sartrean Ethics, Sartre's Two Ethics,* and *A Commentary on Gabriel Marcel's* The Mystery of Being.

J. C. Berendzen, Associate Professor of Philosophy at Loyola University New Orleans. He has published multiple essays on the philosophy of Maurice Merleau-Ponty and Jean-Paul Sartre, and he is a scholar of Frankfurt School critical theory.

John Caputo, David R. Cook Professor of Philosophy Emeritus at Villanova University and Thomas J. Watson Professor of Religion Emeritus at Syracuse University. His noted works on existential phenomenology and postmodern thought include *Demythologizing Heidegger, Radical Hermeneutics, The Prayers and Tears of Jacques Derrida,* and *The Weakness of God.*

Sally Fischer, Professor of Philosophy at Warren Wilson College. Her articles on Merleau-Ponty and Irigaray have appeared in *International Studies in Philosophy,* and in *Merleau-Ponty and Ecology, Intertwinings,* and *Maternal Subjects.*

Thomas Flynn, Samuel Candler Dobbs Professor of Philosophy at Emory University. Among his many notable works on French existentialism are *Sartre and Marxist Existentialism, Sartre, Foucault, and Historical Reason* (two volumes), and *Sartre: A Philosophical Biography.*

Shaun Gallagher, Lillian and Morrie Moss Professor of Excellence in Philosophy at the University of Memphis and Professorial Fellow at the University of Wollongong, Australia. A noted scholar of phenomenology and cognitive science, his many publications include *How the Body Shapes the Mind* and (with Dan Zahavi) *The Phenomenological Mind*.

Gregory Hoskins, Assistant Professor and Assistant Director of the Augustine and Culture Seminar Program at Villanova University. His main research interests concern the philosophy, ethics, and politics of memory and commemoration, especially in regard to specific American historical events and sites.

Adrian van den Hoven, Professor Emeritus of French Studies at the University of Windsor. He has translated Sartre's works *Truth and Existence* and *Hope Now: The 1980 Interviews*. He has also written extensively about Sartre's theater and his literary works and was a founding editor of *Sartre Studies International*.

Geoffrey Karabin, Assistant Professor of Philosophy at Neumann University. His main research interests regard a belief in immortality and its relationship to violence and he has published works on Gabriel Marcel. He is a co-founder of *Marcel Studies*.

William McBride, Arthur G. Hansen Distinguished Professor of Philosophy at Purdue University. His numerous works on existentialism and social and political philosophy include *Sartre's Political Theory*, *Philosophical Reflections on the Changes in Eastern Europe*, *From Yugoslav Praxis to Global Pathos*, and *The Philosophy of Marx*.

Shannon M. Mussett, Professor of Philosophy at Utah Valley University. She has published multiple works on the philosophy of Simone de Beauvoir, and co-edited two works on Beauvoir, *Beauvoir and the History of Philosophy from Plato to Butler* and *The Contradictions of Freedom*. She is also a scholar of Hegel and feminist theory.

Ronald E. Santoni, Maria Theresa Barney Chair Emeritus of Philosophy at Denison University and Life Member of Clare Hall, Cambridge University. Among his many notable works on French existentialism are *Sartre on Violence—Curiously Ambivalent*, and *Bad Faith, Good Faith, and Authenticity in Sartre's Early Philosophy*.

Sally Scholz, Professor of Philosophy at Villanova University. Her works on social and political philosophy and feminist theory include *On de Beauvoir*, *Political Solidarity*, and *Feminism: A Beginner's Guide*. She is currently Editor of *Hypatia: A Journal of Feminist Philosophy*.

Robert Wood, Professor of Philosophy in the Institute of Philosophic Studies at the University of Dallas. His many works include *Martin Buber's Ontology*, *A Path into Metaphysics*, and *The Beautiful, the True, and the Good*. He is a past president of the American Catholic Philosophical Association and past editor of the *American Catholic Philosophical Quarterly*.

Preface

Living Existentialism is a collection of essays in honor of Thomas W. Busch. Busch has been a consistent proponent of continental philosophy in America for half a century. He first encountered continental philosophy as a student of Fr. Robert Lechner, the founder of *Philosophy Today*, a journal that served as a primary forum for disseminating continental philosophy in the United States. Busch then went on to do his graduate studies at Marquette University, where he wrote a dissertation in the early 1960's on Merleau-Ponty. He has been a long-time active presence at various continental philosophy organizations in America, including the Society for Phenomenology and Existential Philosophy, the North American Sartre Society, the Marcel Society, and the International Merleau-Ponty Circle. Further, Busch has taught at Villanova University for over 50 years, serving as department chair in the early 1980's and helping to found the Doctoral Program in Philosophy in 1994.

The author of numerous articles, Busch's essay "Sartre: The Phenomenological Reduction and Human Relationships" was recognized by the *Journal of the British Society for Phenomenology* in a special edition as one of its top essays. Busch is the author of two books—*The Power of Consciousness and the Force of Circumstances in Sartre's Philosophy* (1990), and *Circulating Being: From Embodiment to Incorporation (Essays in Late Existentialism)* (1999). He is the editor of a Gabriel Marcel Reader—*Participant Perspective: A Gabriel Marcel Reader* (1987)—and he co-edited, with Shaun Gallagher (one of the contributors to this volume), a collection of essays on themes in the work of Merleau-Ponty—*Merleau-Ponty, Hermeneutics, and Postmodernism* (1992).

In *Circulating Being*, Busch contends that, "[E]xistentialism made possible in significant ways what occurs in the present forms of continental philosophy, all of which assume the existentialist critique of dualism, essentialism, and totality in modern philosophy, while at the same time, existentialism remains capable of haunting today's scene as an important and relevant critic."[1] The essays in this volume aim to honor Busch's work by exemplifying this insight. In differing ways, they attest to the continuing importance and relevance of existentialist philosophy.

Much of Busch's own work and teaching has involved demonstrating that existentialism is a living movement and does not deserve its reputation as being a "philosophy of the lived experience of highly individualistic subjectivity."[2] Writing in the late 1990's about the tendency of encyclopedists to designate existentialism a finished project—as if it were, "a brilliant flash of lightning across the philosophical sky, both intense and brief"[3]—he cautions that such hasty periodization risks distorting our understanding of the contemporary philosophical scene and of depriving ourselves of vital resources for critiquing contemporary forms of what Gabriel Marcel referred to as processes of dehumanization. Rather than consigning existentialist philosophy to the dustbin of history, we should recognize that the existentialists' views are "invitations, solicitations to think together, and to inevitably transgress their own thinking."[4] Further, he contends that existentialism did not end after the first generation of French existentialists traced out the centrality of embodiment and of lived experience:

> What is far less established and publicized is how [the existentialist's] works, particularly their late works, moved beyond, without denying, embodiment to what I call "incorporation," the transcendence of individual experience in the discursive circulation of Being, a circulation which, while admitting individual differences, calls discussants together ethically and politically.[5]

Busch remarks in the interview that closes this volume that he is a "historian of philosophy." This description is both helpful and potentially misleading. It is helpful because what marks Busch's scholarship is an historian's fastidious attention to the details in the source texts and a refined sense of judgment about what is and what is not alive, or worth rehabilitating, in the work of the thinkers he takes up (thinkers who are primarily, but not

---

1. Busch, *Circulating Being*, x.
2. Ibid.
3. Ibid, ix.
4. Ibid., 129.
5. Ibid.

exclusively, Twentieth Century French philosophers and writers: Gabriel Marcel, Albert Camus, Maurice Merleau-Ponty, Jean-Paul Sartre, Simone de Beauvoir, and Paul Ricoeur). These features of Busch's work are arguably best illustrated in his book on Sartre's philosophy, *The Power of Consciousness and the Force of Circumstances in Sartre's Philosophy*. In the book Busch offers a series of studies of key texts in Sartre's *oeuvre* that trace Sartre's changing conception of freedom, from his initial articulations of a radical freedom, after his discovery of Husserl's phenomenology of consciousness, to his mature, post-war reconceptualization of freedom that attends to *la force des choses*, to the power of circumstances and the affects and effects of social alienation and oppression. (Although they are not his targets, the book serves as a rebuke to those who do not read *Being and Nothingness* closely—Sartre is upfront with the limits of his project in that book, but many commentators simply ignore those remarks—and those who do not read anything Sartre wrote after *Being and Nothingness*.)

What is misleading in the description is that Busch does not have the proverbial historian's disdain for the contemporary situation. On the contrary, Busch is responsive in his scholarship and teaching to contemporary debates, controversies, and topics. To cite two revealing examples: First, in his graduate courses and writings he addresses head on the critique of Merleau-Ponty's work on embodiment put forward in the 1980's by American feminist philosophers such as Iris Marion Young and Judith Butler. Interested neither in defending Merleau-Ponty in a knee-jerk fashion nor in conceding some of the seemingly more dismissive conclusions of the critique, Busch has sought to delineate the terms of a constructive dialogue between Merleau-Ponty and his critics (that nonetheless does not seek to elide important differences). Secondly, in response to calls that began in the final quarter of the Twentieth Century for an ethics and politics of dialogue—a movement most readily associated with Habermas' work on a communicative rationality—Busch offers the notion of "incorporation," a conception of dialogue derived from a response to, and an approach to, the Other that eschews the aspiration for an absolute consensus and that recognizes irreducible differences. There is thus perhaps more in common between incorporation and Merleau-Ponty's conception of the "lateral universal"[6] than between it and Habermas' conception of discourse ethics.

As noted above, Thomas Busch urges philosophers to acknowledge that "existentialism remains capable of haunting today's scene as a important and relevant critic." The essays in this volume support that claim. However, they also go beyond that claim and suggest that existential philosophy

---

6. Merleau-Ponty. "From Mauss," 120.

continues to play a constructive role in the development of contemporary philosophy. This point is surely in keeping with Busch's overall view, and it is in Busch's honor that we offer this overview of some of what is truly living in *living existentialism*.

The authors in this volume responded to the general call for contributions in a variety of ways, and the essays collected here cover a fairly wide range of existentialist thinkers and topics. The contributions are gathered under very large umbrella headings: essays concerning the work of Gabriel Marcel, essays concerning the work of Simone de Beauvoir, Maurice Merleau-Ponty, and Jean-Paul Sartre, and essays on the work of other existentialists. The volume concludes with an interview with Thomas Busch. The editors readily admit that there is an aleatory character to this arrangement and acknowledge that there are other reasonable ways in which these contributions could be organized.

The volume begins with a section of essays that attest to the continuing importance of the thought of Gabriel Marcel. It is particularly appropriate to open with this section, because throughout his career Busch has been a staunch advocate of Marcel's work. Marcel's thought is under-studied and under-appreciated in relation to the work of other existentialists, but the three essays in this section attest to the fact that Marcel's views are relevant to contemporary—and perennial—philosophical concerns. The section opens with an essay by John Caputo on Marcel's influence on Jacques Derrida. Building on Edward Baring's recent intellectual history of the young Derrida[7], Caputo examines the ways in which, although he did not always acknowledge it, Derrida's reading of Marcel influenced his later philosophy. Specifically, he shows that, "Marcel's distinction between problem and mystery belongs to the pre-history of Derrida's distinction between the deconstructible and undeconstructible."

In the second essay, Sally Fischer examines the development in Marcel's thought of a form of embodied and dialogical ethics that turns on being available to others in their differences. Fischer highlights the similarities and links between Marcel's thought and a kind of ethical perspectivism that is prominent in some Twentieth Century feminist thought, but particularly in Luce Irigary's *I love to you*. In the third and final essay in the section, Geoffrey Karabin offers a discussion of Marcel's views on belief in the afterlife. Karabin shows that Marcel's views on the afterlife, which are tied to the experience of love for another, are of particular relevance because of the way they take seriously, and respond to, those who argue that belief in the afterlife amounts to a denial of the value or meaning of this life.

---

7. Baring, *The Young Derrida*.

The second section of the volume, which is the largest, brings together essays that focus on the thinkers that are most commonly associated with French existential philosophy: Simone de Beauvoir, Maurice Merleau-Ponty, and Jean-Paul Sartre.[8] This section displays the depth and breadth of contemporary scholarship on French existentialism by bringing together established and younger scholars who explore a wide variety of philosophical themes. The section opens with an essay by J.C. Berendzen that examines the somewhat conflicting claims made by Merleau-Ponty in *Phenomenology of Perception* regarding the normativity of perception. By weaving together Merleau-Ponty's claims, ideas taken from contemporary analytic philosophy of perception, and a suggestive passage from Busch's dissertation, Berendzen presents an interpretation of Merleau-Ponty's views that works through their seeming contradictions.

Thomas Flynn reconsiders the dispute between Merleau-Ponty and Sartre, focusing on Merleau-Ponty's critique of Sartre's use of the dialectic. Along with a discussion of Merleau-Ponty's well-known critique of Sartre on the dialectic in *Adventures of the Dialectic*, Flynn analyzes Merleau-Ponty's earlier critique of Sartre as it developed in a newly transcribed set of lecture notes from a spring of 1956 course titled *La dialectique* offered at the Collège de France. In the third essay in this section Shaun Gallagher examines Sartre's views on intersubjectivity in connection with his (in)famous notion of the "gaze." Gallagher breathes new life into a much-discussed area of Sartre scholarship by comparing Sartre's views with those of other philosophers (notably Emanuel Levinas) and with recent discussions of intersubjectivity in contemporary cognitive science.

In her contribution to the section, Shannon Mussett offers a discussion of one of the central topics in Sartre's philosophy: radical freedom. She traces the origin of Sartre's thinking on the topic out of his engagement with Edmund Husserl's philosophy of consciousness and then his development of the topic in relation to Simone de Beauvoir's work. Mussett argues for continuity in Sartre's *oeuvre* regarding his views on radical freedom. In the next essay Ronald Santoni takes up another of Sartre's core concepts: bad faith. Santoni provides a concise overview of the concept of bad faith, and argues against recent treatments of the concept, as primarily a matter of intersubjective social relations, that bad faith has epistemological features and implications. Santoni reminds us that bad faith does many things in Sartre's thought, but that, "bad faith often serves as a kind of criterion by which Sartre evaluates not only the actions and views of others but also our

---

8. A glaring omission from this list is Albert Camus. The lack of reference to Camus is due solely to the contingencies of our contributor's topics, and is not meant to indicate that we are taking a particular stand on his works.

individual and collective praxes, mindsets, movements, and socio-political positions."

In the penultimate essay of the section, Sally Scholz reads Beauvoir's novel *The Mandarins* for insights about a cluster of concepts concerning the metaphysics, ethics and politics of groups. Specifically, she uses the novel and other key texts to explore Beauvoir's thinking about the ontological status of political groups, the role of writing in the formation and maintenance of groups, the nature of solidarity, and the responsibilities and duties members owe to groups. The final essay in the section, by Adrian van den Hoven, continues the discussion of literary works. Van den Hoven offers a reading of Sartre's play *The Devil and the Good Lord* that examines the religious and specifically Christian aspects of the work in light of Sartre's avowed atheism.

The essays in the third and final section of the book move beyond the boarders of French existential philosophy, but they continue the work of honoring Thomas Busch by displaying the richness of existential thought and its links to earlier thinkers and to other movements and traditions. In the first essay of the section, Thomas Anderson investigates Søren Kierkegaard's views on the dynamic between faith and reason. As a corrective to a somewhat pat summary of Kierkegaard as dismissive of natural human reason, Anderson demonstrates that reasoning for Kierkegaard plays a unique, positive role as a propaedeutic to faith. Next William McBride reflects on the current status of postmodern philosophy and asks, "Is it now *passé*?" Weaving together reflections on some of Busch's work and on the work and legacy of Richard Rorty, McBride concludes that postmodernism is indeed past (though, perhaps by implication, that existentialism is not). In the final essay in the section Robert Wood explores Edith Stein's experiential critique of Heidegger's pre-*Kehre* existence-philosophy. Following Stein's lead, Wood juxtaposes Stein's critique of Heidegger with a summary of Stein's alternate existential analytic: one drawn from her reading of Teresa of Avila's *Interior Castle* written in 1577.

The final item in the volume is an interview of Thomas Busch by Gregory Hoskins. The interview is roughly divided into two parts, first questions about Busch's intellectual and professional biography, and then questions about the discipline of Philosophy and the subjects and themes of Busch's work.

Near the end of the interview, Busch expresses his conviction that existentialists "will be around to haunt and bother future philosophy in the form of testing, prodding and questioning." The essays in this volume indicate that even if existentialism is dead—a diagnosis that is far from conclusive—the ghost of existentialism is alive and well.

Bibliography

Baring, Edward. *The Young Derrida and French Philosophy: 1945-1968*. Cambridge: Cambridge University Press, 2011.

Busch, Thomas. *Circulating Being: From Embodiment to Incorporation: Essays in Late Existentialism*. New York: Fordham University Press, 1999.

Merleau-Ponty, Maurice. "From Mauss to Claude Levi-Strauss." In *Signs*, 114–25. Translated by Richard McCleary. Evanston, IL: Northwestern University Press, 1964.

Acknowledgments

The editors wish to thank Dr. Sally Scholz, chair, Department of Philosophy at Villanova University, for encouraging us to undertake the project, and for serving as wise counsel and offering a supportive voice throughout. Further, we gratefully acknowledge financial support for the project from Villanova's Center for Liberal Education.

This volume is dedicated to Dr. Thomas W. Busch, our mentor and friend.

PART ONE

Gabriel Marcel in Contemporary Context

1

Marcel and Derrida

Christian Existentialism and the Genesis of Deconstruction

—John Caputo

In *Circulating Being* Thomas Busch defended the thesis that, contrary to the received view, Existentialism was alive and well.[1] Not as such—that much was true. It had suffered quite a shock from a critique of humanism from which it never quite recovered. So as a movement, it was a thing of the past. Instead, he argued, its survival can be seen in the way that so many central Existentialist claims have been assimilated by and become part of the working presuppositions of its very critics—notions like the Existentialist critiques of body/mind dualism, rationalism, essentialism and totalizing thinking. In a perverse sense, Busch has been proven right by the current wave of "Speculative Realism" spurred by Quentin Meillassoux, which today denounces post-structuralism itself for being just another round of humanism, a form of Kantian subjectivism, and for not being radically reductionistic, naturalistic, and scientific. But I am interested in a more philosophically interesting and even more unlikely confirmation of his thesis coming from the recent publication of Edward Baring's *The Young Derrida and French Philosophy*,[2] a careful study of Derrida's early life and studies, going all the way back to 1948 when Derrida was only eighteen years old. Basing his book upon Derrida's unpublished archival papers, Baring argues that the young Derrida was something of a Christian Existentialist with a particular

---

1. Busch, *Circulating Being*, ix–xi.
2. Baring, *The Young Derrida*.

interest in Gabriel Marcel and Simone Weil. Of course, at so early an age, we have all thought thoughts that we have long since abandoned, but in this case I think that what Baring has unearthed is genuinely significant. In the present essay I pursue this surprising and unlikely link between Marcel and Derrida which I hold is both significant for understanding the subsequent development of Derrida's work and further support for the thesis defended in *Circulating Being*.

Heidegger, Sartre, and the Question of Humanism

First, we need to reconstruct the world in which the young Derrida—before Jackie became Jacques—entered philosophy. The issue that was grabbing all the headlines in French philosophy in the 1940s was the controversy over "humanism." Is Marxism the true humanism, the only one that is seriously concerned with the economic well-being of human beings? After all, what could be more basic to human well-being than to have the food, shelter and clothing necessary to maintain human dignity? Or was it the case—as Bishop Sheen was reminding us weekly on a very successful program in the early years of American television—that what the Marxists were proposing was not so much basic as just plain base, nothing but soulless totalitarian materialism? Is not the true humanism found in Christianity, where the notion of the sacredness of each human soul before God was the only sure way to protect human freedom and dignity? Any number of major Catholic philosophers and theologians were engaged by this debate, one of the most significant contributions to which was *Integral Humanism* (*Humanisme integrale*) published by Jacques Maritain in 1936.[3] Maritain and the medieval historian Étienne Gilson were the two sustaining pillars of the revival of Thomistic philosophy, and two of the greatest Catholic philosophers, of the twentieth century.

This was of course the heyday of French "Existentialism." The movement had begun in the 1930s—the term could be traced back to Marcel's *Metaphysical Journal*[4]—when it was dominated by French Catholics who were inspired by Kierkegaard's brilliant if rather Lutheran-Augustinian meditations upon the individual standing before the white light of God. "Atheistic" Existentialism was historically a later inflection defended by Sartre and Camus. So the debate about the true humanism was also a debate about the true Existentialism. Did true humanism require God or did it demand the death of God? As you might expect, questions like that, which

---

3. Maritain, *Integral Humanism*.
4. Marcel, *Metaphysical Journal*.

had been explored in depth by Henri de Lubac's well-known *The Drama of Atheist Humanism* (1945),[5] had among other things made for a great material for the philosophy courses Thomas Busch and I taught back the 1960s and 1970s, when we taught large numbers of Augustinian seminarians who needed to know this material for the theological studies they would undertake after they finished their baccalaureate degrees.

In a 1945 essay entitled "Existentialism Is a Humanism,"[6] Jean Paul Sartre had thought to make a strategic intervention in this debate by arguing that atheistic Existentialism is the true humanism, the true Existentialism and the true Marxism! To pull off such a philosophical trifecta, Sartre had his work cut out for him, because he was anathema twice over—an atheist to the Christians and a bourgeois individualist to the Marxists. So Sartre sought a synthesis of Marxism and individual freedom by arguing that the revolution is impossible without it (shades of Badiou); the Communist decision is an existential one, made in the depths of existential freedom—otherwise we can just sit back and wait for the wheels of dialectical materialism to turn and it will come about all by itself. But to choose for myself (with subjective passion) is to choose for all men, as a collective (shades of Kant). In this way Sartre sought to dodge (1) the totalitarian complaint made by the Christians against the Marxists, (2) the other-worldliness complaint, the neglect of real economic suffering in the present, made by the Marxists against the Christians, and (3) the Marxist critique of him as a subjectivist.

Sartre could not have foreseen what would happen next. Heidegger intervened! He published a landmark essay entitled *Letter on Humanism*,[7] which basically introduced us all to what came to be known as the "later" Heidegger. In those days Heidegger was taken—by Sartre and by everybody else—to be an Existentialist and his *Being and Time* (1927)[8] was considered to be the theoretical masterpiece of the movement, upon which Sartre (and everybody else) had clearly been drawing. Not only was the very title of Sartre's major work, *Being and Nothingness*,[9] something of a riff on Heidegger's landmark book but it actually would have served as a fairly good title of Heidegger's famous 1929 lecture "What is Metaphysics?" which was all about Being and "the" Nothing, a text upon which Sartre was clearly drawing.[10] Heidegger did not dispute Sartre's central claim, that Existential-

---

5. De Lubac, *The Drama of Atheist Humanism*.
6. Sartre, *Existentialism Is a Humanism*.
7. Heidegger, "Letter on Humanism," 213–66.
8. Heidegger, *Being and Time*.
9. Sartre, *Being and Nothingness*.
10. Heidegger, "What is Metaphysics?," 89–110.

ism is a humanism; in fact, he took Sartre at his word and went on to argue that *Being and Time* is not Existentialism and to that extent not humanism. What Heidegger said was absolutely prescient. He did not get into the debate about who is proposing the true humanism so much as to question the truth of humanism itself. In doing so Heidegger anticipated and antedated (1) the widespread critique of human subjectivity that would first prevail in structuralism, to which there were certain similarities in the later Heidegger; (2) contemporary environmentalism, which describes the present age as that of the "Anthropocene," which was a very considerable part of Heidegger's own agenda; (3) the study of evolutionary biology where human exceptionalism, classically embodied in the Aristotelian tree, with rational animals perched at the top, is considered a very misleading paradigm for scientific work on the animals that we all are.

Being and Time, Heidegger complained, is about Being and not about "human being." The "analytic of existence" is not an existentialist analytic, but an existential-ontological one. The thesis defended in *Being and Time* "the essence of Dasein lies in existence" is an ontological one to be distinguished from the anthropological Existentialist thesis proposed in Sartre's "existence precedes essence," of which it seemed to be a clever transcription. Where Sartre wrote that we live on a plane where there is only humanity, Heidegger rejoined, "we live on a plane where there is only Being," and then went on to offer an esoteric gloss on the German idiom "*es gibt*," which literally means "it gives"—hence it gives Being as time, and time as Being. What gives? The "it" itself, which is not a human being, not a being at all, but Being itself, and is not even Being itself, since that is what is given, and so the "it" is what he called the "event" (*Ereignis*) of Being's being given over the epochs from the early Greeks to the age of techno-science. There followed a series of shocking and highly un-Existentialist renderings of familiar terms from *Being and Time*, like Dasein itself, resoluteness, and thrownness—a word seized upon by Camus and Sartre and ingredient in their notion of the "absurd." We are not blindly thrust into the world at birth and blindly cast forward into death, Heidegger said, but thrown into the truth of Being and asked to be its shepherd.

You could have fooled Sartre (and apparently did). In fact, you could have fooled *anyone*. The *Letter on Humanism* was not so much a legitimate complaint about how readers of *Being and Time* have all been misinterpreting this book as it was Heidegger's expression of how he had in the meantime changed his mind about a lot of the very basic claims in *Being and Time*. It reflected the ongoing evolution of Heidegger's thought from 1933 to 1945—the time of the Third Reich—of which no one outside of Germany, and certainly not in France, could have had any inkling. Such was the shock that the Heidegger scholars have been arguing about what happened ever since, literally, for the last seventy years and counting! A few years ago I went to my first Heidegger conference in many years, and they were still arguing about it. My own hypothesis is that this debate will subside only when, with the increasingly accelerating expansion of the universe, our little solar system, and so the partisans in this debate, will all be stardust.

On a strictly exegetical level, one could argue that Sartre's understanding of *Being and Time* was in many ways closer to that book than the *Letter on Humanism*, but Heidegger's thought had mutated during the war years and he was now on to something new. Sartre could be certainly forgiven for taking the "existential analytic" served up in *Being and Time* to be a choice bit of Existentialism, especially with its obvious debt to Kierkegaard. To be sure, Heidegger, in a fit of the "anxiety of influence" tried to tuck away his heavy borrowings from Kierkegaard (especially Kierkegaard's analysis of "anxiety") into the footnotes. Heidegger actually had the audacity to criticize Kierkegaard, to shamelessly bite the philosophical hand that was feeding him some of his best lines in that book. No one before the *Letter on Humanism* saw any harm describing Heidegger's "existential" analysis with the little nominalization existential*ism*. But for reasons of his own, reasons intimately tied up with his disastrous encounter with National Socialism, Heidegger had in the meantime headed out in a different and completely unforeseen direction.

There was, however, even from a strictly exegetical-philological point of view, a "mistake" in the French Existentialist rendering of *Being and Time*, which goes back to the unfortunate translation by Henri Corbin of "Dasein" as *realité humaine*.[11] Heidegger had taken great pains to speak in strictly ontological terms and to avoid anthropological language. That largely went unnoticed in France. French readers more or less breezed by the (fifteen page) "Introduction" to *Being and Time* (420 pages) in which Heidegger made it plain that the published text of *Being and Time* was a torso. The "existential analytic" was propaedeutic to the main point of the book, which was the elaboration of the "meaning of Being" in the section of the book which was still to appear. (It never did appear, thus perpetuating a perpetual discussion.) So Heidegger was right to say in the *Letter on Humanism* that the Existentialist-humanist reading of the "existential analytic" is an "anthropological" interpretation that missed the "ontological" problematic and that he was here setting the record straight. That was true, on strict exegetical grounds and on philosophical grounds—the French had ignored that

---

11. Heidegger, *Qu'est-ce que la métaphysique?* This French collection of writings by Heidegger contains a partial translation of *Being and Time*.

bit of *Being and Time*. The book was not ultimately about human being but about the question of Being, and the question of Being in turn required displacing the centrality of man, overcoming humanism, in order to "let Being be." But it must be added that even those who did not commit the French error had expected some sort of post-Kantian transcendental ontology, that is, a Dasein-oriented rethinking of ontology, to emerge from the missing third part. No one, including Heidegger, expected the u-turn that Heidegger actually took.

This ultimately proved to be quite a blow to Sartre and to Existentialism generally. On the one hand, the (atheistic) Marxists led by Louis Althusser were unconvinced by Sartre and indeed would shortly conclude, that Marxism is not only not Existentialism it is, on the contrary, actually structuralism. The Catholic philosophers, on the other hand, likewise jumped the ship of Christian "humanism" and embraced Heidegger's post-humanism! The whole tone of *A Letter on Humanism*, and this would be a constant feature of everything Heidegger published after the war, was, if not theological, at least mystical, deeply touched by what he himself would call "openness to the mystery" of Being. Classical mysticism has always been marked by a radically theo-centric displacement of any possible anthropocentrism, by a self-effacing mystical humility, a critique of human hubris, which moves the ego out of the way in order to let God take over the workings of the soul. The relationship of human being to Being reminds anyone literate in the writings of the great Catholic Rhineland mystics of the relationship of the soul to God.

That in fact was my first scholarly project—*The Mystical Element in Heidegger's Thought*.[12] Heidegger unapologetically used the language of the mystics, most notably the word *Gelassenheit*, which in ordinary German meant "composure," but literally meant "letting-be-ness." Heidegger had borrowed the term from Meister Eckhart—God desires nothing of you so much as that you let go of your ego and let God be God in you—and used it to mean, by an unmistakable analogy, to let go of our anthropological-humanist-Cartesian subject and let Being be Being in us. Thinking, he said, is letting Being be. Thinking is letting go of concepts, propositions and syllogisms and letting Being be thought in us.

The Catholics were fascinated! Indeed, the most important book in English to get the word out to the Anglophone world about the "later" post-Existentialist Heidegger and the "turn" that had taken place in Heidegger's thought was written by William Richardson, an American Jesuit priest. Richardson had followed Heidegger's 1955–56 course on "The Principle of

---

12. Caputo, *Mystical Element in Heidegger's Thought*.

Reason" in Freiburg,[13] and taken his doctorate at the Catholic University of Louvain under Alphonse De Waelhens, a Catholic philosopher and himself the author of a major work on *Being and Time*. Marcel would later on express his admiration for Heidegger after meeting him in 1957 at Cerisy and even Gilson was to add a very respectful disagreement with Heidegger in an appendix to his landmark *L'Être et l'essence*.[14] By the same token, the German Protestants were struck by the later Heidegger's enigmatic pronouncements about "Language," which sounded like the "Word" of God, and so they saw an opening for a renewal of biblical hermeneutics!

All of this was to leave Sartre, Existentialism, and humanism back at the station. Sartre's days were numbered. He had tried to synthesize the two sides and ended up losing both of them. I think Sartre's *Being and Nothingness* was a brilliant bit of philosophy that stands or falls on its own merits. It is a creative reading of *Being and Time*, and one of Heidegger's points in *Being and Time* is that this is exactly how history works, how interpretation works, how hermeneutics works—as an ongoing series of "repetitions." The German word that Heidegger was using is *Wiederholung*, which more literally means fetching-back or "retrieving." *Wiederholung* was the title of the German translation of a book that Kierkegaard had written, which was entitled *Gjentagelse*, which literally meant to "take again," which is translated into English under the title *Repetition*. The problem is that if Sartre's repetition/retrieval of *Being and Time* stands or falls on its own merits, it fell and with quite a thud. "Humanism" was about to be shown the door—by both the Communists *and* the Catholics, and with it Existentialism. While Sartre continued to dominate the French philosophical scene for many years, he had bet on the wrong horse and is today largely the object of historical studies.

Derrida, Marcel, and the Critique of Humanism

Although it was Existentialism that got first Jackie Derrida interested in philosophy, he, too, signed on to the critique of humanism—and although he had reasons of his own (big surprise) he came down closer to the Catholic-Existentialist side than the Marxist! He could never be content with the Marxist Leninist Dialectical Materialist account of History, all capitalized and in the singular, as if there were One Big Thing called History and One

---

13. Heidegger, *The Principle of Reason*.

14. Marcel, "Ma Relation avec Heidegger." Gilson, *L'Être et l'essence*, 365–377. Unfortunately, this appendix is not included in the partial English translation, *Being and Some Philosophers*.

Big Theory that covered it, as if history, language, and thinking were all monoliths and all programmed to one result. The Communists were making a pretense to the one true blue interpretation of everything, which put itself forth as Science, *the* objective Science of History, which neutralized "ideology," a distortion of History by subjective "human" passion from which the Communist Science of History was immune. This Interpretation of History, as we learned from the Soviet Union, its chosen incarnation, dealt harshly with dissenters. Dialectical Materialism was a perfect storm for Derrida, a nightmare. It was a paradigm of what Lyotard called a *grand récit*, a Big Story, an overarching theory of history, when Lyotard famously described "postmodernism" as "incredulity towards *grands récits*,"[15] which means incredulity towards One Big Interpretation. The only way we get One Big Interpretation, in politics or religion, is with one big dose of violence. The reason Derrida made trouble for structuralism, while keeping his counsel about Karl Marx, was that it purported to be Science, and when science was joined with politics, that spelled terror and trouble of an unmistakably totalitarian type. Derrida was a life-long man of the left but, like his Algerian compatriot Camus, he was a post-Communist, post-Dialectical Materialist man of the left. So instead of signing on to the structuralist critique of humanism, he launched instead a post-structuralist one.

This much we all knew, but Baring gives us some hints about just where Derrida's post-structuralism was coming from. Jackie Derrida was interested in ethics, and he saw belief in God as an ingredient in ethics, and so he had a pronounced proclivity for the Catholic Existentialists. That helps to explain the serious sympathy he had for Heidegger's critique of humanism with all its religio-mystical overtones. He distrusted Structuralism and he shared Heidegger's critique of "metaphysics," of a big theory that reduced Being to "presence"—hence the critique of the "metaphysics of presence"—and reduced difference and temporality to variant deviations from presence. He shared Heidegger's appreciation of the limits of rationality, of Heidegger's respect for what he called the concealment (*lethe*) in the un-concealment (*a-letheia*) of truth. Derrida liked to call this the "secret," not only later on but, as Baring shows, way back in the late 1940s, not the human secret that one person keeps from others, but the structural secret built right into the make of up things that prevents us from constructing totalizing theories. Derrida, like Heidegger, wanted to inscribe a zone of "mystery" in being that would always slip away from the reach of conceptual thinking. In the end, Derrida's critique of humanism would be post-structuralist, post-Heideggerian, post-Christian, post-religious. But "post"

15. Lyotard, *The Postmodern Condition*, xxiii–xxiv.

here does not mean "past" or "against" but "passing through" and moving on to the next step—and the crucial thing to bear in mind here is that he had importantly passed through Christian Existentialism.

This helps explains why Derrida would early on take an interest in Levinas' *Totality and Infinity*, where totalizing thought is delimited by the coming of the *tout autre*, and later on show signs of a certain odd but unmistakable congeniality of his own with religion, with a certain "religion without religion." This is an expression he coined in 1992 in a book about Kierkegaard, which I defended in my *The Prayers and Tears of Jacques Derrida: Religion without Religion* (1997). For Derrida there was always—Baring shows its nascent beginning—an irreducible undecidability in things, something unconditional which eludes the concrete conditions under which life is lived, something "undeconstructible" haunting the provisional historical constructions of life. We always and already live in the distance between the conditional and the unconditional, pulled at on one side by the *unconditional* demand for justice (or democracy or hospitality), and on the other side by the concrete *conditions* in which democracy or justice or hospitality can actually exist, can be brought about in reality. We pass our lives in the distance between these two, which is our inescapable hermeneutic situation. The "unconditional" is neither the God of the Bible nor the Ideas of Plato, neither the Categorical Imperative nor the Pure Reason of Kant, nor is it the pure structure of the structuralists. It is the open-ended promise that is lodged in the heart of words of elemental force that are handed down to us by the tradition and call upon us in moments of ambiguity and undecidability.

Derrida was interested in a concretely exercised freedom, neither the pure freedom of Sartre nor the determinism of Marxism. This took the form of a decision made under the condition of undecidability, which was not the enemy of decision, as his critics charged, but the condition of possibility of a genuine decision, rather like Kierkegaard's Abraham's impossible choice. Otherwise decisions and interpretations would be programmed, run on automatic pilot, by inertia, drifting along with the current stream, our personal oars resting in the boat, or eventually—and this is what we worry about today—made by computer programs. Enter IBM's "Watson"! What Derrida's critics missed is that the opposite of what he called undecidability was not a decision—it was programmability, absolutely rule-governed decisions. Undecidability is not the opposite of a decision; it is genuine condition of possibility—otherwise we can let a computer program make the decision. The question of freedom, framed by Heidegger, Sartre and Kierkegaard, a classic "Existentialist" genealogy, figured importantly in the young Derrida's decision to pursue philosophy in the first place. Without Existentialism,

Derrida might have gone on to study literature. A decision cuts off (*de* + *cidere*) other paths and sticks to the one chosen although the ones not chosen continue to lure us even after the decision is made. The thing to avoid here is decision*ism*, the idea that just so long as you decide resolutely and passionately, it does not matter what you do. That is the "anything goes" theory of interpretation Derrida had addressed in *Of Grammatology*, where the standing objection made against existential decision was answered in advance of being made.

By the time Heidegger's *Letter* was absorbed in France, in the 1950s, the terms of the debate between Christian Existentialists like Marcel and atheistic Existentialists like Sartre and Camus, had broken down. It no longer made much sense to describe the author of *A Letter on Humanism* as an "Existentialist" but it was also very questionable whether he was an "atheist," which was the label he wore in the old debate. On the contrary, like the theologian Paul Tillich, Heidegger had opened the door to what we call today "postmodern theology" by displacing the distinction between theism and atheism. The account of the openness of Being in the *Letter* had clearly opened the way to God and the gods, the holy and the divine, as dimensions of Being, and had the Catholic thinkers throwing their theological hats in the air. Existentialism had been left behind and atheism—be it of an Existentialist or a garden variety—was reductionistic. Atheism closes Being down, cuts it down to fit human-scientific proportions, deprives it of its depth and *mystery*. The Catholic philosophers of the day were fascinated by this new Heidegger whom they saw as offering a critique of "ontotheology." Heidegger emancipated them, he emancipated me, from the Neo-Scholastic ontotheology that had dominated Catholic theology and philosophy since the days of Pope Leo XIII. Far from being an atheist, Heidegger showed the way to the God beyond ontotheology, to the truly divine God, which reminded us all of the powerful tradition of apophatic theology.

What we did not know before Edward Baring's book appeared is how and that this all links up with the young Derrida's sympathies for the Christian side of the debate about humanism and in particular for Gabriel Marcel. From very early on, Baring says, Derrida "demanded a type of philosophical humility that Christian scholars thought appropriate to our human limitations."[16] Whatever roots this sentiment did or could have had in his Jewish upbringing, which is where most of us were inclined to find it, it can be explicitly documented in the interest he took in two Catholics, Simone Weil and Gabriel Marcel. To be sure, he was not interested in Catholic theological doctrine, but he did see in the Christian Existentialists the resources

16. Baring, *The Young Derrida*, 5.

for a critique of "the pretensions of human thought," of human hubris and arrogance.[17] The roots of Existentialism lay in the radical Christianity of Søren Kierkegaard, in his analysis of the singularity of the self before God, in fear and trembling. Although Kierkegaard himself had roots deep in his own Lutheranism and in Luther's Augustinianism, his work had been seized upon in France in the 1930s by the Catholics. While Marcel resisted the solitary self individualism of Kierkegaard, and on that point, as Busch would point out, is to be compared to Levinas, Kierkegaard had made the opening move which engaged the Catholic philosophers. Kierkegaard made personal experience—"subjective truth"—fair game for "philosophy." After Kierkegaard, "my life" was not for after-hours discussions or for memoirs late in life; it was the proper subject matter of philosophy. Marcel in particular had argued that without the openness of the soul to God humanism would inevitably reverse itself into an anti-humanism of the absurd, a "refusal to be saved," as he called it. Marcel was the central figure in "Christian Existentialism," which is pretty much what "Existentialism" was before the World War Two, having published his books in *"Philosophie de l'Esprit*," a book series run by Louis Lavelle and René le Senne.

It was to these philosophers that Derrida was drawn. But why Marcel in particular?

Marcel on Problem and Mystery

Marcel had captured the attention of the young Derrida because of the distinction Marcel made between problem and mystery. To understand the difference between the two we must first understand the distinction Marcel draws between objectification and participation, between the constitution of objects of reflective thought and pre-reflective participation in being. This distinction had been prefigured in Kierkegaard's distinction between objective truth and subjective truth, but Marcel's formulation was cast in richer and less misleading language.[18] The object of reflection is the work of the thinking subject, of its discursive tools—concepts, propositions and arguments—which give the world analytic clarity. Without it, we would enjoy none of the advantages of higher thought characteristic of human life, all of which require reflective analytic work. But objectification presupposes a pre-objective stratum of lived experience, what Husserl called the "pre-predicative," which would be accordingly pre-conceptual, pre-propositional

17. Ibid., 7–9.
18 Marcel, *The Mystery of Being*; Marcel, *Being and Having*, 25–27, 100–123. See Busch, *Circulating Being*, 28–42.

and pre-argumentative. There life is lived in the living, *in actu exercitu*, as the scholastics said, in all its immediacy and corporeality. Pre-objective life is the buzzing blooming world of William James, the "life-world" of Husserl and the phenomenologists, the being-in-the-world of Heidegger's Dasein. It is concrete and sensuous, material and carnal, flowing and temporal, active and operative, intimately interwoven with the things of the world and with other people. If it is "our" world, it is not because it belongs to us, but because we belong to it. We do not have it (*avoir*); it has us. We do not own it or master it but participate in it; it is our participation in being (être).

So everything turns on a fairly clear distinction between the objectification of being carried out by reflective thought and our pre-reflective participation in being. But making a fairly clear distinction like this is itself the work of reflective thought. So is not "participation" just another object, not a scientific one, like the speed of light, or a literary one, like the concept of epic poetry, but a philosophical object? This is just the kind of conceptual construction and more or less technical vocabulary typical of a philosopher, and we can even identify its pedigree in a particular sort of philosophy called Phenomenology and Existentialism. Up to a point that is undeniably true. Otherwise we would be at a loss to explain what sort of books Gabriel Marcel writes, the librarians would have no idea where to shelve them, and college registrars would not know how to credit courses on the work of Marcel on a student's transcript.

But it is only true up to a point, and to clarify that, Marcel says that we must make another conceptual distinction, between primary reflection and secondary reflection. Primary reflection is objectifying all the way down; it abstracts from lived experience, dials down all personal involvement, filters out the subjective and engages in an objective account of things as if we were not there at all. There is every good reason to do such a thing, and we should not denounce it as the work of the devil, otherwise our lives would be dominated by primitive superstitions and ignorance. But primary reflection calls for a "secondary" and properly philosophical reflection. The latter is characterized by the fact that it knows that objectifying reflection is the objectification of a world that precedes it, indeed that also follows it, that can never be turned off, and so is never reducible to objectifying reflection. Marcel calls this sense an intuition of being, an expression which is as likely to get our attention as it is to mislead us, and was taken up by Jacques Maritain as a way to expound Thomas Aquinas' idea of *ipsum esse*. Secondary reflection is not a mystical intuition like a soul caught up in the seventh heaven of beatific union. It is the lived sense, the pre-conceptual realization built into our bones, that the lived world is always-already there, always-already given, radically pre-given. It is in virtue of this sense that we know there is a *limit* built right into any possible objectification, any possible attempt to distinguish the objectified from the pre-objectified world. Such a realization would require non-objectifying language to succeed, a power of evocation of something we know but have trouble saying because the moment we reflect upon the pre-reflective it becomes an object of reflection. We need a way to think something that is not simply thinking *about* it as an object of thought but *from out of it* as from a pre-given world. We need to come up with a non-objectifying language, a language to be variously found in the inventive locutions of existential-phenomenological philosophers, the mystics, the later Heidegger, as also in literature, which is why Marcel himself was not only a philosopher but a dramatist.

Put in an affirmative way, secondary reflection has the task of catching life in the act before reflection arrives on the scene. But that inevitably involves a negative operation, which is why secondary reflection invites comparison with negative theology, where the apophatic language corrects the kataphatic. Secondary reflection points out that whatever we say about the pre-reflective world will fall short of that world, but knowing *that* is knowing something important, something significantly "Socratic," a term that Marcel embraced. That bit of Socratic or apophatic non-knowing (non-objectifiability) is the learned ignorance that is crucial to secondary reflection. The non-objectifiable is not so much the bit that objectification leaves out as it is the whole to which it never gained access in the first place, a whole which we do not grasp so much as it grasps us, a whole *in* which we find ourselves without being able to objectify it. We "know" it by knowing we participate *in* it and can never get our head or our philosophical vocabulary around it. So secondary reflection is restorative or corrective of the distortion that could set in if we considered primary reflection the last word. Primary reflection is primary not because it is the prime value. It is primary because it is but the first word, not the last.

The distinction between problem and mystery is a distinction between the difficulties that arise in sorting out objects and the more unfathomable depths of our primordial participation in being, which we are never going to sort out. Objects get entangled in problems, but participation is steeped in mystery. A problem can be solved, in principle, if not now, then later, down the road, like finding a cure for cancer. A mystery cannot be solved, now or later, in fact or in principle. Treating cancer, postponing death, extending life—those are medical problems. But what, if anything, lies beyond the grave? Why do innocent young children die? That is a mystery. Furthermore, if I have a problem, like a failure in the power grid that causes my lights to go out, the local electrical power company can send technicians to solve the problem. It has entirely to do with power wires and transformers and the like, and there are people trained to solve such problem. But if I ask myself what I should do with my life, there are no experts whom we can call in to resolve the question, no one who can run a software program that will analyze and resolve that problem. This is not a problem but a mystery of my freedom and I will never really know if I have chosen properly or even if there is any such thing the one right thing to choose. Problems yield to methods, software programs, systematic examination; mysteries do not.

In a problem, my very being is not at stake. A problem requires dialing down my own participation to zero, so that the emphasis is on the object not the subject. If my computer does not work this morning, that is a technical problem in need of a fix; it may make my day difficult, but it does not make my life meaningless. I may be annoyed but it does throw me into despair or result in what Kierkegaard calls the sickness unto death. I am inconvenienced by a problem but my authenticity as a human being is not on the line or in any way dependent upon solving the problem. I myself, in my singularity as an existential subject, am pushed face to face with a decision that is, as Kierkegaard said, the truth that is true for me. But the technician who checks out my computer is a strictly epistemological subject, a skilled subject scrutinizing a detached object. The technician is existentially neutral—to the point that he or she is to a large extent replaceable by the software program that would run a check on the system.

The technician might find my problem interesting or tantalizing and it may well excite his curiosity until he finds the solution. But the existential subject standing before a mystery is more deeply engaged than any epistemological subject reviewing a technical difficulty that will eventually be resolved. The existential subject is not curious but struck with awe and wonder before a permanent and impenetrable mystery. Science may not find a cure for cancer in time to do me any good, but my being-towards-my-death lies in the courage and dignity with which I face the inevitability of death, if not from cancer then from something else, which lies in the depth of my freedom. Death is not only or ultimately a medical problem.

The source of every mystery is participation: I cannot ultimately step outside of my own skin and make myself or the world an object for myself. The ultimate mystery is the mystery of being itself, in which I participate without have been consulted, from whose meaning and destiny I cannot detach, abstract or subtract myself. I participate in the mystery of being and I cannot saturate being with objectifying thought. I can think from within being but I cannot stand outside being and objectify it. Once the question of being is raised, my own being is put in question and I say with St. Augustine, *quaestio mihi magna factus sum*; "I became a great enigma to myself."[19]

Derrida on the Mystery of the Undeconstructible

According to Baring Derrida's attraction to Marcel's distinction between problem and mystery lay at the center of his sympathy for the Christian Existentialists and their receptivity to the later Heidegger. Like them, he treated Sartre's atheism as an exercise in hubris, because atheism presumes to have the last word, claiming to dispel what Karl Rahner called the mystery we call God. The youthful Derrida (1949–52) believed in God and was concerned about the questions of ethics, which he described in terms of the "transcendence of value" and a moral need for God as a ground for moral decision making.[20] Materialism is nihilism, he thought, because it undermines value; it is an exercise in human arrogance and a denial of our finitude. The two years Derrida spent in the *Khâgne* were passed under the tutelage of Étienne Borne, a defender of Christian Existentialism. Like Marcel, Borne thought that the "problem of evil" was not ultimately a problem but a mystery, testimony not to the atheistic "absurdity" of life but to the "mystery" of evil. Sartre's atheism was written off as a personal choice he made, not the inevitable result of an Existentialist analysis of human experience. Given such mystery, proving the existence of God was every bit as arrogant and profane as undertaking to disprove it.

The young Derrida was no less interested in those days in Simone Weil and her notion of a "purifying atheism."[21] He thought that philosophy, left to its own resources, ended up in nihilism, either that of the pure decisionism of Sartre's absolute freedom or that of a materialism that determined human choices. He sought a way out in Marcel and Weil, beyond philosophy, beyond nihilism, one that adheres closely to an analysis of experience and is not lost in a debate about abstract ideas. Experience exacts a movement of faith in God, but one that has been purified and has passed through the fires of atheism, losing God, as Weil said, in order to find God. Faith requires an existential-experiential choice, beyond the reach of rational proof and disproof. In Marcel's terms, God is not a problem but a meta-problematic mystery, and the decision for God is not arbitrary but, rooted as it is in an experience of our insufficiency, the only authentic one.

19. Augustine, *Confessions*, 55.
20. Baring, *The Young Derrida*, 57–63.
21. Ibid., 63.

But if Borne accepted Marcel's distinction between problem and mystery he rejected their opposition and sought ways to knit the two together.[22] The mystery does not excuse us from analyzing the problem as far as we can before we leave off and assign the rest to mystery. Derrida followed Borne on this point, which looks a bit like an anticipation of his later critique of "binary oppositions," meaning that after we make a distinction, the next thing to do is to make trouble for it. God is indeed a mystery, but that does not relieve us of the need to understand our faith in God. Nowadays, we might be inclined to add that this works both ways, that contemporary speculative physics finds itself face to face with self-acknowledged mysteries, with equations whose intuitive fulfillment it cannot imagine, with a universe which seems intent on confounding its every advance. Left to its own devices, Marcel's distinction is too clean and it shows an inclination to settle comfortably back into the old humanism, a way of promoting the humanities and of casting suspicion on the natural sciences and mathematics as dehumanizing.

Adopting the title of a book about the Christian philosopher René le Senne, Derrida labeled his position "existentiel spiritualism." By this he meant to describe a position that steers its way between the oppositions of Idealism versus Materialism, or of mysticism versus absurdity, or of pantheism versus atheism, by cutting a path closely hewn to concrete experience. In the ongoing analysis of experience, "obstacles" would be removed and experience would gain in clarity, even as an ultimate "value" would emerge that would lie forever beyond the reach of analysis. Every determination would yield to an ultimate indeterminable value, a hidden God.

Still, one might object, even if all this is true, so what? Has not everyone entertained thoughts as a twenty-year-old that they have long since jettisoned? The reason I think this is not to be written off as a passing fancy of a very young man is what comes next. The most important point that Baring makes, in my view, is that Derrida's interest in Marcel is also found—even though Marcel is not mentioned by name—in his 1954 thesis *The Problem of Genesis in Husserl's Philosophy*,[23] hitherto the "earliest" Derrida known to his readers. The Derrida who wrote this thesis as Jackie would publish it years later (1990), long after he had been forced to abandon his birth name to become Jacques. Baring argues that the word "problem" was actually chosen with Marcel's distinction in mind, having replaced "studies on the notion of" in the title of the original proposal. Where there is a problem, a residual mystery abides. Every effort Husserl made to solve the problem of genesis

22. Ibid., 64–67.
23. Ibid., 113–145.

left an insoluble mystery standing, and not because of any limitations on Husserl's part but for structural reasons endemic to phenomenology. Phenomenology, Husserl said, must be a perpetual beginning, always renewing itself and starting over again. Phenomenology itself resists the attempt to make it over into a scientific method of solving problems. This was in essence the argument that Derrida made against the then regnant interpretation of Husserl by the Marxist-Structuralist Tran Duc Thao, who was trying to break up the marriage of phenomenology and "Existentialism" and enter phenomenology into a second marriage with materialism and scientific structuralism. That debate also sparked the considerable interest shown in the work of Merleau-Ponty, who while retaining an existential analysis, had pursued phenomenology in collaboration with the natural sciences. In those days, for example, the word "genesis" was more closely linked to Piaget than Husserl.

The problem of genesis, Derrida says, turned on an abiding aporia: unless the genesis is undergirded by a logic, it cannot lay claim to the constitution of objectivity; but any such logic would require a prior constitution.[24] If consciousness, in a passive genesis, is guided by the constituted world, how did the constituted world get constituted in the first place? There is clearly some sort of "dialectic" between the constituting and the constituted, Derrida says, but by this he did not mean to concede the ground to the dialectical materialism of Tran Duc Thao, which places matter absolutely first and submits consciousness to mirroring it. To speak of a "dialectic" for Derrida, who soon abandoned this word, is to describe an unresolved problem, not to propose a solution. It simply stood in as a short-hand for an aporia that was understood as such. Genesis was formally a problem, but materially a mystery.[25] Problems can be solved, but mysteries can only be recognized. Problems arise and are resolved within fixed and already constituted presuppositions, but the genesis of the presuppositions belongs to a mysterious field that lies prior to the constitution of a problem. Derrida had a life-long interest in aporias, in insoluble problems, and double binds.

Given that, as Baring holds, Derrida's interest in phenomenology was linked to his interest in the Christian Existentialists, for him the constitution of objectivity can only be resolved so far before it yields to mystery. It is difficult to exaggerate the importance of this point. As Derrida said in the beginning of *Of Grammatology*, the science (*logos*) of writing (*gramme*) depends upon the prior possibility of the writing of science.[26] Writing sup-

---

24. Baring, *The Young Derrida*, 131; citing Derrida, *The Problem of Genesis*, 108.
25. Baring, *The Young Derrida*, 136; citing Derrida, *The Problem of Genesis*, xlii.
26. Derrida, *Of Grammatology*, 27.

plies the condition of possibility of science while also making it impossible to formalize writing by way of a *logos*. There is always and in principle something prior to and lying behind any constituted science or scientific object. But this a priori is not a pure "transcendental" a priori or principle, which gives rise to predictable and fixed objects, but a "quasi-transcendental" one. By this Derrida meant a genetic source that precedes the constituted object but that cannot *itself* be regulated, closed or formalized, so that the genesis gives rise to unpredictable effects. In the beginning is not the Transcendental Ego but an anonymous quasi-transcendental field. The quasi-transcendental gives rise to open-ended differential interweavings, not to closed systems. The origin, as Derrida said, is always a non-origin, since in classical terms origins are supposed to be unitary principles not a differential play. The condition under which objectivity is possible also makes pure objectivity impossible, and with that statement we have arrived at the central theorem of deconstruction.

I submit that, given what Baring is saying—I have not examined these unpublished manuscripts myself—Marcel's distinction belongs in an essential way to the pre-history of deconstruction.

Put in its most general form, deconstruction turns on the distinction between the conditional and the unconditional. The conditional is what constituted under the concrete conditions of space and time; it is factual and historical, concrete and particular; contingent and reformable. In short, the conditional is deconstructible. The conditional belongs to the constituted horizons of expectation, to the predictable, calculable, and foreseeable, which Derrida calls the "future present," the future we can foresee becoming present. None of this means the conditional can be dismissed. We are responsible for the foreseeable future. We can calculate its coming and we are obliged to prepare for it, the way we are obliged to provide for the education of our children, or for the debts we incur, or for our retirement, or for a designated driver if we intend to pass the evening celebrating. This is the sphere in which we cannot complain that we did not see this coming. If we were ignorant of this future, we should not have been and our ignorance is culpable. *The conditional is the sphere of the problematic*, of the problems that admit of *calculable solutions* within the prevailing presuppositions. It is the sphere of the "possible," what we have every reason to expect or hope within the current horizon of expectation.

The unconditional, on the other hand, is what we cannot see coming, the incalculable, the unforeseeable "event," *the* impossible, not a simple logical impossibility, like a contradiction in terms, but a phenomenological impossible, which shatters our horizon of expectation. The unconditional or the impossible leaves us stunned and asking, "how was that possible?" The impossible is accordingly risky business. But to eliminate this risk, to try to make everything safe, to bring everything under the rule of the foreseeable, the calculable, is riskier still. Were we to succeed (which we would not) in guaranteeing that all there is to life is the foreseeable and the calculable, then at the end of life we would be forced to conclude that life has passed us by. The unconditional is the "absolute future," the absolutely unforeseeable, the one that breaks in upon us uninvited, that takes by surprise. But it is our openness to the unforeseeable that keeps the future open, that allows all things to made new. Openness to the future is sustained by a fidelity to the future that runs deeper than any doctrinal faith, and by a hope against hope that runs deeper than confessional hope. *Openness to the future is an openness to the mystery.*

The absolute future calls us like a lure; it has a fetching quality, like an absolute promise. A promise of what? Of something, I know not what, like a democracy-to-come whose contours I cannot make out, of which what is presently called democracy is a faint foreshadowing. Or a justice to come, or a work of art to come, or a science to come. When it arrives we will ask, what is this? Is this even art? Or science? Is it not mad? The structure of the to-come destabilizes any and every order of human activity with the promise of what is coming which is attached to it like a co-efficient of infinity. This is not an actual infinity, but an infinitival one, which turns every nominatival X into an in-finitival X, an X-to-come. So the impossible, the unconditional, is the undeconstructible, not because it is an eternal being or an imperishable essence but because it has not been constructed yet. It is the promise of what is coming that puts pressure on what is present to yield to its promise, which never comes, not quite, not for beings in space and time.

The absolute future is incalculable, meta-problematic. The democracy or the work of art or the science to come make up the subject matter of a hope against hope, even I would say of a prayer. They float before us like ghosts, remain enshrouded in a cloud of unknowing and unforeseeability, like an essential undisclosable and structural secret, an irreducible *mystery* that destabilizes the present.

In short Marcel's distinction between problem and mystery belongs to the pre-history of Derrida's distinction between the deconstructible and undeconstructible.

I am sure that Thomas Busch, who has spent years reading Marcel, did not see this coming. None of us did. It is at least as much a surprise for him as for the specialists who have spent years reading Derrida. At most we might have been tempted to make this comparison purely in the abstract, as a structural matter, probably in a conference hotel bar late at night with only a minimal memory of it in the morning. Without Baring's archival research, we would never have known that the young Derrida—who says his interest in philosophy was stimulated by a radio broadcast by Camus that he heard while growing up in Algeria—was importantly, I am tempted to say, decisively influenced by Marcel. This confirms, strengthens and elaborates Busch's hypothesis in *Circulating Being*, that certain underlying features of Existentialism are an irreducible component in poststructural, postmodern theory, in particular, its critique of totalizing thought.

Allow to me to add in conclusion that, on a personal note, this is a point in which both Tom Busch and I can take some satisfaction. The two of us, having come of age intellectually in an American Catholicism that was inching its way towards Vatican II, pressed the case of Existentialism and Phenomenology upon a philosophy department that, still steeped in mid-twentieth century revival of Scholasticism, was not a little skeptical about what these two young upstarts, newly arrived at Villanova, were trying to sell them.

Bibliography

Augustine. *Confessions*. Translated by F. J. Sheed. Indianapolis: Hackett, 1970.
Baring, Edward. *The Young Derrida and French Philosophy: 1945–1968*. Cambridge: Cambridge University Press, 2011.
Busch, Thomas W. *Circulating Being: From Embodiment to Incorporation: Essays on Late Existentialism*. New York: Fordham University Press, 1999.
Caputo, John D. *The Mystical Element in Heidegger's Thought*. Athens, OH: Ohio University Press, 1978; 2nd edition. New York: Fordham University Press, 1986.
———. *The Prayers and Tears of Jacques Derrida: Religion without Religion*. Bloomington: Indiana University Press, 1997.
Derrida, Jacques. *Of Grammatology*, corrected edition. Translated by Gayatri Spivak. Baltimore: Johns Hopkins University Press, 1997.
———. *The Problem of Genesis in Husserl's Philosophy*. Translated by Marian Hobson. Chicago: University of Chicago Press, 2003.
Gilson, Etienne. *Being and Some Philosophers*, 2nd edition. Toronto: Institute of Medieval Studies, 1952.
———. *L'Être et l'essence*, 2nd edition. Paris: J. Vrin, 1962.
Heidegger, Martin. *Being and Time*. Translated by John Macquarrie and Edward Robinson. New York: Harper & Row, 1962.
———. "Letter on Humanism." Translated by Frank A. Capuzzi and J. Glen Gray. In *Basic Writings*. Edited by David F. Krell, 2nd edition, 213–266. New York: Harper & Row, 1993.
———. *The Principle of Reason*. Translated by Reginald Lilly. Bloomington: Indiana University Press, 1991.
———. *Qu'est-ce que la métaphysique?* Translated by Henri Corbin. Paris: Gallimard, 1938.

———. "What is Metaphysics?" Translated by David F. Krell. In *Basic Writings*, edited by David F. Krell, 89–110. 2nd ed. New York: Harper & Row, 1993.

Lubac, Henri de. *The Drama of Atheist Humanism*. Translated by Edith Riley et al. London: Sheed & Ward, 1949.

Lyotard, Jean Francois. *The Postmodern Condition: A Report on Knowledge*. Translated by Geoff Bennington and Brian Massumi. Minneapolis: University Of Minnesota Press, 1984.

Marcel, Gabriel. *Being and Having: An Existentialist Diary*. Translated by Catherine Farrer. New York: Harper Torchbooks, 1965.

———. "Ma Relation avec Heidegger." In *Présence de Gabriel Marcel*, 25–38. Paris: Aubier, 1980.

———. *Metaphysical Journal*. Translated by Bernard Wall. Chicago: Regnery, 1952.

———. *The Mystery of Being, Vol. 1, Reflection and Mystery*. Translated by G. S. Fraser. Chicago: Regnery, 1960.

Maritain, Jacques. *Integral Humanism, Freedom in the Modern World, and A Letter on Independence*, revised edition. Translated by Otto Bird et al. Notre Dame, IN: University of Notre Dame Press, 1996.

Sartre, Jean Paul. *Being and Nothingness*. Translated by Hazel E. Barnes. New York: Philosophical Library, 1956.

———. *Existentialism Is a Humanism*. Translated by Carol Macomber. New Haven: Yale University Press, 2007.

2

Reading Marcel's Philosophy of Dialogical Inter-subjectivity in a Contemporary Light

—Sally Fischer

Gabriel Marcel developed a rich body of phenomenological thought that places particular emphasis on a description of embodied and dialogical relations that has relevance today toward fostering ethical respect for difference. In a world of often inhuman, technocratic thinking that appears both in social institutions and in interpersonal experiences, Marcel's notions of availability and creative fidelity offer correctives to a contemporary society that is witness to a disappearance of joy in favor of more egocentric and instantaneous "satisfactions" that are so central to our age of technics. His notion of "availability" as a central value-concept entails a receptive yet active attitude, in other words, a dialogical attitude, which calls for a freely chosen commitment, a "creative fidelity," or a lived, active, and open response to the situation at hand. His works include an insightful critique of instrumental rationality and its mode of the reduction of the other, both other persons and nature. From his rich body of work, we can elicit an ethics that calls for a shift in the way we think about and live our lives, opening us to a way of being in which we can construct dialogical situations through lived commitments. While his philosophical works are often woven together with a phenomenology of spiritual and religious consciousness, Marcel's work can, and I think, ought to be opened up again to consider his fruitful philosophical insights in a light that sets aside its religious aspects. In this chapter, I discuss an existential, dialogical ethics as a mode of being with others, based on an obligation to maintain an availability in which one remains open to the perspective of the other as a *real* other, and through which one attempts to get beneath or beyond what Marcel terms the spirit of abstraction, an attitude that yields objectification and domination. In stark contrast to the quasi-solipsism of contemporaries such as Sartre, Marcel offers an interpretation of joy and wisdom as an existential attitude that necessarily involves an openness or availability. Many of the concerns and ideas he addressed from the early 1920s to the 1960s—for example, a critique of technics or instrumental rationality, and a historicized, embodied, and decentered subject—were written before they were addressed, for example, by Heidegger in *A Question Concerning Technology*, or by Merleau-Ponty in *Phenomenology of Perception*. Merleau-Ponty once credited Marcel with allowing his contemporaries to understand perceptual experience in a new way in terms of his reflections on embodied participation in the world.[1] Eighty years later, I think that there is much in Marcel's philosophy of embodied participation that is still very relevant and fruitful toward an ethics of dialogical respect. My interest in this chapter is to highlight the connections between a Marcelian dialogical perspective that insists upon respect for the irreducible other, and an ethical perspectivism found in late Twentieth Century feminist thought. I am particularly interested in drawing connections to the ideas of ethical relations found in Luce Irigaray's *I love to you*. Because I purposefully ignore most of the religious aspects of Marcel's work, my goal in this reading of Marcel is obviously not an all-encompassing retrieval, but rather to do justice to an aspect of his philosophy in a way that brings to light the lasting fecundity of much of what he had to say, and that bears upon ethical and social issues in our contemporary world.

My idea to go back to Marcel's works and to reread them in a new light first occurred when I read Luce Irigaray's *I love to you* in the late 1990s and was startled by the similarity of many of their ideas and concerns. The fact that Marcel was a Christian existentialist and that Irigaray is a postmodern, deconstructivist feminist might make them appear to be an unusual pair. While critical of the methodology of phenomenology itself, Irigaray radically deepens the existential phenomenologists' critique of the sovereign, rational subject of Modernity by recognizing that the traditional understanding of the subject has been ontologically, discursively, and historically gender-biased. Yet many of her ethical aims are remarkably similar to Marcel's. Particularly in *I love to you*, she writes about the need for a perceptual relation that does not renounce the sensible to the universal/abstract,

---

1. Merleau-Ponty, "Etre et Avoir."

but is rather a material and a spiritual contemplation. Like Marcel, she is critical of the emphasis on instrumental and technocratic rationality and distinguishes (as does Marcel) wisdom from this kind of rationality. Both share an ethical concern with the fundamental irreducibility of the other, while at the same time call for a dialogical inter-subjectivity. Furthermore, both philosophers have attempted, as Irigaray says, to "recommence everything," to go back to experience and re-articulate the categories by which we understand our selves, subject-object divisions, our relations to others and to the natural world. While each effects their philosophical critiques of Modern subjectivity differently, and with somewhat different goals, there are, nevertheless, many shared ideas and values regarding the way that they both call for a general shift in the way we live our lives and relate to other humans and to the non-human world. Both, in strikingly similar ways, are critical of Modern conceptions of interpersonal relations, especially those inherited from Descartes and Hegel. Below I discuss the aspects of their respective philosophies that are relevant to a dialogical ethics, and suggest how Marcel's ideas might benefit from a critical reconsideration in terms of gender and racial perspectives.

Recuperating Dialogical Life in a World of Abstraction

Some of Marcel's most passionate writing can be found in his analysis and critique of the spirit of abstraction and its accompanying framework of technics—socio-economic, discursive, and personal—through which we understand and relate to the world and to others in terms of impersonal functions and objectifying attitudes. In the spirit of abstraction, our desires and our fears serve as the wellspring from which we invent appropriate techniques. But Marcel is no Luddite—he is aware of naïve intellectual attacks on technical progress, and he clearly recognizes that much of our technical progress should be welcomed as a liberation from the forces of nature. The problem, rather, is when a spirit of abstraction in general pervades our contemporary societies. As early as 1933 he claims: "man is *at the mercy of his technics*. This must be understood to mean that he is increasingly incapable of controlling his technics, or rather of *controlling his own control*."[2] According to Marcel, to be caught up in and defined by this spirit of abstraction represents a degradation of our very being. In his work, *The Decline of Wisdom*, he offers examples from medicine, educational and mental health testing, the lives of workers, particularly factory life, and the rise of big business. He describes how "small enterprises, that is to say those

---

2. Marcel, "Ontological Mystery," 31; Marcel's emphasis.

which are really on a human scale, are systematically penalized in favor of enormous and dehumanized concerns. Still another [example] is the danger to such professions as medicine when they are run by functionaries."[3] The systemic nature of technics and the spirit of abstraction can lead to despair. In his essay, "On the Ontological Mystery," he states: "from this standpoint, despair consists in the recognition of the ultimate inefficacy of all technics, joined with the inability to change over to a new ground . . ."[4]

To better understand what Marcel might mean by this new ground, let us consider briefly the distinction he makes between having and being, and likewise between the realm of the problematical, and the realm of mystery or the meta-problematical. Having involves a relationship where the self is set apart from or over against the other. This involves objective, or abstract thought, e.g., the impersonal thinking and the kind of relationship to the object we would like the mechanic to use when we need the engine fixed. But having can become a general mode of living as well: we can relate to a meal as a function to quickly fuel our bodies rather than as an occasion to really be with another; an artwork can be valued only as an economic investment, rather than a site of beauty or contemplation. Epistemologically, in the mode of having, one defines thinking as the concept constituted in consciousness, considered from a third-person perspective. Marcel calls this the realm of the problematical, which implies a contrast between within and without. There is an obvious connection, then, between this mode of having and our larger, lived framework of technics. But not all of our relations with things and with persons are possessive, abstract, or purely functional. Not all of our possessions "swallow us up."[5] In his book, *Being and Having*, Marcel recognizes that at the other end of the spectrum, our relationship with things, e.g., a beloved garden or violin, may be aspects of the world with which we are vitally and creatively bound in a personal, emotional, and perhaps spiritual sense.[6]

In contrast to having-as-possession, being involves openness, a kind of hospitality, what Marcel calls an "availability" that transcends the mode of having and instead implies a dialogical openness and respect for the other who remains irreducible. Being, for Marcel, is always a being-with, and it is precisely being *involved* in a relation, not simply taking the spectator view, that undercuts the Cartesian subject-object bifurcation. It is also at this level of being that we find ourselves confronted with a mystery, or the

---

3. Marcel, *Decline of Wisdom*, 47.
4. Marcel, "Ontological Mystery," 30.
5. Marcel, *Being and Having*, 152.
6. Ibid., 165.

meta-problematical, since we are reflecting from our site of involvement, rather than attempting an objective, theoretical stance. While Sartre and Heidegger focus on anxiety or angst as the premiere existential moods that disclose our being, for Marcel, love is the essential ontological datum that opens up this mode of being-with. Love is the condition of possibility for the spiritual bond of presence with another, irreducible to my grasp. Love not as erotic possession, but as agapeic love, applicable to both human and non-human being. In fact, in his essay, "Life and the Sacred," Marcel writes of an experience he had in a sacred grove in Japan—an encounter with the forest that involved neither the objectifying Sartrean gaze nor the abstract materialist reduction of the biologist, but rather a material and spiritual contemplation. Here we must give the term "spiritual" a broad definition. In fact, in that same text, where Marcel discusses what he sees as the essential problem of the "desacralization of life" he is clear that "something sacred, whose nature remains yet to be determined, can exist for an individual who refuses all ritualism and belong to no church."[7] When, in this example, non-human beings become the objects of or the opening to contemplation, they are not related to solely in terms of their functions, material aspects, nor are they simply regarded as valuable for evoking an affective response. He writes: "If the reactions evoked are affective only, then they cannot be regarded as relevant in this context. But we are in fact beyond simple affectivity here. The sacred is such only if it determines a course of action. This course of action is contrary to everything resembling technique, or, even more concretely, to everything that might be mere know-how or manipulation."[8] Marcel goes on to discuss the central role of respect here, which, manifested perhaps in silence, recognizes the integrity or dignity of the other human or non-human being. It is here that we find ourselves at the level of an ontological mystery—as he says: "life is, as it were surprised at its center; and must it not be said that this center is revealed only to love?"[9] Here, as elsewhere in Marcel's texts, we find the seeds of a care ethic: describing what he means by "love," he gives examples of caring for babies, animals, and even flowers. Such loving care is an art, not reducible to a technique, and "this art implies a gift of self, a reverential attitude designated by the term "piety." This attitude is inconsistent with the pretension of mastering something in order to exploit it."[10] But such an ethics of care cannot be reduced or abstracted into universal maxims.

7. Marcel, "Life and the Sacred," 109.
8. Ibid., 110.
9. Ibid., 113.
10. Ibid., 114.

So, if ethical being-with arises out of my involvement in a situation, it is only because from the start I am an embodied subject in-the-world, and not a constituting consciousness shut off from the world. In his 1925 essay, "Existence and Objectivity," he rejects both an idealist and a mechanistic notion of the body, instead claiming, "I am my body," meaning that I am this situated body-subject, and thereby undercutting the Cartesian bifurcation of mind and body, and self and world.[11] Similar to Merleau-Ponty and Heidegger, Marcel thus begins from a notion of incarnate existence, or embodied participation in the world with others as a fundamental aspect of our being. Existence begins with the "I am" rather than with the Cartesian "I think." In volume one of *The Mystery of Being*, he accuses idealism of "thingifying the self," and is clear throughout that text that he is not aiming to do a phenomenology that reduces the self or experience to an object.[12] Marcel's understanding of the self, then, includes those aspects of "withness" when he claims: "the personal pronoun 'I' should be taken here in its widest sense. For it is not a matter only of that finite individuality that I myself am . . ."[13] In fact, Marcel thinks that it is only by use of a contemplative secondary reflection, not a logical analytical argument, that we can shed some light on the "disquieting ambiguity"[14] of the self and its exigence of being, which is always already an exigence of being-with.[15]

The difficulty both in life and in philosophy is to try to understand and to recuperate this possible mode of being-with or ethical inter-subjectivity and to shift away from the spirit of abstraction. Marcel's term "secondary reflection" describes a reflective activity that tries to elucidate experience in a non-objectifying, non-fragmenting way—i.e., a reflection in which I am not a spectator but rather in which and through which I am involved. While Paul Ricoeur and others say his attempts at secondary reflection border on mysticism, Marcel defends his attempts at a *philosophical* secondary reflection in such little-read works as *The Decline of Wisdom*. In this text, he tries, somewhat successfully, to describe wisdom as an ongoing practice, a way or mode of being that opposes a hubristic spirit of abstraction. Secondary reflection, here, implies a meta-technical reflective activity that arises out of a habitual stance of "gratitude"—a "wakefulness, a vigilance of the

---

11. Marcel, "Existence and Objectivity," 65.
12. Marcel, *Mystery of Being*, 61.
13. Ibid., 52.
14. Ibid., 103.
15. In "On the Ontological Mystery" Marcel describes this exigence of being-with as fundamental, otherwise despair would not be such a pervasive response to our era of technics and its mode of having-as-possession.

soul attentive not to lose what it regards as of lasting value."[16] Furthermore, secondary reflection involves a creative and not simply passive receptivity as a way of being, and this requires an openness, gratitude, and what Marcel calls consciousness of the sacred.[17] Ultimately, secondary reflection is a recuperative process (in thought and practice), requiring an existential mode of "ingatheredness," a re-collection of oneself. There are tones here of Nietzsche's notion of becoming who you are, as well as Heidegger's anticipatory resoluteness, but for Marcel, the emphasis of this experience is one which opens up my being in relation with others in a much deeper sense than we find in Heidegger's *Mitsein*. Ingatheredness requires a listening, but Marcel distinguishes different kinds of listening: one that may hear the words but effectively shut oneself off from the other, and an attentive listening that opens up a presence *with* the other. It is obviously the latter that sets the stage for both understanding and living a more genuine inter-subjective relation with the other.

Constructing Dialogical Life in a World of Sexual Indifference

Irigaray's critique of much of the Western tradition of philosophical discourse—a discourse that has shaped the categories and concepts that we use, not only in philosophy, but in other knowledges as well, such as law, biology, psychology, etc.—centers around exposing the implicit (and sometimes explicit) logic of the hierarchical binary structure which often has caged gender-biased concepts (including subjectivity, rationality, citizenship) as "neutral" or universal. What Irigaray calls the "fraternal" economy (exchange between members of the male sex) has taken place empirically in history in terms of embodied experience, where for example, women have largely been commodities (objects) of exchange (in marriage laws, for example) between male subjects. However, the sense in which Irigaray exposes this economy cuts deeper; it is part of the very structure of our language in the general discourse of the West. She correctly claims: "Language and its values reflect the social order and vice versa."[18] (She argues that subjectivity, in its many social, cultural, and religious manifestations, has not been represented in terms of real, sexed speaking subjects, but has instead been predicated on one morphology and one style of embodied experience.) While thinkers like Nietzsche, Marcel, Merleau-Ponty, and Heidegger cri-

---

16. Marcel, *Decline of Wisdom*, 26.
17. Ibid., 32–33.
18. Irigaray, *I love to you*, 66.

tiqued the Cartesian notion of subjectivity defined as a rational subject and juxtaposed with the body-object, philosophers such as Irigaray, building on earlier work from Simone de Beauvoir, argue that subjectivity in the West has also been ordered around male morphology and masculine parameters yet it is caged as "neutral." Thus, according to Irigaray, there has been no place for the subject *as* woman, since this so-called "neutral" subjectivity is already represented and structured as that which is not female/feminine. Most liberal feminists, she thinks for example, "describe what a woman is within the horizon of a male subject's culture."[19] While her focus is thus on the pervasive discursive power of patriarchy, my understanding of a Marcelian dialogical ethics, which I will discuss in the last section of this chapter, will include ethical recognition for racial, ethnic, and non-binary sexual differences. Nevertheless, I think that Irigaray's approach can be useful toward envisioning necessary conditions for ethical recognition of multiple and intertwining sets of differences, even if her own work remains stuck in a binary notion of sexual difference.

The creative aspect of Irigaray's task centers around envisioning the beginnings of a new symbolic order, a new ontology of embodiment, and rethinking the necessary conditions of genuinely dialogical relations that include a recognition of real differences. While her focus has generally been on critiquing the sexual *in*difference in the discourses of philosophy, psychoanalysis, and law, we can witness the pervasive ignorance of or lack of respect for sexual difference in art, religion, politics, and in general culture. *Asserting* sexual difference, she thinks, is a necessary strategy if we are going to suppose that we can have an inter-subjectivity which arises out of two subjects, speaking from the perspective of their own respective morphologies, and their own differently situated experiences. In other words, asserting sexual difference means asserting a place for the woman-subject to speak as a woman on her own terms, and not as that falsely neutral (pseudo-masculine) subject.[20] Through the use of metonymy, Irigaray finds a way to

---

19. Ibid., 61. A perfect example of this in the United States would be Sheryl Sandberg's book, *Lean In*. While ostensibly supporting feminism, the book advises women to strive harder to succeed by the norms of an "ideal-worker," the model of which was set by a patriarchal family structure in a society without universal paid family leave or quality subsidized childcare. The background assumptions in the book are those of privileged wealth and dual parenting.

20. For example, towards this new ontology of embodiment, Irigaray's uses metonymic devices such as what she calls "the two lips" and "the mechanics of fluidity" to serve as concepts meant to disrupt the traditional categories of Western thought by blurring the dichotomies of subject/object, inside/outside, active/passive, unity/plurality, etc. (Irigaray, "When Our Lips Speak Together"). Her concept of fluidity represents the contiguous, fluid, and dynamic relation between the two lips/leaves, as the

represent the female/feminine in a manner that links a discursive order with sexed embodiment, and that can serve as a starting point for the construction of new myths, fictions, of a new female imaginary, which, she thinks, could perhaps assist in the birth of a new social order beyond patriarchy. It is important to note that Irigaray is asserting the *connection* between discourse and embodiment, but does not think that connection is ahistorical or static. "For the generic universal is not transhistorical."[21] Embodiment and discursive concepts are undoubtedly historical, and asserting sexual difference requires women of different races and ethnicities, in all kinds of fields, within all kinds of discourses to speak their experiences in a way that ruptures and transforms masculinist discourse and its assumptions. Since the subject is historical, embodied, situated in terms of class, race, etc., as well as sexed, the call for a recognition and creation of sexual difference is not an essentialism, but an ongoing process. In other words, this utopic ideal is not static, but rather an ongoing goal of attaining genuinely dialogical rather than monological relations, as well as a social-linguistic situation that fosters dialogue through the recognition of full personhood of differently embodied persons.

In her book, *I love to you*, Irigaray argues that in order to have genuinely inter-subjective and dialogical relations, two things must obtain: First, we must create and represent new symbolic orders of sexed identity. She claims: "[I]f the other is not defined in his or her actual reality, there is only an other me, not real others."[22] And secondly, in terms of lived experience, we must also approach the other with the acknowledgement that "I am not everything."[23] This is an important facet of Irigaray's ethics—what she calls the role of the "negative," that interval between myself and other that is protective of the reduction of myself to the other, and of the other to me. A central feature of *I love to you* involves a critique of Hegelian dialectics, hence her rereading of the role of the "negative" as a locus of respect and irreducibility, rather than as a site of overcoming that subsumes the Other into the Same. Marcel's works, too, struggle with the dangers that lie in Hegelian and Cartesian idealism. In *Being and Having*, he writes: "The world of the

---

dual aspect of ourselves as body-subjects in its redoubling as two sensing-sensibles, neither side solely subject or object. Irigaray uses the notion of the "two lips" as a metonymic device that links a new discursive and ontological order to the female body, and furthermore, as a way to rethink relations *between* embodied subjects. Her use of metonymy and her attempts to link ontology to the female body are not meant to be the complete and final definition of a woman's identity or ontology.

21. Irigaray, *I love to you*, 112.
22. Ibid., 61.
23. Ibid., 51.

Same and the Other is the world of the identifiable. Insofar as I remain its prisoner, I surround myself with a zone of separation . . . according to the category of Having."[24] For both Marcel and for Irigaray, we must move toward both a new economy of relations—practically, epistemologically, and ontologically—in order to move beyond master-slave dialectics and towards a more fecund and dialogical understanding and practice of inter-subjective personhood. The negative in sexual difference means an acceptance of the limits of my gender and recognition of the irreducibility of the other.

Irigaray thinks that this acceptance of the limits of my gender (and I would add other culturally significant limiting differences) is a necessary condition for cultivating oneself and humanity. She writes: "It is significant that in our culture, man thinks or prays by estranging himself from his body, and that thinking or praying do not assist him in becoming incarnate, becoming flesh."[25] For Irigaray, rather, "sacrifice [of one's embodiment, of the awareness of one's natural immediacy] is a sign of a lack of contemplation (*recueillement*)."[26] She claims that this attempt to estrange himself from his body, in general, and from his morphology as *limited*, in particular, is an error: "[Man] should rather understand that he represents only half of humanity but it is this condition that permits him to postulate the infinite without an *anti-natural* labor of the negative. The fact of being half enables the whole to be constructed without denying what it is."[27] Here, Irigaray understands *recueillement* as "ingathering," connoting a returning to or re-collecting the embodied self as a ground for its cultivation: "It remains for us to go beyond the [dualistic, phallocentric, and masculinist] origin so as to learn how to ingather ourselves within ourselves and to think."[28] Her intention is to assure the cultivation of our differently sexed identities so that we may "become who we are." "Equally, it is to spiritualize my nature in order to create with the other."[29] Cultivation of oneself and of one's relations with others goes hand in hand, and both require a non-imperialist attitude of accepting the limits of one's gender (and race, class, ethnicity, etc.). Similarly, in *Man Against Mass Society*, Marcel says: "the spirit of abstraction can in certain respects be regarded as the transposition of the attitude of imperialism to the mental plane."[30] The danger of sexual indifference in the

24. Marcel, *Being and Having*, 153.
25. Irigaray, *I love to you*, 40.
26. Ibid.
27. Ibid., 41.
28. Ibid., 40.
29. Ibid., 39.
30. Marcel, *Mass Society*, 155.

discourses of the West that Irigaray sees is that those discourses and their truth claims precisely claim to estrange thinking from corporeal existence at the same time that they have actually predicated thinking and speaking (and the institutions built on them) upon one sexed identity: male morphology[31] and historically masculine experience. Marcel was keenly aware of the dangers of a false universality and its estrangement from embodied experience that comprise a spirit of abstraction, and he also recognized that meaningful, lived experience arises contextually out of certain intelligible background structures of which the expressive subject is not aware. In his essay, "Gabriel Marcel: Reflection as Interpretation," Thomas Busch argues that, for Marcel, the situated self "is constrained to use expressive capacities, the contingent categories of meaning, borrowed from (or produced by) that very situatedness."[32] Busch notes that: "The traditional puzzle about mind and body, for example, must include, in determining its intelligibility, the experience of one who is embodied. An account of society must include reference to the lived experiences of its members, who belong to it as a shared form of life. But, as noted, all expressions of lived experience involve interpretation and a rejection of translation into the 'impersonal.'"[33] It is not surprising for the time period that Marcel did not investigate (even after de Beauvoir's *Second Sex* was published in 1949) the patriarchal logic of those very discursive, social, and, institutional intelligible background structures that rendered invisible and unheard the potential expressiveness of subjects whose embodied experiences lie outside (or served as the tain in the mirror for) the conceptual and institutional norms. The translation into the impersonal, "borrowed from (or produced by) that very situatedness"—masculinist and Eurocentric—also rendered the majority of lived experiences, to borrow Charles Mills' phrase, "subpersonal."[34] We have seen that Marcel was critical of the attitude of imperialism and of the estrangement from embodied experience that comprises a (false) universality in the spirit of abstraction. In Marcel's philosophy we find an unbreakable connection between ontology, social criticism, and interpersonal ethical relations, but this will have to be taken-up and reconsidered in contemporary terms in order to remain a living existentialism.

---

31. "Morphology" is not simple sexed anatomy, but rather the way the sexed body is taken up in culture.

32. Busch, "Reflection as Interpretation," 32.

33. Ibid., 33.

34. In his book, *Blackness Visible*, Mills carefully demonstrates the way the ontology of experience is caged such that: "White experience is embedded as normative, and the embedding is so deep that its normativity is not even identified as such" (10).

"You, who will never be mine": Dialogical Life as Lived Commitment

An important aspect of Irigaray's philosophy, as we have seen, is the writing of a new ontology of female embodiment with the larger aim of fostering genuinely inter-subjective relationships, so that each person's subjectivity is articulated along the lines of their own lived morphology: "She should . . . gather herself within herself in order to accomplish her gender's perfection for herself, for the man she loves, for her children, but equally for civil society, for the world of culture . . ."[35] While Marcel obviously does not touch on this topic of asserting difference in his philosophy of being, there are nevertheless many interesting points of striking overlap between other aspects of their accounts of ethical being and its emphasis on the dialogical, and these shared themes highlight important facets of a contemporary Marcelian ethics of dialogical recognition. One of these themes is a non-instrumental relation with nature. It is no surprise that throughout many of her works, Irigaray interprets interpersonal relations in a way that does not depend upon an exchange of human commodities, but in *I love to you*, there is also a central focus on re-interpreting a relation with non-human nature that does not involve commodification and instrumental reason. Marcel's interpretation and description of the ontology of the self coincides with his social criticism of technics and our relationships of abstraction, mostly toward human beings, yet even regarding our relation with non-human nature he also describes the mode of wonder and contemplation of the natural world in ontological terms: "Even leaving aside any belief in a divine creator, the naturalist experiences a kind of wonder before the fineness and complexity of he structure he observes . . . Sanctity here does not refer to a quality of moral disposition in the properly rational sense of this word. We are rather on the level of ontology."[36] It is on the level of being, not having, that the person may overcome the current separation between human and nature. Irigaray gives a similar example of a shift from instrumental reason to a kind of contemplation that involves respecting the integrity of the other being. She gives the example of the Buddha gazing at the flower: ". . . Buddha's gazing at the flower is not an inattentive or predatory gaze, nor the decline of the speculative flesh. It is both material and spiritual contemplation . . . This contemplation is also a training in finding pleasure while respecting what does not belong to me."[37] Both Irigaray and

---

35. Irigaray, *I love to you*, 27.
36. Marcel, "Life and the Sacred," 117.
37. Irigaray, *I love to you*, 24.

Marcel, then, are concerned about turning human and non-human beings simply into objects of the predatory gaze, a possible result of our notion of the imperialist, rational subject in its mode of having-as-possession. Marcel writes: "[C]ontemplation insofar as it cannot be simply equated with the spectator's attitude, and in a deep sense is even in an opposite pole from that attitude, must be considered as a mode of participation, even as one of participation's most intimate modes."[38] This is what Irigaray meant when we saw that she claimed that sacrifice of one's natural immediacy of embodied participation is a sign of *lack* of contemplation: "Take this as an example: do we have to fell a tree before cultivating it? If that were the case, what would we cultivate? An idea of the tree, but not the tree itself."[39]

Connected to this notion of a non-objectifying contemplation, Irigaray and Marcel are each critical of the traditional Western epistemologies' reliance on oculocentric metaphors, which tend to freeze the object and preclude a dialogical relation with other human and non-human beings. In his text on Marcel, Sam Keen claims: "Marcel's philosophical stance is essentially auditory rather than optical. He is not the spectator who looks for a world of structures that may be clearly and distinctly seen. He listens to and responds to 'voices' and 'calls' that make up the symphony of being."[40] Notions of listening are central to both philosophers' accounts of situated inter-subjectivity. Irigaray, like Marcel, places deep listening as an inherently necessary facet of ethical recognition:

> Thus, *I am listening to you* is not to expect or hear some information from you, nor is it the pure expression of sentiment . . . *I am listening to you* is to listen to your words as something unique, irreducible, especially to my own, as something new, yet unknown. It is to hear them as the manifestation of an intention, of human and spiritual development . . . I am listening to you not on the basis of what I know, I feel, I already am, nor in terms of what the world and language already are, thus in a formalistic manner so to speak. I am listening to you rather as the revelation of a truth that has yet to manifest itself . . . If I am to be quiet and listen, listen to you, without presupposition, without making hidden demands—on you or on myself—the world must not be sealed already, it must still be open, the future not determined by the past.[41]

---

38. Marcel, *Mystery of Being*, 152.
39. Irigaray, *I love to you*, 40.
40. Keen, *Marcel*, 14.
41. Irigaray, *I love to you*, 117.

This kind of deep listening is the foundation for the art of care that Marcel says implies a gift of self, an availability towards the other, and which can only be understood through secondary reflection involving a creative receptivity within, as Irigaray says, "a world [which] must not be sealed already."

Additionally, Irigaray places a special emphasis on the relation of touch to her rereading of inter-subjective perceptual relations. Touch tends to both blur the subject-object distinction, as well as represent a contiguity between body-subjects, whereas visual metaphors (which we find in most of the tradition, from Plato to Freud and Sartre) tend to emphasize distance and subject-object relations. Touch can yield violence and erasure when it reduces the other to an object, but in the mode of being rather than having, it also can yield a dialogical contiguity, essential to the art of care. In her essay, "When Our Lips Speak Together," the lips are a metonymic expression of contiguity and of dialogical relations between two women (she leaves it unclear whether they are friends, lovers, mother-daughter, or author-reader) with the exigency to speak, in their own terms, their own embodied participation, and to open up a place for the other in her becoming. This becoming requires language beyond or outside of patriarchal norms and concepts: "If we keep on speaking the same language together, we're going to reproduce the same history ... The same difficulties, the same impossibility of making connections."[42] Deep listening and availability are necessary facets of a kind of secondary reflection as a *creative* enterprise—one that could possibly be the site of constructing difference, of constructing perspectives that have hitherto been marginalized. Later, in the same essay, she writes: "If we don't invent a language, if we don't find our body's language, we will have too few gestures to accompany our story. We shall tire of the same ones, and leave our desires unexpressed, unrealized. Asleep again, we shall fall back upon the words of men."[43] Both Irigaray and Marcel describe agapeic love, or at least a non-possessive love, as the site or opening of embodied inter-subjectivity as dialogical, and both understand dialogical relations as the ground for cultivation of the self, and for creative building-together. We have seen that for Marcel, love thus offers a way to get inside a dialogical relation with another. "[L]ove as the breaking of the tension between the self and the other, appears to me what one might call the essential ontological datum. I think ... that the science of ontology will not get out of the scholastic rut until it takes full cognizance of the fact that love comes first."[44] The experience of love, then, opens up a unique way inside a deeper presence with

---

42. Irigaray, "When Our Lips Speak Together," 205.
43. Ibid., 214.
44. Marcel, *Being and Having*, 167.

another, who is at the same time irreducible to my grasp, in other words, the other as "thou." The meaning of Irigaray's title, "I love *to* you" suggests an offering of love as a gift. Rather than using "I love *you*" (you, as direct *object*), she uses the indirect voice, suggesting that I offer to you, another subject, this gift of love, listening, openness. Love in this way symbolizes inherent respect for the loved one's being as full personhood, as a thou who speaks from their own (perhaps differently) embodied perspective.

The consonant approach of these two thinkers, emphasizing deep listening and a non-imperialist attitude as vital to both the cultivation of the self and to developing and maintaining ethical relations with others, is a good starting-point for a dialogical recognition of difference in contemporary terms. We have seen that, for Marcel, expressions of lived experiences ought to involve "a rejection of translation into the impersonal," as Busch correctly notes, but we also can see that many marginalized voices have been rendered subpersonal as well—in law, social and economic sanctions, and in their political voices. It is not simply a general spirit of abstraction that, in the United States, has yielded the "new Jim Crow," kept women's wages at around 80 percent of men's, or rates of gender and racial violence high. Social, political, and institutional relations of subjugation and inequity play out in individual terms and vice versa. If we take Irigaray's critique of sexual indifference seriously (as I think we should, in all its intersectional dimensions of difference), then the "impersonal" has a two-fold danger that a Marcelian dialogical ethics must overcome in order to be relevant to a contemporary ethical world: first, the general abstraction from a personalist perspective in a technocratic, digital world, where bureaucracy and social media are as likely to close off as open up deep listening; second, larger and generally unacknowledged biases in discursive concepts and social institutions. The latter are the culmination of millennia of patriarchal, heteronormative, and Eurocentric norms that preclude personalist expressions of the experiences of non-whites, women, and LGBTQ persons having social and economic power and political relevance on their own terms, according to their own morphologies and experiences. The "irreducible other" that Marcel values in his time period often seems fairly reducible to a patriarchal, hetero-normative, and Eurocentric worldview from our own vantage point. So, here we see the crux of the matter: Can a Marcelian philosophy of dialogical inter-subjectivity be "updated" to include multiple kinds of other embodied perspectives (here, through Irigaray, we mostly considered sexed others, but also race, class, gender-orientation, etc.)? I think that the necessary conditions for ethical inter-subjectivity that Irigaray lays out are helpful here for also reconsidering a Marcelian dialogical ethics in our contemporary world. It seems to me that these conditions must obtain: (1) others are recognized as *real* others, expressed in discourses and in institutions on their own terms, grounded in their own embodied experience, rather than as so-called universal or neutral subjects, and that (2) the kind of availability and irreducibility he describes requires a reciprocal *recognition*, a stance that maintains "I am not everything" in terms of both personal expression and in larger institutional and discursive background structures.[45] In terms of his examples and his particular assumptions at that time about men and women, Marcel certainly was guilty of not only what Irigaray calls sexual indifference, but of old-fashioned empirical sexism and patriarchal religious dogma. He sometimes advocates a return to the patriarchal family order (which he saw disintegrating in the 1950s!) and includes rants about the abominable use of birth control. He is horrified by gender roles in Soviet communism, and finds it outlandish that a colleague would even suggest that women be paid for their work as homemakers. But rather than critique Marcel for obvious blind-spots arising out of his own historical situation as well as his occasional lapsing into Catholic ideology, I think that a Marcelian notion of dialogical participation is amenable to sexual, racial, and ethnic differences. Because Marcel rejects the individualist and solipsistic subject in favor of a decentered and dialogical subject, already we have a subject "poised" for the possibility of constructing and respecting difference, as long as there is an open commitment to maintaining availability and deep listening on individual and social levels.

It might be helpful to briefly consider what might be some Irigaryan concerns (since, to my knowledge, she has written no direct critique of Marcel's thought) regarding Marcel's *phenomenological* approach that may hinder a deeper recognition of difference. In her work, *The Ethics of Sexual Difference*, Luce Irigaray critiques the philosophy of Merleau-Ponty, whose philosophy of embodied subjectivity bears some resemblance to Marcel's, since they both understand the body-subject as decentered, hermeneutical, and dialogical. In her chapter on Merleau-Ponty, Irigaray is wary of a hermeneutics that closes in on its object, and precludes real respect for difference: she sees the danger of sexually indifferent language as that whereby the subject, "closes his circle, his bubble"—i.e., that "the speaking body of the subject is in some way archeologically structured by an already spoken

---

45. An example of the failure of these two conditions currently in the United States is the reaction among a large percentage of the white community on social media to the *Black Lives Matter* campaign. Responses such as "All Lives Matter" have missed the very point of the importance of hearing perspectives from black Americans who have systematically and institutionally been categorized as "subpersons," often with violent outcomes. The "all" in the "All Lives Matter" response only reifies the unacknowledged white privilege in the name of a false universal.

language . . ."⁴⁶ For Merleau-Ponty, there is a dialectic between sedimented and creative language, and this must be understood as an *open* hermeneutics and as diachronic movement. Thus, in a nutshell, I would argue that her criticism of Merleau-Ponty's thought here is not valid.⁴⁷ But her concerns are nevertheless useful to consider for the purpose of more closely examining Marcel's thought, and whether Marcel's notion of the subject as embodied participation is caught up in a closed hermeneutic "bubble." In other words, is Marcel's notion of secondary reflection one where its re-collective and recuperative functions are inherently conservative; one that would preclude a historical, perspectivist understanding grounded in cultivating diverse participant expressions that are inclusive of non-dominant embodied perspectives?

In *The Decline of Wisdom*, Marcel paints a picture of the sage, who is not caught up in an egoistic, materialistic life, and who maintains a creative openness, an availability towards others, opening up a possible inter-subjective presence with the irreducible other as "thou." An important feature of this ethical life involves a different kind of reflection, secondary reflection, which, as we have seen, entails creative interpretation arising out of an inner grip (ingatheredness) of the self. Unlike Aristotle's *phronimos*, the wisdom of Marcel's sage is existential-historical. Secondary reflection aimed at one's own being can be recuperative, or recollective in terms of an existential calling of oneself to oneself in a creative commitment, as a counterpoise to losing oneself in a world of abstraction and technics where we are reduced to functions.⁴⁸ But it's not re-collective in the sense of being static, or accomplishing a complete return. His understanding of the self is a hermeneutic temporality, and secondary reflection is, as we have seen, a creative process. On a larger scale, even if we acknowledge the relationship with the "vertically" transcendent (which I have largely excluded in my reading), we find in Marcel's phenomenology a diachronic element to subjectivity, since secondary reflection arises out of our being involved in a situation, which is historical. In the previous section, we saw that Thomas Busch argues that secondary reflection is "inevitably interpretive," since, as Marcel says in *Man Against Mass Society* (and Busch quotes in *Circulating Being*): "The very note of our human condition, is, in fact, that it is not assimilable to some kind of objective and already existing structure which we have merely to uncover and explore. The human condition, whatever may be the foundations on which it ultimately rests, seems to be in some ways

---

46. Irigaray, *Sexual Difference*, 176.
47. I offer a more thorough argument in "Social Ecology and the Flesh."
48. Marcel, *Man Against*, 174.

dependent on the very manner in which it is understood."⁴⁹ Like the Marcel's picture of the sage, the intelligible background structures through which we understand the human condition are also existential-historical, and can be reconstructed to include multiple perspectives, but that requires a creative commitment. Here, I think Marcel would agree with Nietzsche: "There is *only* a perspective seeing, *only* a perspective "knowing"; and the *more* affects we allow to speak about one thing, the *more* eyes, different eyes, we can use to observe one thing, the more complete will our "concept" of this thing, our "objectivity" be."⁵⁰ Marcel recognizes that the human condition is "in some ways dependent upon the manner in which it is understood" and so if we are to have a richer understanding of ourselves, and be able to cultivate our selves personally (even those positioned in privilege), we need these different eyes, different voices.

Unlike the individualism of Nietzsche, however, throughout Marcel's thought we find the ground for an existential, *dialogical* ethics that rests upon fidelity as participation *with* the other—fidelity to maintain availability. Central to a Marcelian ethical shift from having to being is thus a *commitment* to try to approach dialogue with others who are irreducible to me; it is to try to engage in deep listening in a way that would allow my own perspective to bend or stretch to be able to begin to understand those whose *own* embodied experiences are quite different from mine.

Moving from the context of interpersonal relations to a consideration of larger perspectives, might allow us to see the relevance of a Marcelian dialogical ethic writ large. Patricia Hill Collins, in her work, *Black Feminist Thought*, begins her epistemology of the politics of subjugation and of empowerment from the participant perspective:

> Living life as an African-American woman is a necessary prerequisite for producing Black feminist thought because within Black women's communities thought is validated and produced with reference to a particular set of historical, material, and epistemological conditions . . . However, [Black women's] tenuous status in academic institutions led them to adhere to Eurocentric masculinist epistemologies so that their work would be accepted as scholarly. As a result, while they produced Black feminist thought, those African-American women most likely to gain academic credentials were often least likely to produce

---

49. Ibid., 98.
50. Nietzsche, *Genealogy*, 119.

Black Feminist thought that used an Afrocentric feminist epistemology.[51]

Here, within an academic context, we can understand the weight of dominant perspectives in reducing or erasing difference, often unknowingly through white-privilege and male-privilege. Mills writes: "[T]he relation to the white Other is crucial, an other not on an equal plane but with the supervisory power to determine whether one appears to (public) view and how one (privately) appears in one's own eyes."[52] This kind of "ontological elimination" that Mills describes is difficult to overcome because it requires not only "asserting difference" from non-dominant groups, but moreover a commitment among privileged groups aligned with the normalizing view—here, white and masculinist—to acknowledge and to remember that their perspective is as *situated* as much as black, feminist, and Afrocentric. From a Marcelian ethics, we must ask: what sort of vigilance is needed to maintain an openness or availability—not to relativism, but rather, as Hill Collins says, to "bring Black women's [and other marginalized group's] standpoint to larger epistemological dialogues"? In an academic, as well as in a larger and more general political context, this requires an ethical perspectivism between participants, irreducible to the other, but with a simultaneous commitment to dialogue. In her chapter of *I love to you* titled, "You Who Will Never Be Mine," Irigaray writes: "Recognizing you means or implies respecting you as other, accepting that I draw myself to a halt before you as before something insurmountable, a mystery, a freedom that will never be mine . . . I recognize you is the one condition for the existence of the *I, you and we*."[53] The lived, rather than abstract, commitment to dialogue within a perspectivist approach, grounded in a respect for "you who will never be mine" is necessary—even if never fully realizable—whether in an academic classroom or in a police department suffering from institutionalized racism. In "Life and the Sacred," Marcel says: "values are rooted in the concrete, in life, which we must affirm. And this affirmation must not remain purely theoretical."[54]

Existential thought is relevant to our lives, and it is never outdated when it remains creatively open and unfinished in its richness. In a Marcelian dialogical ethics, if the ingathering or contemplative experience of the situated participant involves a *creative* availability and respect for the irreducible other, then that very notion of human being is open to an

---

51. Hill Collins, "From *Black Feminist Thought*," 443.
52. Mills, *Blackness Visible*, 11.
53. Irigaray, *I love to you*, 104.
54. Marcel, "Life and the Sacred," 114.

ethical recognition of difference, providing that difference gets asserted, and eventually *incorporated* into discourses and institutions. The latter is obviously a larger, creative and constructive enterprise, but there is nothing in a Marcelian ontology of the self that precludes a deeper recognition of difference within social and institutional structures, although it requires a commitment to a mode of being, rather than having, and to maintaining an ethical stance of: "I am not everything". Given his ongoing social concerns regarding the spirit of abstraction, in conjunction with a phenomenology of embodied inter-subjectivity that emphasizes respect for the irreducibility of otherness—I think that we can elicit from Marcel's thought a contemporary relevance towards an existential, dialogical ethics in general, and for ethical considerations concerning racial and sexual difference in particular.

Bibliography

Busch, Thomas. "Gabriel Marcel: Reflection as Interpretation." In *Circulating Being: From Embodiment to Incorporation. Essays on Late Existentialism*, 28–42. New York: Fordham University Press, 1999.

Busch, Thomas, Ed. *The Participant Perspective: A Gabriel Marcel Reader*. Lanham, MD: University Press of America, 1987.

Fischer, Sally. "Social Ecology and the Flesh: Merleau-Ponty, Irigaray, and Ecocommunitarian Politics." In *Merleau-Ponty and Environmental Philosophy: Dwelling on the Landscapes of Thought*. Edited by Suzanne Cataldi and William Hamrick, 203–15. New York: SUNY Press, 2007.

Hill Collins, Patricia. "From *Black Feminist Thought*." In *Feminist Theory*, edited by Wendy Kolmar and Frances Bartkowski, 442–46. 3rd ed. New York: McGraw Hill, 2010.

Irigaray, Luce. *Ethics of Sexual Difference*. Translated by Carolyn Burke and Gillian Gill. Ithaca, NY: Cornell University Press, 1993.

———. *I Love to You: Sketch for a Felicity within History*. Translated by Allison Martin. New York: Routledge, 1996.

———. "When Our Lips Speak Together." In *This Sex Which Is Not One*. Translated by Catherine Porter, 205–218. Ithaca: Cornell University Press, 1985.

Keen, Sam. *Gabriel Marcel*. London: Carey Kingsgate, 1966.

Marcel, Gabriel. *Being and Having*. Translated by Kathleen Farrer. New York: Harper & Row, 1965.

———. *The Decline of Wisdom*. Translated by Manya Harari. London: Harvill, 1954.

———. "Existence and Objectivity." In *The Participant Perspective: A Gabriel Marcel Reader*, edited by Thomas W. Busch, 49–72. Lanham, MD: University Press of America, 1987.

———. "Life and the Sacred." In *Tragic Wisdom and Beyond*, 104–19. Translated by Stephen Jolin and Peter McCormick. Evanston, IL: Northwestern University Press, 1973.

———. *Man against Mass Society*. Translated by G. S. Fraser. South Bend, IN: Gateway, 1962.

———. *Mystery of Being*. Vol. 1. Translated by G. S. Fraser. Chicago: Gateway, 1968.
———. "On the Ontological Mystery." In *The Philosophy of Existentialism*, 9–46. Translated by Manya Harari. New York: Citadel, 1968.
Merleau-Ponty, Maurice. "Etre et Avoir." *La Vie Intellectuelle* 45 (1936) 98–108.
Mills, Charles. *Blackness Visible*. Ithaca, NY: Cornell University Press, 1998.
Nietzsche, Friedrich. *Genealogy of Morals*. Translated by Walter Kaufmann. New York: Vintage, 1967.

3

Reflections on Gabriel Marcel's Belief in the Afterlife

—Geoffrey Karabin

Marcel, the Afterlife, & Critics of the Beyond

This essay explores Gabriel Marcel's love-based conception of afterlife belief. Marcel locates the source of afterlife belief in the experience of love. The belief germinates from an encounter with value that is communicated through love. While Marcel denies that love offers proof of the afterlife's existence, he does argue that the value experienced in love provides hope for immortal life. That Marcel's belief in the afterlife emerges from a hope that is itself generated from an experience of incarnate life's value is significant insofar as a belief in the afterlife has been criticized as life-denying. In this essay, my aim is to comment on this long-standing critique of afterlife belief. I argue that Marcel's vision of afterlife belief serves as a response to those who view afterlife belief in particular and religious belief more generally as life-denying. The response is significant because it does not contest the life-denying critics on abstract conceptual grounds nor on the grounds of theological ideology. The life-denying critics are offered a response that germinates from the very life that they view as being denigrated by religious and afterlife belief.

To believe in the afterlife is, according to the life-denying line of critique, to transfer the value of present life—the incarnate, worldly life in which human beings are enmeshed—and shift that value to an otherworldly abode. To believe in the afterlife is to value something other than this life. Whether a believer looks forward to the promise of an afterlife because of his/her anguish in "this vale of tears,"[1] or whether the expectant glories of post-mortem bliss reduce temporal life to a shadow world, the salient point for those who adopt this line of critique is that a belief in the afterlife is intertwined with a devaluation of present existence.

Among others, Ludwig Feuerbach,[2] Sigmund Freud,[3] Karl Marx, and Friedrich Nietzsche view a hope for the beyond as life-denying. Nietzsche states the case unambiguously:

> If one shifts the centre of gravity of life *out* of life into the 'Beyond'—into *nothingness*—one has deprived life as such of its centre of gravity. The great lie of personal immortality destroys all rationality, all naturalness of instinct, all that is salutary, all that is life-furthering.[4]

Placing the reality of life in the "nothingness" of some "Beyond" operates against the affirmation of life in the present. Because "the great lie of personal immortality" shifts the "gravity of life *out* of life," a commitment to incarnate existence is undermined by a focus on, awe of, and subservience to the next life. To believe in life beyond death is, for Nietzsche, to betray incarnate life. While Marx's critique of afterlife belief is aimed at a different victim than that with whom Nietzsche is concerned, both construe a belief in the beyond as a betrayal of the present.[5] Marx's famous dictum that "the mortgage held by the peasants on the heavenly estates guarantees the mortgage held by the bourgeoisie on the peasant estates" is emblematic.[6] The

---

1. Taken from the Christian, Rosary prayer, "Hail, Holy Queen."

2. James Massey speaks for Feuerbach: "If it can be proved that the individual human totally ends at the close of his natural life here, then human sights can be lowered back to realistically attainable ideals, to sharing in the goals of this life" ("Feuerbach and Religious Individualism," 372).

3. Freud points to "a new era of maturity" that humanity can enter once "religious realities are [recognized as] merely the projection of human—predominantly unconsciousness and infantile—needs" (Elder, "The Freudian Critique of Religion," 369, 350).

4. Nietzsche, *Twilight of the Idols*, 167–168.

5. Ishay Landa, in a provocative essay entitled "Aroma and Shadow: Marx vs. Nietzsche on Religion," distinguishes a fundamental difference with regard to Nietzsche's and Marx's critique of religious belief. Landa highlights how Nietzsche views afterlife belief as undermining those who are naturally strong. The belief thereby becomes a tool of aggression used by the weak against the powerful. Marx comes to the opposite conclusion. He interprets the belief as a tool used by the strong against the weak. He sees it as a way in which those in power better ensure the passivity of the oppressed.

6. Marx, *The Class Struggles in France*, 85.

peasant's temporal life is stripped of value and, given that there is nothing to defend in this world, the peasant gives up a claim on his/her current existence. Suffering, marginalization, humiliation, and poverty become the means by which the peasant purchases an existence worth his/her while.

Against those that view afterlife belief as an evacuation of incarnate value, the origin of Marcel's afterlife belief offers an antidote. When grounded on the experience of love, on the experience of the beloved's unsurpassable worth, one is provided a belief that originates in value. It originates in a value located in the incarnate other whom one loves. Against religious critics who view religious belief in general and hope for the afterlife in particular as life-denying, Marcel offers a vision of the beyond that affirms the present. As opposed to equating finitude with futility, Marcel offers his readers a way to look to finite life and discover a fullness of value. As opposed to "shift[ing] the . . . gravity of life out of life," Marcel's afterlife belief encourages believers to shift their attention to the fullness of value that resides within one's present relationships.[7]

A Love-Based Belief in the Afterlife

Beginning with a vision of what I name a love-based belief in the afterlife, Marcel announces simply, but provocatively, that "to love a being is to say, 'thou, thou shall not die.'"[8] Expanding upon the sentiment, he writes:

> The more each one of us takes himself for a center, considering others only in relation to himself, the more the idea of the beyond will be emptied of all meaning, for this world beyond will then appear as a senseless prolongation . . . On the contrary, the more the other, or others, will have become an integral part of my experience, the more I will be led to recognize their irreducible value as well as the difficulty *for us* of achieving a lasting harmony here below; and the more necessary it will be

---

7. It is worth mentioning the way in which the thought of Tom Busch interacts with the particular argument. In both *The Participant Perspective: A Gabriel Marcel Reader* and his essay "Gabriel Marcel on Existence, Being and Immortality," Busch explores the ways in which Marcel's conception of the afterlife is intimately linked to the experience of love. In exploring this link, Busch juxtaposes Marcel's thought to that of the absurdist philosophies of Jean-Paul Sartre and Albert Camus. While this essay does not take up Busch's analysis of Sartre and Camus, Busch's juxtaposition involves a distinction between a philosophical perspective that begins with the experience of value versus a perspective that sees in reality an absence of value, at least an absence in an ultimate sense.

8. Marcel, *The Mystery of Being*, vol. 2, 153; quoted in Anderson, *A Commentary*, 168.

to conceive a mode of existence which is different from the one we have known, and which will lead us toward the real and *pleromatic* unity where we will be all in all.[9]

"The idea of the beyond" is enlivened by an experience where other people increasingly penetrate the boundaries of, and thereby become "integral" to, one's life. The more one loves, which means the more one allows oneself to enter into communion with other persons, the more a belief in the beyond is filled with, as opposed to "emptied of," meaning. The living reality of afterlife belief has its vital source in the experience of love and the *telos* of the belief points to the fullest fruition of love. This fullest fruition is what Marcel refers to as "the real and *pleromatic* unity where we will be all in all." Absent a foundation in love, which Marcel equates with an egotistic desire for personal preservation, one is left with the desiccated remnant of afterlife belief.

The same insight is elegantly expressed in Fyodor Dostoevsky's masterpiece *The Brothers Karamazov*. In response to a woman distraught by the lack of certainty surrounding the post-mortem existence of her recently deceased husband, the character Father Zosima offers the following advice:

> Try to love your neighbors actively and tirelessly. The more you succeed in loving, the more you'll be convinced of the existence of God and the immortality of your soul. And if you reach complete selflessness in the love of your neighbor, then undoubtedly you will believe.[10]

This brief yet incredibly rich insight is an emblematic vision of a love-based belief in the afterlife. What is of interest, and this is true of both Marcel and Dostoevsky, is not whether Zosima's advice constitutes a convincing proof of life after death, but rather, the way in which Dostoevsky utilizes Zosima to trace a belief in the afterlife to the active expression of love. Put simply, a belief in the beyond is proportionate to the degree one loves. Love and the afterlife are intimately linked; hence, a belief in the afterlife is portrayed as an outgrowth of the fullest possible expression of love. To believe more fully in life beyond death is to love those who live more completely.

To investigate why love and a belief in the afterlife should be interlinked in a profound and intimate manner—as opposed to being an arbitrary connection born from romantic sentimentality—one can explore Marcel's conviction that the experience of love is connected to a revelation of value. Marcel explicitly asserts that a lover responds to an "irreducible,"

---

9. Marcel, *The Existential Background*, 141.
10. Dostoevsky, *The Brothers Karamazov*, 56.

"unconditional" and "overwhelming" value experienced in the beloved.[11] Thomas Busch notes how, for Marcel, love is "the personal encounter with a being that has 'depth' and presents itself as eternal, irreducible value."[12] The lover encounters the beloved *as* value and Marcel is convinced that this encounter is ontological in nature: "The ontological weight of human experience is the love which it is able to bestow."[13] The lover, in other words, gains access to the genuine nature, to the very being of the beloved.

Marcel's association of love with the revelation of the beloved's fundamental, ontological value removes love from the purely emotional or psychological dimension of human experience. Love, for Marcel, cannot be reduced to a transitory feeling. Nor can love be understood in terms of a lover's psychological needs. Love is better understood as a revelation regarding another person and, in its most complete sense, as a revelation regarding the nature of intersubjective as well as divine relationships. Busch notes that, for Marcel:

> In the experience of love the value of the beloved is not presented as a projection onto the beloved from some extrinsic source, but is rather recognized to be there intrinsically ('love is revelation'). The act of love does not create the value of the beloved; this value was present on the level of existence in the form of appeal, prior to love as a personal act.[14]

Rather than creation and projection, response and revelation are the avenues through which the beloved's value emerges. Value is not, for Marcel, a product of a psyche divorced from an atomistic and inhuman universe that lacks intrinsic value. Rather, love brings one into contact with that which is valuable.

As an ontological experience, love reveals the beloved to possess a value that is freed from whatever use he/she may have for the lover. In fact, it is only when the beloved is released from a use-value that one truly loves and it is only upon such a release that the value of the beloved becomes fully manifest. Rather than an encounter where my desires and needs are projected onto a lover whose value is then determined by whether he/she can fulfill these desires/needs, Marcel identifies the process of love as that whereby the beloved's singular worth becomes manifest. Whereas the ego imposes barriers and generates a distance between myself and others, love

---

11. Anderson, "Personal Immortality," 401.
12. Busch, "Existence, Being and Immortality," 81.
13. Marcel, *Existential Background*, 79.
14. Busch, "Introduction," 16–17.

names a process that is best associated with grace. It is the process whereby the lover is freed from his/her own self so as to recognize the intrinsic goodness constituted by the beloved.

For Marcel, the beloved's value cannot be reduced to what the beloved does. Love reveals that there is something about the nature of the beloved that is inextricably worthwhile. The beloved is, of course, able to betray his/her value by living in a way that does not exhibit the dignity of his/her person. At times, the dichotomy between the beloved's value and his/her actions can be extreme. Still, according to Marcel, "to love one's brothers is above all to have hope in them, that is, to go beyond that in their conduct which almost always begins by bruising or disappointing us."[15] To love is to continually renew one's hope that the beloved will more fully manifest the worthiness that defines his/her very being. To love is to continually remind oneself that the beloved's status as a person, rather than his/her actions, are the ultimate source of the beloved's value.

At this stage in the essay, the connection between the experience of love and a belief in the afterlife becomes evident. Love reveals the beloved's unconditional value and, due to the unconditional nature of that value, the cessation of the beloved's existence is put into question. Joe McGown makes explicit the Marcelian logic: "Unless we posit a radical separation of being and value, we must know that the *being* of the loved one is as perennial as his value."[16] In a similar manner, Thomas Anderson references Marcel's conclusion that "love centers on others insofar as they are bearers of eternal value and so transcend the temporal order of things."[17] When love reveals the beloved's "unconditional" and "overwhelming" value, love reveals a being whose worth surpasses a term limit that finitude would impose upon that worth.[18] Poetically, but perhaps most incisively, Marcel describes value as "the very substance of exaltation."[19] The "substance of exaltation" is found in love because in love one discovers a fullness of value that points beyond the limits of temporality.

Keeping in mind that Marcel views love as a response to, rather than as a projection of value, Busch writes of a refusal to relinquish the beloved to death: "Marcel does not consider this refusal a cowardly or unrealistic act, but a most realistic recognition of the intrinsic value of the beloved."[20]

---

15. Marcel, *Existential Background*, 148.
16. McCown, *Availability*, 58.
17. Anderson, "Personal Immortality," 401.
18. Ibid.
19. Marcel, *Homo Viator*, 143.
20. Busch, "Existence, Being and Immortality," 81.

The lover encounters the beloved as possessing an unconditional value and, for Marcel, the lover is right to remain faithful to that encounter by holding out hope for immortality. To not hold out hope would be to say that the value of the beloved—at least in so far as one considers his/her value to be unconditional—is a projected, constructed value. To not hold out hope is, for Marcel, to reduce the beloved to the status of a thing. It is to say that, like all physical things, the beloved possesses existence only insofar as he/she is physically present.

Marcel elaborates on the juxtaposition of love to death. He categorizes love as "an ontological counterweight to death."[21] Death, if taken as the preeminent ontological experience—which would mean that death would define the beloved's being—would proclaim that the value of the beloved is restricted to his/her temporal duration. The value that, as McGown and Anderson note, is identified with the very being of the beloved would perish with the cessation of his/her life. And, even if one nonetheless wished to claim that the value of the beloved existed beyond his/her death, it would be a value restricted to a memory kept alive by those left behind. Marcel surmises that if "the departed is no longer there—or, which comes to the same, is reduced to some dry bones or to a handful of cinders—presence is reduced to a purely subjective feeling."[22] If the beloved "exists" only in an act of memory, then value is only temporarily attached to the beloved. The beloved is valued rather than possesses value and this derivative value depends upon the lover keeping the beloved in mind. For Marcel, the experience of love suggests that the beloved possesses value and that the possession of such value entails that its preservation is not dependent upon the one who loves. To reiterate the central claim, Marcelian love entails a recognition/revelation of value, rather than a bestowal of value. That the revelation refers to an "inexhaustible" value is why love's revelation is opposed to death and distinguished from a merely psychological form of endurance.

For Marcel, all persons must grapple with the question of whether one's insight into human existence is predicated upon love or death. Is one's insight predicated upon an experience where another human person is affirmed as unconditionally valuable or upon an experience where human persons perish in every aspect of their existence? Is there more to the person than his/her finite appearance—as the notions of "unconditional" and "overwhelming" value suggest—or can one only speak about the person's value in terms of his or her temporal duration? For Marcel, the choice

---

21. Marcel, *Creative Fidelity*, 143.
22. Marcel, "Presence and Immortality," 240.

comes down to whether one recognizes and thereafter cultivates a belief in love's revelation of the beloved's value.

The Marcelian Afterlife: Fidelity & Intersubjectivity

More fully exploring Marcel's belief in the afterlife, along with the affirmation of life upon which the belief is grounded, requires that one examine his notion of fidelity. Marcel explicitly connects love not only to a revelation of value but to an act of fidelity. Anderson notes that, in Marcel's mind, "love and fidelity are inseparable."[23] Marcel himself categorizes love without fidelity as a kind of pretense.[24] For Marcel, an authentic form of love involves an offer of self never to be renounced:

> It is possible for there to be an unconditional love of creature for creature—a gift which will not be revoked. Whatever may occur, whatever disappointment experience inflicts on our hypotheses, our cherished hopes, this love will remain constant, this credit intact.[25]

"Whatever may occur"—and this "whatever" includes death—the lover offers his/her self as a "gift [that] will not be revoked." Busch articulates Marcel's position as follows: "The Thou is experienced as irreducible value, while at the same time my own life is touched in a depth relationship which calls me into a loving, lasting concern (fidelity) for the Thou."[26] Having experienced the beloved as fundamentally worthwhile, the lover is called to an unceasing concern for the beloved. The lover is called to be available for the beloved and to be so in perpetuity.

Based upon a commitment that does not take heed of temporal boundaries, the invocation of fidelity further intertwines a belief in the afterlife with the experience of love. Marcel writes of "the spirit of fidelity" and how he became "more and more convinced that what this spirit demands of us is an explicit refusal, a definite negation of death."[27] Sam Keen echoes this sentiment: "In faith, which [for Marcel] . . . is the paradigm of fidelity, we reach the assurance that human relationships of love and fidelity are eternally significant."[28] To love another is not to say that I am with you until

---

23. Anderson, "Personal Immortality," 401.
24. Marcel, *Existential Background*, 48.
25. Marcel, *Creative Fidelity*, 136.
26. Busch, *The Participant Perspective*, 144.
27. Marcel, *Homo Viator*, 147.
28. Keen, "The Development of the Idea of Being," 110–111.

death do us part. To love another is to say that I am with you and reality is structured in such a way that death will never part us.

So to summarize, a belief in the afterlife has been construed as the progeny of love. But from an even earlier genealogical vantage point, both love and a belief in the afterlife can be seen as a response to the tremendous worth manifest in the beloved's existence. Love serves as an active recognition of that worth and in that recognition calls forth fidelity to the absolutely irreplaceable other. The afterlife would eternally sustain the inexhaustibly worthwhile loved one while also allowing the lover to fulfill his/her unconditional commitment to the beloved. The message to be gleaned is that a belief in the afterlife is, at bottom, a belief in the revelation made possible by love. A belief in the afterlife is a belief in the beloved's "unconditional" and "overwhelming" value and it expresses the hope that the unconditional pledge characteristic of love can be fulfilled.

Having made these claims, the implication is that love demands the survival not merely of the beloved, but the love relation itself. This demand, it must be repeated, is not offered as proof of the afterlife. The demand may well go unfulfilled. But Marcel's point is that the demand grows stronger as the experience that gives rise to it is entered into more fully. More fully entering into a love-based belief in the afterlife occurs when the relationship itself becomes the basis of one's belief. Marcel writes that "hope . . . is always hope for us."[29] The invocation of "us" is critical. Busch writes that "Marcel's approach . . . will not be to 'prove' immortality, but rather to elucidate the sense of death within the context of the peak intersubjective experience—love."[30] Intersubjectivity, which entails a communion with others, is not only the truest representation of love, it is that which constitutes the fullest challenge to death's finality.

Given Marcel's emphasis on intersubjectivity, one must not understand a love-based belief in the afterlife in atomistic terms. This is true both with regard to the beloved's and the lover's post-mortem fate. Marcel draws out the point in relation to the lover: "As a rule, nothing is easier at a certain time of life than to accept death for oneself if one considers it a dreamless sleep without awakening; what cannot be accepted is the death of the loved one: more deeply still the death of love itself."[31] Once again, death is challenged by the lover's recognition of value in the beloved, but the most profound challenge is found *in the relationship* in which that value becomes manifest.

29. Marcel, "Presence and Immortality," 232.
30. Busch, *The Participant Perspective*, 245.
31. Marcel, "Theism and Personal Relationships," 41.

The Marcelian lover's potential afterlife is disassociated from an egotistic concentration on the value of his/her life. The lover is preserved because he/she is involved in a communion that harbors a fullness of life. This fullness, in turn, is increasingly diminished as persons become isolated and atomized. Such diminishment is what Marcel referred to when he declared that:

> The more each one of us takes himself for a center, considering the others only in relation to himself, the more the idea of the beyond will be emptied of all meaning for this world beyond will then appear as a senseless prolongation.[32]

The more one conceives of the afterlife in terms of atomistic survival, the less desirable it becomes. It is not in an isolated I, but in the experience of we, that reality becomes meaningful. Hence, Marcel places limited value in an afterlife belief that is predicated upon a desire for individual survival—a predication for which the Spanish philosopher Miguel de Unamuno could be taken as emblematic[33]—whereas an afterlife belief that emerges from and promises to sustain the inexhaustible richness of relationships is worthy of belief.[34]

A belief in the beyond is construed as a response not only to intersubjective communion, but to the joy it generates. Marcel describes how love gives witness to "a primordial existential assurance, which is finally perhaps nothing other than a very mysterious radiation of the *gaudium essendi*. And this radiation is hope."[35] The "*gaudium essendi*," translated as "the joy of existing," is connected both with the experience of love and the hope that leads beyond death. In this view, the afterlife not only fulfills the deepest yearning of inter-personal relationships, it responds to the joy found within these relationships. The afterlife responds to one who finds, in the experience of love, so much value and so much joy that the cessation of this joy appears increasingly less intelligible the more one experiences it. Busch references

---

32. Marcel, *Existential Background*, 141.

33. Unamuno's masterpiece, *Tragic Sense of Life*, is a sustained reflection on his need for immortality. In a passage that perhaps best encapsulates the basis for an afterlife based on personal preservation, Unamuno exclaims: "I do not want to die—no; I neither want to die nor do I want to want to die; I want to live for ever and ever and ever. I want this 'I' to love-this poor 'I' that I am and that I feel myself to be here and now, and therefore the problem of the duration of my soul, of my own soul, tortures me" (*Tragic Sense*, 45).

34. Busch notes, "In Marcel's philosophy of intersubjectivity it is not *my* death (as in Heidegger's philosophy) but the death of the beloved that calls the self to its most significant ontological decisions" ("Introduction," 12).

35. Marcel, "Authentic Humanism," 43.

Marcel's hope for "an eternal communal fullness . . . [which] . . . Marcel refers to being-as-fullness as 'the Pleroma which is Being' or the 'symphony of being.'"[36] The metaphor of the "symphony" not only captures a sense of fullness and community, but of beauty. The experience of intersubjectivity that gives rise to a hope for life beyond death, while first predicated on the beloved's "unconditional" value, opens the lover to a richness of life that manages to expand its "unconditional" starting point. As Marcel reflects on his own philosophic journey, he writes that "it has become more and more clear to me . . . that there could be an existential experience of joy and fullness."[37] Not only did it become increasingly clear to Marcel, this experience of joy and fullness increasingly becomes the bedrock of Marcelian hope, faith, and belief in the afterlife.[38]

To those who frame religious and afterlife belief as life denying, the fact that Marcel intertwines afterlife belief with a revelation of value and the experience of joy constitutes a powerful response. With his invocation of the *gaudium essendi*, a belief in the afterlife is ultimately founded on a primordial, Genesis-like notion that, "God saw everything that he had made, and behold, it was very good."[39] There is something fundamentally worthwhile about life and the more fully this affirmation becomes manifest, the more fully does one come to believe that the boundaries of finitude are porous. The elemental affirmation that life is good, so good, in fact, that one is led to hope for its never-ending continuity is inseparable from love and that is why love is the gateway to the beyond. It is love that reveals inexhaustible value, constitutes communion, calls forth fidelity, and is marked by a profound source of joy. These are moments of incarnate goodness that provide the springboard to the beyond and they are far from Nietzsche's beyond, a beyond that "shifts the center of gravity out of life." Whereas the life-denying critics contend that afterlife belief is inseparable from a denial of this life, Marcel offers a vision where afterlife belief gains strength to the degree that one affirms this life. To such critics, Marcel responds that it is not flight from the world but the embrace of it that leads to a hope for life beyond death.[40]

---

36. Busch, "Introduction," 15.

37. Marcel, "A Conversation Between Paul Ricoeur," 290.

38. One could turn to Marcel's late essays in *Tragic Wisdom and Beyond* as emblematic of this position.

39. Gen 1:31 (RSV).

40. In a book devoted to the work of Thomas Busch, a comment on the man himself is in order. What strikes me about Tom is that he is a good man. He is kind, he is available, and he exudes a sense of warmth. He fosters the development of his students and, by all accounts, he is an extraordinary colleague. Tom is a man who cherishes both his immediate and his extended family at Villanova. He is as happy to discuss Sartre

Bibliography

Anderson, Thomas. *A Commentary on Gabriel Marcel's* The Mystery of Being. Milwaukee: Marquette University Press, 2006.

———. "Gabriel Marcel on Personal Immortality." *American Catholic Philosophical Quarterly* 80 (2006) 393–406.

Busch, Thomas. "Gabriel Marcel on Existence, Being and Immortality." *Proceedings of the American Catholic Philosophical Association* 52 (1978) 77–86.

———. "Introduction." In *The Participant Perspective: A Gabriel Marcel Reader*, edited by Thomas Busch, 1–24. Lanham, MD: University Press of America, 1987.

———, ed. *The Participant Perspective: A Gabriel Marcel Reader*. Lanham, MD: University Press of America, 1987.

Dominican Fathers. "Hail, Holy Queen." http://www.rosary-center.org/howto.htm.

Dostoevsky, Fydor. *The Brothers Karamazov*. Translated by Richard Pevear and Larissa Volokhonsky. New York: Farrar, Straus & Giroux, 2002.

Elder, Charles R. "The Freudian Critique of Religion: Remarks on Its Meaning and Conditions." *Journal of Religion* 75 (1995) 347–70.

Keen, Sam. "The Development of the Idea of Being in Marcel's Thought." In *The Philosophy of Gabriel Marcel*. Edited by Lewis Edwin Hahn and Paul Arthur Schlipp, 99–120. La Salle, IL: Open Court, 1984.

Landa, Ishay. "Aroma and Shadow: Marx vs. Nietzsche on Religion." *Nature, Society, and Thought* 18 (2006) 461–99.

Marcel, Gabriel. "Authentic Humanism and Its Existential Presuppositions." In *Tragic Wisdom and Beyond*. Translated by Stephen Jolin and Peter McCormick, 33–44. Evanston, IL: Northwestern University Press, 1973.

———. "A Conversation between Paul Ricoeur and Gabriel Marcel." In *The Participant Perspective*, edited by Thomas Busch, 283–93. Lanham, MD: University Press of America, 1987.

———. *Creative Fidelity*. Translated by Robert Rosthal. New York: Fordham University Press, 2002.

———. *The Existential Background of Human Dignity*. Cambridge: Harvard University Press, 1963.

———. *Homo Viator: Introduction to a Metaphysic of Hope*. Translated by Emma Craufurd. New York: Harper Torchbooks, 1962.

———. *The Mystery of Being*, Vol. 2. Translated by Rene Hague. South Bend, IN: St. Augustine's, 2001.

———. "Presence and Immortality." In *Presence and Immortality*. Translated by Michael A Machado, 22–244. Pittsburgh: Duquesne University Press, 1967.

———. "Theism and Personal Relationships." *CrossCurrents* 1 (1950) 35–42.

---

as is he is to chat about Villanova basketball and perhaps nothing gives him more joy then when one of the graduate students or Villanova professors brings in their kids. His availability to others may well be Tom's defining feature and, in conjunction with that availability, he is humble to a fault. In a profession where scholars often draw attention to the grandeur of their intellects, Tom avoids any hint of pomposity. As one of Tom's graduate students, I can unequivocally say that to work with Tom is a blessing and to get to know him is an honor. Many a Villanova student, both graduate and undergraduate, has been blessed.

Marx, Karl. *The Class Struggles in France, 1848–1850*. Translator unknown. New York: International, 1964.
Massey, James. "Feuerbach and Religious Individualism." *Journal of Religion* 56 (1976) 366–81.
McCown, Joe. *Availability: Gabriel Marcel and the Phenomenology of Human Openness*. Missoula, MT: Scholars, 1978.
Nietzsche, Friedrich. *Twilight of the Idols and The Anti-Christ, or How to Philosophize with a Hammer*. Translated by R. J. Hollingdale. Reissue ed. Edited with an Introduction by Michael Tanner. London: Penguin Classics, 1990.
Unamuno, Miguel de. *Tragic Sense of Life*. Translated by J. E. Crawford Flitch. New York: Dover, 1954.

PART TWO

Living French Existentialism

Beauvoir, Merleau-Ponty, Sartre

4

Picking Out the "Right" Color

Perceptual Normativity in Merleau-Ponty

—J. C. BERENDZEN

In his 1966 doctoral dissertation on the work of Maurice Merleau-Ponty, Thomas W. Busch makes the claim that for Merleau-Ponty "lived-perception is more a matter of aesthetics than of mechanics."[1] This point is made as Busch draws an analogy (which he takes from Merleau-Ponty) between perception and painting, and the main point of the overall passage is to summarize Merleau-Ponty's perceptual holism. In the midst of making this analogy, Busch touches on, without elaborating, the idea that perception contains a normative element. "The colors in a painting" he notes, "all have a 'place' and the painter is at pains to pick out the 'right' color," and just as there is a "right" way for things to hang together within the painting, there is a "right" way for things to go together in perception such that the object can be perceived.[2] Perception, for Merleau-Ponty, is normative.

As will be discussed in more detail below, the notion that perception is normative is not that unusual. In standard views on perception, this normativity is cashed out in terms of veridicality, or the way in which our perception does or does not correctly represent the actual state of the distal environment. But it is important to note that the type of normativity alluded to in Busch's discussion cannot be cashed out in terms of veridicality as in

---

1. Busch, "The Role of the Cogito," 55.
2. Ibid., 55.

the standard view. This is because the kind of normativity in painting that Busch is referencing is not analogous to veridicality.

Busch says that the painter is at pains to pick out the "right" color, but he does not explain what standard is applied to judge this rightness. One might apply to painting a representational standard that would mirror veridicality in perception, such that the right color would be the color that correctly matches the distal (painted) object. But it is unlikely that Busch intends this representational standard. For one thing, it does not fit well with Merleau-Ponty's discussions of painting from which Busch is drawing.[3] It also does not fit well with the rejection of a "mechanical" view of perception that motivates Busch's discussion. The idea here is that perception is not made up of bits of sensory information that match up via a one-to-one correspondence with objects or qualities in the world. On the other hand, one might assume (though Busch does not make this clear) that the rightness of the color is dependent upon the painter's aesthetic vision or aims. Or the rightness might be dependent upon the painter's ability to elicit an aesthetic experience in the viewer of the painting (and/or these two might be combined). In either case, the sense of "rightness" here is ambiguous, as it depends not on some clear relation to an objective reality but on a concatenation of factors in the painting, painter, and/or viewer that might change with different contexts. This ambiguity is perhaps why Busch puts "right" in scare quotes in the quoted passage. There is a sense in which the painting could go right or wrong, but this is fluid and bound to shift.

But this leaves the analogy with perception somewhat unclear. What would the correlate to the painter's, or the viewer's, aesthetic sense be in perception? What is the standard for rightness in perception, if it is not veridicality? And does it make sense to claim that perception is normative, but in the ambiguous sense alluded to in Busch's discussion? Perhaps Busch is not completely elaborating on what it really means to draw the analogy between painting and perception, but his analogy is, I think, apt, and this will be shown below.

Merleau-Ponty does want to hold that perception is normative, but he rejects the standard veridicality view, and he maintains that there is ambiguity at the heart of this normativity. The rest of this paper will focus on elaborating on Merleau-Ponty's views on the normativity of perception, and vindicating Busch's painter analogy. This will also provide the opportunity to critique a prominent recent view on the normativity of perception that also draws on Merleau-Ponty—that of Sean Kelly. While Kelly describes a

---

3. One of the upshots of Merleau-Ponty's discussions of Cezanne in *Phenomenology of Perception* is that painting does not represent objects in the world in the fashion of direct correspondence. See, for instance, Merleau-Ponty, *Phenomenology,* 332–333.

view that in many ways fits Merleau-Ponty's thought, he does not properly account for Merleau-Ponty's insistence that perception can be systematically ambiguous. The extension of Busch's painter analogy that is developed in this paper can, on the other hand, account for that ambiguity. Before diving into the discussion of ambiguity, however, it should be helpful to clarify in more basic terms what it would mean to take perception to be normative, and it is easiest to do this by starting with the standard view.

Perceptual Normativity: A Standard View

It is common, both within contemporary philosophy of perception and perceptual psychology, to define perception as aiming at the representation of the distal external environment. Key to understanding the nature of "representation" in this sense is the idea that perception has accuracy conditions and so can represent the environment veridically or non-veridically. Tyler Burge summarizes this idea as follows:

> Explanatory practice in psychology grounds appeal to representational states. Such states are type-individuated partly in terms of their conditions for being veridical. For example, a perceptual state is the type of perceptual state it is partly by virtue of being a state that purports to pick out various particulars in a scene and to attribute to those purported particulars such attributes as being cube-shaped, being green, being in certain directions and at certain distances. If there are particulars causing the perceptual state in the right way and those particulars have the attributes that are attributed, the perceptual state is veridical.[4]

As Burge goes on to elaborate, on such a view of representational accuracy and veridicality, perception is norm-guided in the sense it has "a standard or level of possible performance that is in some way adequate for fulfillment of a function or purpose."[5] The purpose or function of perception is representational, and veridicality is the standard of performance that is adequate to that function.[6]

---

4. Burge, *Origins*, 308.

5. Ibid., 311.

6. It is worth noting that Burge's discussion of these issues is somewhat unique in that he describes functional performance in terms of "norms" and "normativity." This is merely terminological, however; the general view he describes—that the representational function of perception involves accuracy conditions—is a very common one. As Burge notes, it is also reasonable to use the term "norm" in this context; see Ibid., 311, n. 34 (which is a citation to the OED definition of "norm").

Such representational norms are, as Burge puts it, natural norms, which is to say that they hold independently of the individual recognizing them or acceding to them. While there seem to be clear instances where individuals recognize that their perception is not veridical and experience that as a failure of their perceptual functioning, this need not be the case. Furthermore, "natural norms apply even if an individual cannot understand or be guided by them"; it is not required that one be able to (to paraphrase Kant) act in accordance with a conception of the norm in order for it to be a norm.[7] All that is necessary for natural normativity is that the individual has capacities (in this case, perceptual) that have a function the performance of which can be evaluated according to a standard.

There are passages in *Phenomenology of Perception* that might lead one to think that Merleau-Ponty would agree with this standard view. For example, in chapter II of the introduction ("'Association' and the 'Projection of Memories'") he discusses the so-called proofreader's illusion (he gives the example of reading "'deduction' where the paper bears the word 'destruction'").[8] Of the illusion he writes:

> The illusion tricks us precisely by passing itself off as an authentic perception in which signification is born in the sensible and does not come from elsewhere. The illusion imitates this privileged experience in which the sense fits over the sensible perfectly, is visibly articulated or enunciated in it. The illusion presupposes this perceptual norm.[9]

Taken out of context, at least, it is not hard to interpret "this perceptual norm" as referring to veridicality. The "sense fitting over the sensible perfectly" might just be another way of saying that the representation corresponds accurately with the object, and the illusion's trick is just that one takes the inaccurate perception to be veridical. This is a fairly simple point that would correspond with standard descriptions of illusion.

On the other hand, there are passages that seem to run entirely counter to the standard view. Consider Merleau-Ponty's discussion of the Müller-Lyer illusion, wherein auxiliary "arrow" lines cause equal parallel lines to be seen as unequal. The standard view's description of this illusion should be fairly clear. Those who succumb to the illusion see the two main parallel lines as unequal when they are not; the character of the perceptual representation differs from the character of the actual environmental stimulus. Thus the perceptual representation is inaccurate and the norm

7. Ibid., 314.
8. Merleau-Ponty, *Phenomenology*, 21.
9. Ibid., 22.

of veridicality is not met. But Merleau-Ponty asserts that the "two straight lines in the Müller-Lyer illusion are neither equal nor unequal" and that the visual field is an "indeterminate" and "strange milieu in which contradictory notions intertwine."[10] Whatever this might mean, it seems to clearly run counter to the standard view. The standard view entails that the two straight lines are in fact equal and that they are (for those who experience the illusion) represented as unequal. If their possible equality or inequality merge in an "indeterminate field" it seemingly would be impossible to state that the illusory perception is in fact inaccurate.

If we focus just on these two passages on illusion taken out of *Phenomenology of Perception*, it looks as though Merleau-Ponty holds two conflicting views. On the one hand, he wants to hold, along with standard views on (visual) perception, that the illusions involve a non-veridical experience that thus fail the (representational) norm of perception. On the other hand, he seems to reject this conception of veridicality as it relates to illusion as being connected (in the Müller-Lyer case, at least) to a mistaken form of "objectivism" which denies the indeterminacy that is inherent in perception. Given this apparent conflict, one must sort out Merleau-Ponty's view on perceptual normativity and show how it fits with elements of the standard view while at the same time going beyond the standard view. The discussion of indeterminacy will be crucial to this task, and will eventually lead us back to Busch's painter analogy.

Merleau-Pontyian Perceptual Normativity

Perhaps the best passage for assessing Merleau-Ponty's views on perceptual normativity occurs near the beginning of the chapter in *Phenomenology of Perception* titled "The Thing and the Natural World." There he discusses the phenomenon of size constancy (the fact that our perception of the size of objects can remain relatively constant despite changes in distance which would change the size of the image of the objects on our retinas). Without denying the phenomenon of size constancy, Merleau-Ponty rejects the idea that the size remains absolutely constant as the "product of distance multiplied by apparent size."[11] Instead, the constancy comes from the fact that "there is an optimal distance from which it [the object] asks to be seen," and this optimal distance, which could perhaps be said to reveal the object's true size, then factors, as a kind of norm, in the changes of distance. Merleau-Ponty sums up this idea by saying that "the distance between me

10. Ibid., 6.
11. Ibid., 315.

and the object is not a size that increases or decreases, but rather a tension that oscillates around a norm."[12] The "norm" mentioned in the last sentence cannot be veridicality, at least as it is typically understood. Size constancy, as Burge notes, involves a capacity to "track given environmental attributes under . . . very different types of proximal stimulation," which entails that constancy involves a relation between different representational states.[13] Veridicality, on the other hand, attaches to individual representational states, so it is not well fit to be a norm for judging the relation between those states. Perhaps more importantly, the constancy capacity can come into play in cases where perceptions are inaccurate; one could have a series of illusory representational states that are tracked for size constancy. So for the standard view, Merleau-Ponty's discussion of perceptual normativity here is not likely to fit.

In order to begin to get a sense of what it could mean for perception to involve a "tension that oscillates around a norm" we should examine more fully the passage from which that phrase is taken:

> For each object, just as for each painting in an art gallery, there is an optimal distance from which it asks to be seen—an orientation through which it presents more of itself—beneath or beyond which we merely have a confused perception due to excess or lack. Hence, we tend toward the maximum of visibility and we seek, just as when using a microscope, a better focus point, which is obtained through a certain equilibrium between the interior and the exterior horizons . . . The distance between me and the object is not a size that increases or decreases, but rather a tension that oscillates around a norm. The oblique orientation of the object in relation to me is not measured by the angle that it forms with the plane of my face, but rather experienced as a disequilibrium, as an unequal distribution of its influences upon me. Variations of appearance are not increases or decreases of size, nor real distortions; quite simply, sometimes its parts mix together and merge, sometimes they are clearly articulated against each other and reveal their riches. There is a point of maturity of my perception that at once satisfies these three norms and toward which the entire perceptual process tends.[14]

Merleau-Ponty's language in this passage is a bit unclear. On the one hand, the norm being discussed here must be the "maximum of visibility";

12. Ibid., 316, emphasis added.
13. The discussion of size constancy can be found in Burge, *Origins*, 387–389; quote on 388.
14. Merleau-Ponty, *Phenomenology*, 315–316.

perceptual experiences are to be judged according to the extent to which they attain this maximum. Note, however, the reference in the last sentence of the passage to the satisfaction of three norms. While the passage is not entirely clear on this point, it seems that the "three" refers to "the distance between me and the object," the "oblique orientation of the object in relation to me," and the "variations of appearance." Each of these are presumably "norms" in the sense that they are three aspects of the perceptual process that need to be dealt with for visual perception to function properly. In order to achieve the "maximum of visibility" we need to be at the proper distance from the object, the proper angle to the object, and catch its appearance in its most "clearly articulated" state. Merleau-Ponty is perhaps using the term "norm" too loosely in the case of the "three norms." The actual norm is the "maximum of visibility" and those three things would not be norms so much as crucial elements for the fulfillment of the norm.

What is clear, though, is that Merleau-Ponty intends to highlight a kind of activity; his view is not that when the three elements are fulfilled one has achieved a kind of static state (i.e. the single point where correct angle, correct distance, and articulated appearance converge). This is, again, suggested by the reference to "oscillation," but this point really becomes clear when one puts this passage in the overall context of the views developed in *Phenomenology of Perception*. Along these lines, one should note two key (and well known) elements of Merleau-Ponty's views that operate in the background of this passage.[15]

First, the reference to the "equilibrium between the interior and exterior horizons" is connected to Merleau-Ponty's general holism regarding perception (which, as is noted above, is the main topic of the passage where Busch makes the painter analogy). Merleau-Ponty applies the figure/background relationship that Gestalt psychologists find in certain key instances of perception to perception as a whole. Taken to its extreme end, Merleau-Ponty says that perception "is not even an act or a deliberate taking of a stand; it is the background."[16] Thus perception, for Merleau-Ponty, is not thought of primarily in terms of discrete states that accurately (or inaccurately) represent discrete objects. This fits with Merleau-Ponty's much discussed views on the indeterminacy of perception, which we encountered earlier in the reference to the "indeterminate" in the discussion of the Müller-Lyer illusion. Perception is in part indeterminate because it is dependent upon a holistic context which is not clearly bounded and which can shift.

15. The following discussion borrows heavily from, and expands on, my discussion of veridicality and illusion in Merleau-Ponty in "Disjunctivism," 274–279.
16. Merleau-Ponty, *Phenomenology*, lxxiv.

This is why Merleau-Ponty wants indeterminacy to be taken as a "positive phenomenon" and to be seen as a constitutive element of our perceptual experience.[17]

The second closely related point is that Merleau-Ponty conceives of perception as a dynamic process. Regarding indeterminacy, the point here is not that there is no possibility of determinacy, but that determinacy is not predetermined. It rather requires an activity of carving determinate moments of perception out of a holistic system, and the determinacy of elements in the holistic network is dependent on relations with other elements. Strictly speaking there are no atomic units of perception. Insofar as we carve determinacy out of indeterminacy, perception is both holistic and active. Note the reference above to the "perceptual process" and note the extent to which the optimum view is discussed as being obtained via a kind of activity. An important point that is not directly conveyed by the above passage, though, is that this activity might be continuous. Ultimately, Merleau-Ponty does not just want to say that a process is required in order to reach a veridical state that would be more or less stable, but rather that the optimum view itself is a part of a dynamic process.

It should be noted that Merleau-Ponty's view described above is not entirely different from the standard view. Insofar as the object "asks to be seen" optimally, there is some trace of the idea that there are objective standards according to which the perceived environment is presented in our perception. So it would not seem totally wrong to speak of perception having accuracy conditions on Merleau-Ponty's view. But the holistic and dynamic nature of Merleau-Ponty's view marks an important point of distinction with the standard view, because veridicality is usually thought of as attaching to discrete perceptual states and such states are not dynamic. Veridicality is a fact about individual representational states, and can be thought of as applying to static individual time-slices of our perception. Also, one other divergence with the standard view should be mentioned. Merleau-Ponty says that the equilibrium or disequilibrium is felt; we have some experience of the perceptual experience as being optimal or suboptimal. On the other hand, as was noted above, Burge emphasizes the fact that veridicality is a natural norm that need not be experienced by or guide the subject who undergoes the relevant perceptual states.

So while Merleau-Ponty's view is not wholly different from the standard view, there are crucial differences, and veridicality has perhaps been replaced by the perceptual process's dynamic relation to some optimal state. At this point, however, there is a big hole in the discussion: the character

17. Ibid., 7.

of this optimal state, or "maximum of visibility," has been largely left unexplained. Following this, it is still unclear how that optimal state could itself be dynamic.

To explain the nature of the optimal perceptual state, we can begin with an idea that Busch discusses just prior to the painter analogy, which is that we "come to grips" with the perceived object. The optimal perceptual state is often referred to, in the literature on Merleau-Ponty, as "maximum grip." That phrase (in French, *maximum prise*), which is especially favored by Hubert Dreyfus, is not actually used by Merleau-Ponty in *Phenomenology of Perception*. There are, however, passages that use similar phrasing that highlights our "grip on" or "gearing into" (depending on the translation of "*prise*") the environment.[18] For example:

> My body is geared into the world when my perception provides me with the most varied and the most clearly articulated spectacle possible, and when my motor intentions, as they unfold, receive the responses they anticipate from the world. This maximum of clarity in perception and action specifies a perceptual ground, a background for my life, a general milieu for the coexistence of my body and the world.[19]

While they are not fully separable (per the point above that perception requires dynamic activity), we can abstractly think of such "gearing in" as containing a properly perceptual and a properly actional element. Perceptually, we get clear articulation, which we might think of in terms of the determinacy mentioned above. We perceive the various elements of the scene clearly and distinctly. Actionally, full gearing in happens when our intended actions fit the elements of the perceived scene properly. This latter element clearly distinguishes Merleau-Ponty's view from the standard view. Veridicality takes into account representational accuracy only, not accuracy for some actional purpose. But these are two sides of the same coin for Merleau-Ponty; perceptual articulation unfolds as our actions receive the appropriate responses, and the one depends on the other.

As noted above, something akin representational accuracy is not entirely missing from Merleau-Ponty's view, because he takes perception to present the external environment to us, and to do so with more or less

---

18. I will primarily use "gearing in" rather than "grip" because the former is used more frequently in the relevant passages in the 2012 translation of *Phenomenology of Perception*. In a translator's note (Merleau-Ponty, *Phenomenology*, 496-497 n.47) Donald Landes provides a helpful explanation of the translation of "*en prise*" and notes that it is connected to "grip" and "gearing in."

19. Merleau-Ponty, *Phenomenology*, 261.

clarity and articulation.[20] But this view is construed in terms of his holistic and dynamic conception of perception, which is intertwined with bodily action. But at this point a question arises—does he really think that there is some attainable "maximum grip" that is operative in normal perception? How does this fit with his insistence that indeterminacy is a positive element of our perceptual experience?

"Gearing in" and Indeterminacy

In "The Normative Nature of Perceptual Experience" Sean Kelly argues for a conception of perceptual normativity that draws heavily on the Merleau-Pontyian view that is initially described in the previous section.[21] While I agree with much of what Kelly writes about Merleau-Ponty's view, there is an important way in which his interpretation of Merleau-Ponty is incorrect. Examining the fault in Kelly's discussion—which does not take the notion of indeterminacy seriously enough—can help us elaborate a difficult nuance in the Merleau-Pontyian conception of perceptual normativity, and to understand his references to a maximal state in perception. This will also help us make sense of Busch's painter analogy.

Kelly makes much of Merleau-Ponty's notion that the perceiving subject feels the need to attain a better perceptual grip on the environment. He helpfully describes this in terms of moving from a nongestalted to a gestalted presentation of the perceptual scene and this further makes sense of what the Merleau-Pontyian optimal perceptual state is supposed to be. Kelly draws on the following passage in *Phenomenology of Perception* (which I quote more extensively):

> If I am walking on a beach toward a boat that has run aground, and if the funnel or the mast merges with the forest that borders

---

20. This point opens up a very large question regarding whether Merleau-Ponty thinks perception is representational or has "content" in the manner that those terms are currently used in philosophy of perception. Merleau-Ponty makes numerous criticisms of the concept of representation, though his targets obviously predate the specific current use of that concept. But the general point being made here should largely swing free of this bigger issue.

21. Kelly, "Normative Nature," 146–159. I am perhaps being ungenerous to Kelly when I say, in what follows, that there is an error in his interpretation of Merleau-Ponty because his essay is clearly not meant to be an exegesis of Merleau-Ponty's views. Rather, he is using Merleau-Ponty as an inspiration for developing his own view. However, I think there is the fairly clear suggestion in the text that Kelly takes Merleau-Ponty to generally agree with him on the points I am considering here. At the very least, Kelly does not note the important way in which Merleau-Ponty's view is different from the view he ultimately develops in this essay.

the dune, then there will be a moment in which these details suddenly reunite with the boat and become welded to it. As I approached, I did not perceive the resemblances or the proximities that were, in the end, about to reunite with the superstructure of the ship in an unbroken picture. I merely felt that the appearance of the object was about to change, that something was imminent in this tension, as the storm is imminent in the clouds. The spectacle was suddenly reorganized, satisfying my vague expectation. Afterward I recognized, as justifications for the change, the resemblance and the contiguity of what I call "stimuli," that is, the most determinate phenomena obtained from up close and with which I compose the "true" world . . . But these reasons, drawn from having properly perceived the boat, were not given as reasons prior to correct perception. The unity of the object is established upon the presentiment of an imminent order that will, suddenly, respond to questions that are merely latent in the landscape.[22]

Initially the scene described here is nongestalted in the sense that its form is indeterminate; the subject does not perceive all of the parts of the ship unified in an "unbroken picture." This is felt by the subject, and "there is something immanent"—presumably the felt, but not reasoned, experience that some determinate form is there waiting to be seen—in the "tension" that the subject feels when confronted with the nongestalted scene. It is through the activity of coming to grips with the "three norms" referenced above that the subject eventually comes to see the full form of the ship. When this happens, it is as though truth is achieved.

Building on passages like this, and the earlier quoted passage where Merleau-Ponty mentions the "maximum of clarity" in perception, Kelly argues that it is inherent to perception that the perceiving subject is motivated to come to a clearer perception; "I always experience myself to be drawn toward a maximal grip on an object."[23] This point is implied by the passages quoted from *Phenomenology of Perception* above, and the action in perception does seem to entail the motivation to gear into the world better. Kelly goes further, however, and argues that one is motivated in this way because any perceptual experience is "an openness onto the world that in itself eschews lack of clarity."[24] For Kelly, the motivation toward clarity is a constitutive part of all perceptual experiences. This suggests that for every perceptual experience there is clarity to be had; there is some actual state

22. Merleau-Ponty, *Phenomenology*, 17–18.
23. Kelly, "Normative Nature," 152.
24. Ibid., 152.

of "maximal grip" that can be attained. It is this latter point that I believe Merleau-Ponty would disagree with, because it does not take indeterminacy seriously enough as a positive phenomenon.[25]

We can begin to see the point that some perceptual experiences might not include any graspable optimum state by considering Merleau-Ponty's discussion of color constancy. This is the phenomenon (similar in many ways to size constancy) whereby an object's perceived color remains relatively constant despite changing lighting conditions (for example, the color of paint on a wall is perceived as constant despite the presence of shadows). Merleau-Ponty notes:

> The table is and remains brown throughout all of the plays of light . . . what is this real color and how do we have access to it? It will be tempting to respond that it is the color according to which I most often see the table, the one that it takes on in daylight, at close proximity, under "normal" conditions, in short, the most frequent conditions. When the distance is too large, or when the lighting has a color of its own (such as at sunset, or beneath an electric light), I displace the actual color to the benefit of a color from memory which is predominant because it is inscribed in me by numerous experiences. The constancy of the color would thus be a real constancy. But here we have merely an artificial reconstruction of the phenomenon.[26]

This passage seems to lead to a rejection of the existence of some "real color" that is there to be perceived. On the one hand, what Merleau-Ponty is objecting to here as an "artificial reconstruction" is the idea that the phenomenon of color constancy depends on the imposition of the "actual color" by memory. As the text continues, however, Merleau-Ponty sheds doubt on the idea that, the role of memory aside, there is even such a thing as the experience of the "actual" color. The upshot of the pages that follow the above quote is that color perception is thoroughly dependent on specific characteristics of both the environmental context and the perceiving subject; "lighting and the constancy of the illuminated thing, which is its correlate, depend directly upon our bodily situation."[27] So there is no "real color" if

25. It is worth noting that Romdenh-Romluc in "Hallucination," 76–90 makes a very similar argument to Kelly's regarding Merleau-Ponty's views on perceptual normativity. As is the case with Kelly's consideration, I think Romdenh-Romluc's description is mostly correct, but she also overstates the extent to which Merleau-Ponty thinks that there is some optimal perceptual state available, and she underplays the role of indeterminacy.

26. Merleau-Ponty, *Phenomenology*, 318.

27. Ibid., 324.

by that one means some fully objective, entirely context independent color. Of course the emphasis on context-dependence does not itself rule out the notion of optimal perceptual conditions that afford maximal grip. It would only entail that those optimal conditions could not be specified apart from the context. Each possible perceptual context might have its own "maximum of clarity"—the point at which the "three norms" are fulfilled—that could be attained within that context. But even this construal of the optimal condition strains Merleau-Ponty's views. The bodily situation that makes up the perceptual context is dynamic and constantly varies such that Merleau-Ponty claims that any "color-quale is thus mediated by a color-function and is determined in relation to a level that is variable."[28] The idea that there is a maximum of clarity attainable within a particular context implies that different contexts are discrete and have discrete optimal states that are attached to them. But for Merleau-Ponty there are no discrete contexts, there is a perceptual field and a bodily situation which is dynamically variable. The idea of a maximum of clarity loses some of its force if what clarity is constantly shifts and the norm becomes a continually moving target.

Furthermore, for Merleau-Ponty it is the case that the contextual dynamism of perception leads there to be at least some perceptual experiences that are fundamentally ambiguous, and thus would seem to entirely lack any sense of maximum clarity. This is a key element of his discussion of the Müller-Lyer illusion mentioned above. What Merleau-Ponty is specifically objecting to there is the "scientific" or "objectivist" view that the perception of the illusion must in fact first entail a determinate perception of two equal lines. On this view the illusory perception would then be layered onto the initial determinate perception as another determinate element (first we have the perception of equality, then we have the mistaken perception of inequality). Merleau-Ponty chides this view for not "noticing that the nature of the perceived is to tolerate ambiguity, a certain 'shifting' or 'haziness.'"[29] The perceptual experience of seeing the Müller-Lyer illusion is not made up of determinate moments of equality and inequality; rather it is a dynamic process of viewing an ambiguous object which gives itself to be seen in differing ways depending on varying contextual elements.

To be fair to Kelly, he is clearly not committing the objectivist error that Merleau-Ponty is arguing against. He takes perception to involve a dynamic process of coming to grips with the environment. But insofar as he argues that such a process is necessarily oriented toward reaching clarity, he misses Merleau-Ponty's insistence that the nature of the perceived

28. Ibid., 324.
29. Ibid., 11.

is to tolerate ambiguity. Importantly, the French word that is translated as "'shifting' or 'haziness'" is *bougé*, which comes from *bouger*, which means "to move"; a common use of *bougé* is to refer to movement blurring in photography (due to something like camera shake).[30] The suggestion here is that "blurring" or indeterminacy is inherent in the experience because of the dynamism in perception. Thus Merleau-Ponty could not agree with Kelly that our perceptual experiences "simply do not like to be unclear."[31] Perhaps certain theoretical meta-perspectives on perception want to eschew lack of clarity, but perception itself is far more tolerant.

Norms, Context, and Optimum Conditions in Perception and Painting

This last point leaves the present interpretation of Merleau-Ponty in a difficult position. If one takes the idea that perception tolerates ambiguity too far, it would seem to completely undo the idea that Merleau-Ponty takes there to be normativity in perception. Where is the sense of ought in this indeterminacy?

Merleau-Ponty's emphasis on the context dependence of perception can provide us with a clue here. It is completely in keeping with Merleau-Ponty's views that some perceptual contexts might offer a greater "maximum of clarity" than others. The perception of the Müller-Lyer illusion is in some sense a special case, after all, as the illusory figure is designed to play on ambiguities in our visual processing. Perhaps not all instances of perception are quite that ambiguous, and many contexts provide us with the opportunity to gear into the perceived environment quite fully. This could be the case, for instance, when the perceiver in Merleau-Ponty's example comes to recognize the mast of the boat that has run ashore.

And for contexts where there is no obvious optimum state, there can still be more or less optimum conditions. We might not be able to say, for instance, that there is some ultimate "true" perception of a color, but we can tell that certain lighting conditions or distances can give us a better sense of the color of an object. Furthermore we can feel this, and can be motivated to seek out more optimal conditions. So when Merleau-Ponty says that there is a "maximum of clarity in perception and action specifies a perceptual

---

30. I am here elaborating slightly on a point helpfully made by Donald Landes in his translator's notes; see Merleau-Ponty, *Phenomenology*, 500.

31. Kelly, "Normative Nature," 152.

ground," we should interpret this not as referring to a discrete state that can always be obtained, but to an ideal toward which we strive.[32]

This way of thinking about normativity fits well with Busch's claim that the painter is at pains to pick out a "right" color, and can explain why Busch would put "right" in scare quotes. On the one hand, it should seem clear that a painter could use color incorrectly, and this is one element that could distinguish good from bad painting. Consider the following advice regarding matching clothing with skin tone from the 17th Century Dutch master Gerard de Lairesse:

> if I may give my opinion, a red and fiery-faced person, dressed in red, seems to me like a red painted statue; and a pale-looking person in a light or yellow dress, as sick or dead. Wherefore, if we would be artful, we must manage otherwise; to wit, that those whom we would represent healthy or sickly, ought to appear such by contrary colours; as lively colours for a sick or unhealthy person; and weak and faint ones for a healthy person.[33]

It makes plain prima facie sense to say that in some cases color can be used incorrectly (as when colors that represent illness, like yellow, are matched with a pallid skin tone). On the other hand, though, it would seem that the painter's choice of color is highly dependent on the context. For a photorealistic painting, for instance, the correct choice of color would be guided by the norm of representational accuracy because of the attempt to copy the photo. But the case would clearly be different for a color-field painting, where perhaps an emotion is indirectly represented by the color, or maybe nothing is represented at all. The relevant color-norm would shift in these cases depending on the nature of the thing being depicted and the aims of the painter (not to mention the perspective of the audience, the lighting of the gallery, or the numerous other factors that could influence the way the color might be presented in the painting). And de Lairesse even notes that his suggestions regarding color are not a "positive law, without exception" but are rather more like tips for beginners.[34]

Again, this context-and-aim dependence does not rule out any sense of normativity; if the point is to realistically represent a healthy child, there are right and wrong colors for the painter to use. We might note that even in

---

32. See also Merleau-Ponty, *Phenomenology*, 332, which refers to "full coexistence with the phenomenon at the moment when it would be in all relations at its maximum articulation" as being the experience of "absolute reality." The "absolute" suggests that it is a kind of ideal.

33. de Lairesse, *A Treatise*, 23.

34. Ibid., 23.

this case the norm is not entirely free of ambiguity, however, because while one might fairly say that it is wrong for the painter to paint an otherwise vibrant, healthy child with a pallid yellow-green face, there are artists who have found meaning in this seemingly odd juxtaposition (the works of the early German expressionists, such as E.L. Kirchner, provide a good example of this). Thus it is not a "wrong" choice in some absolute, context free sense. And given other aims, there might be contexts where there really is no sense of right or wrong color, but just different possibilities that could elicit different responses (and this might be akin to the painting correlate to the perception that thoroughly tolerates ambiguity).

If construed in this way, Busch's analogy is fitting. For Merleau-Ponty, the normativity in perception is like the discussed normativity in painting in certain key ways. There is a clear sense in which perception can go right or wrong, but exactly how this works is dependent on contextual elements in both the perceived environment and within the perceiver. Furthermore, the normativity in perception can vary with the perceiver's aims. Recall the earlier mentioned actional role in perception: how one comes to grips with the world is going to change depending on what, exactly, one intends to do with that grip (to extend the metaphor). Perhaps there is a bit of a disanalogy here, because the aims of the painter may play a bigger role than the aims of the perceiver (perception is, after all, going to be prominently determined by the condition of the external environment). But for Merleau-Ponty it is nevertheless important that how we gear into the world depends on what we are trying to do in that world.

In many cases, the context may be such that the optimal normative state is fairly clear (and in many forms of painting and perception, some degree of representational accuracy may be very important here). But it is also in the nature of perception, as it is for painting, that there will always be more ambiguous contexts, including some where the language of right and wrong might not apply very well. Perception must tolerate this ambiguity, which must always sit alongside normativity. It is this point that I think Busch's analogy can capture.

Bibliography

Berendzen, J. C. "Disjunctivism and Perceptual Knowledge in Merleau-Ponty and McDowell." *Res Philosophica* 91 (2014) 274–79.

Burge, Tyler. *Origins of Objectivity*. Oxford: Oxford University Press, 2010.

Busch, Thomas W. "The Role of the Cogito in the Philosophy of Maurice Merleau-Ponty." PhD diss., Marquette University, 1966.

Kelly, Sean D. "The Normative Nature of Perceptual Experience." In *Perceiving the World*, edited by Bence Nanay, 146–59. Oxford: Oxford University Press, 2010.
Lairesse, Gerard de. *A Treatise on the Art of Painting, in All Its Branches*. Translated by W. M. Craig. London: Orme, 1817.
Merleau-Ponty, Maurice. *Phenomenology of Perception*. Translated by Donald A. Landes. London: Routledge, 2012.
Romdenh-Romluc, Komarine. "Merleau-Ponty's Account of Hallucination." *European Journal of Philosophy* 17 (2007) 76–90.

5

Misadventures of the Dialectic

Merleau-Ponty and Sartre[1]

—Thomas Flynn

> [Sartre] seldom speaks expressly of the dialectic.
> —Maurice Merleau-Ponty[2]

Merleau-Ponty's most extended discussion of Sartre's use of the dialectic is found in *Adventures of the Dialectic*, published in 1955, the year before his lectures on the dialectic at the *Collège de France* were delivered and five years before the first volume of Sartre's *Critique of Dialectical Reason* appeared.[3] This brief chronology is important because I wish to discuss the "pre-history," the "actuality," and especially the aftermath of the controversy between Merleau-Ponty and Sartre on the nature and function of dialectical thinking. I shall also consider the notes for the *Collège de France* course "*La dialectique*" in the spring of 1956. Though its explicit treatment of Sartre is rather brief, the preceding lectures prepare the way for Merleau-Ponty's critique of what he takes to be the Sartrean dialectic.

---

1. A French translation of this essay will appear in a volume entitled "Merleau-Ponty et la dialectique" co-edited by David Belot and Jean-Pilippe Narboux.

2. Merleau-Ponty, *La dialectique*, 93. I thank the editors David Belot and Jean-Philippe Narboux for allowing me access to their transcription of this text, which I cite in my own translations.

3. Merleau-Ponty, *Adventures*. Sartre, *Critique*.

As Merleau-Ponty points out at the start of these lectures, a dialectical relation between dialectical philosophy and its history such as he is presenting at the *Collège* must navigate between a procrustean dogmatism and a skeptical nominalism. As with any interpretation, one begins with presuppositions that must be articulated in order to frame a plausible hypothesis to be tested by the philosophers and texts to be examined. Whether Merleau-Ponty's treatment is dialectical, or rather "bifocal," synthesizing or simply reciprocating, is something I shall discuss toward the end. But it is clear that Merleau-Ponty is addressing the history of dialectic in order to clarify his own use of a kind of dialectical method. This is what brings him into philosophical contention with his erstwhile friend, Jean-Paul Sartre.

The Dawning of a Dispute

The controversy, which was gradually building despite or perhaps because of the common philosophical background of each in the writings of Hegel, Husserl, and Heidegger, came to a head the year before the lectures, on which these notes are based, were given. It is likely that *Adventures of the Dialectic* and these notes grew out of the same research.[4] In *Adventures*, Merleau-Ponty devoted an inflammatory chapter to "Sartre and Ultrabolshevism" where he claimed, among other things, that Sartre's use of the dialectic is basically incompatible with that of the Communists. So when Sartre remarks in *Communists and Peace*,[5] the text that attracts Merleau-Ponty's attention in this chapter, that he is arguing from *his* principles and not theirs, Merleau-Ponty urges that we take this admission at face value because it will reveal, he insists, that a philosophy based on the *Cogito* is in fact unsuited for a dialectical philosophy, certainly not for a dialectical "materialism." But Sartre, in fact, had rejected dialectical materialism since "Materialism and Revolution" (1946) and even as early as *The Transcendence of the Ego* (1936). He concluded the latter with the observation: "It has always seemed to me that a working hypothesis as fruitful as historical materialism never needed

---

4. Merleau-Ponty's attention in *Adventures* and *Course sur la dialectique* is directed toward Sartre's *Being and Nothingness* and *The Communists and Peace*. The latter appeared in *Les Temps Modernes* between October 1952 and April 1954—at the height of Sartre's "fellow-traveling" with the French Communist Party. Clearly, the Sartrean portion of *Course sur la dialectique* was written soon after, if not along with, *Adventures* (though published in 1955, the original French edition lists its dates of composition as extending from July, 1953 to April–December, 1954). Merleau-Ponty had resigned from the Editorial Board of *Les Temps Modernes* in January of 1953.

5. Sartre, *Communists and Peace*, 68.

for a foundation the absurdity which is metaphysical materialism."[6] Though the word "dialectic" is not mentioned, it is clearly implied in this early work. But if Merleau-Ponty is correct, in order to render his philosophy of the *Cogito* compatible with dialectical materialism, Sartre will have to modify either his understanding of "dialectic" or his concept of "materialism"—or both.

The source of Sartre's troubles with the dialectic, Merleau-Ponty argues, is fourfold. First, his ontology as formulated in *Being and Nothingness* is built on rationalist dichotomies that ignore the ambiguities in which politics and history navigate.[7] That same ontology, second, relies on a stark and unpromising looking/looked-at model of interpersonal relations. Third, Sartre seems insensitive to the phenomenon of "objective contradiction" that generates dialectical processes. Finally, Sartre adopts a reductively "individualist" approach to social wholes and a correspondingly "pointillist" theory of time. In each of these cases, Merleau-Ponty claims, what Sartre lacks is a concept of *mediation*, in the sense of Hegel's "*negation of the negation.*"[8] The generic Sartrean response was offered by Simone de Beauvoir in an equally acerbic essay, "Merleau-Ponty and Pseudo-Sartrianism."[9] The substance of her reply is that Merleau-Ponty knew perfectly well that Sartre was reassessing his social theory and that many of Merleau-Ponty's objections had already been addressed, at least initially, in Sartre's published work. In effect, Merleau-Ponty was writing in bad faith.

The Pre-History

To chart the preparation for this dispute let us consider several texts where Sartre either introduces concepts such as "a becoming truth" (*une vérité devenante*), "objective possibility" (or its equivalent) and especially "praxis" or where he speaks of the dialectic either explicitly or by implication via reference to the distinction between analytical and "synthetic" reasoning. I wish briefly to examine four texts (of which there are many) published prior to *Adventures of the Dialectic* for evidence that Sartre was moving towards a form of dialectical reasoning to be formulated *in extenso* in the *Critique of Dialectical Reason* (1960), even as he held firmly (if perhaps not too consistently) to the epistemology of the *cogito* as a foundation for epistemic and

---

6. Sartre, *Transcendence*, 105.
7. Sartre, *Being and Nothingness*.
8. Merleau-Ponty, *Themes*, 54; and *la dialectique*, 93.
9. Beauvoir, "Pseudo-Sartreanism."

moral thinking.[10] Of course, one may well question whether this "evidence" answers Merleau-Ponty's objection or merely confirms it.

The first text to be considered, *Anti-Semite and Jew*, was written in 1944 but not published till 1946.[11] The next two date from 1947, namely, the essays "Materialism and Revolution," published originally in *Les Temps Modernes* and "Consciousness of Self and Knowledge of Self" (the only address Sartre ever delivered to the *Société françise de Philosophie*, June 2 of that year).[12] The fourth is *The Communists and Peace*, from 1952. If we set quotations from each of these texts opposite objections leveled by Merleau-Ponty in *The Adventures of the Dialectic* against Sartre's would-be dialectic, we shall observe a growing amount of evidence to support Beauvoir's contention that Sartre was indeed expanding his basic conceptual scheme, if not changing his mind completely, to accommodate a dialectical form of reasoning and the ontology to support it. So let us cite an example from each of Sartre's earlier works to indicate how they had already addressed a criticism leveled against him by Merleau-Ponty. I will cite additional criticisms from *La dialectique* in the following section, where these objections are repeated but with a greater emphasis on the perceived weaknesses that Sartre's "dialectic" shares with those of its 19th-century predecessors.

(1) The first criticism to be considered is Merleau-Ponty's assertion that Sartre lacks a concept of *objective possibility*.[13] After pointing out in *Anti-Semite and Jew* that one cannot act "directly" on another freedom—a fundamental existentialist tenet—Sartre proposes as the only remedy for this limitation that one address the *bases and structures* of choice so that the option of anti-Semitism is rendered practically impossible:

---

10. Elsewhere, I have discussed what I take to be Sartre's two epistemologies, mutually exclusive but simultaneously employed in his later work (see Flynn, "Praxis and Vision," 21–43). This could be read as lending support to one half of Merleau-Ponty's contention, namely, that Sartre must abandon the *Cogito* as his starting point if he wishes to embrace a genuine dialectic. The question that demands to be answered is whether one can preserve a place for what Sartre in *Being and Nothingness* calls a "pre-reflective *cogito*" in a dialectical context. Merleau-Ponty is skeptical whereas Sartre undertakes to do so by moving from "consciousness" to *"le vécu"* (lived experience) in the 1950s. As he remarks in an interview given in 1969: "The conception of 'lived experience' (*du vécu*) marks my change since *L'Être et le Néant*. My early work was a rationalist philosophy of consciousness" (Sartre, "Itinerary," 41). I shall weigh the significance of this "conversion" later in the essay.

11. Sartre, *Anti-Semite*.

12. Sartre, "Materialism and Revolution" and "Consciousness of Self."

13. Merleau-Ponty, *Adventures*, 166. The same criticism appears in *Course sur la dialectique*.

> Since [the anti-Semite] like all men, exists as a free agent within a situation, it is his situation that must be modified from top to bottom. In short, if we can change the perspective of choice, then the choice itself will change. Thus we do not attack freedom, but bring it about that freedom decides on other bases, and in terms of other structures.[14]

The explicit premise of his argument is that there exists a close reciprocal relation between human reality and the "material conditions" of its "situation." In effect, Sartre is calling for *structural* change in society to render the "choice" of anti-Semitism virtually impossible.

(2) Secondly, Merleau-Ponty insists that Sartre's philosophy is *individualistic and consciousness-centered*.[15] Yet it was in order to change the bases and structures of choice that Sartre in 1948 joined briefly a political nonparty of the non-Communist left, *Le Rassemblement Démocratique Révolutionaire (Revolutionary Peoples' Assembly)*. Speaking of the role of "situation" in a quasi-manifesto for that group, after insisting that it was a concept that Marxist and non-Marxist alike could accept, Sartre observes:

> Above all, we consider it of little importance whether or not a human be endowed with an unconditional or metaphysical freedom. What does matter is that a human is defined by his social situation, by his belonging to one class or another, . . . that he is defined by the whole of his interests and techniques that form him such that there is no eternal human to save but that *the sole means of freeing humans be by acting on their situations*.[16]

We should note that Lukács had modified Weber's notion of objective possibility by appealing to the "interests" of a class and its members while Sartre in *Being and Nothingness* had added the concept of "techniques for appropriating the world" such as the directions in the Metro system or language itself to underscore the inherently social nature of our being-in-situation.[17]

(3) On Merleau-Ponty's reading, Sartre favors "equivocity" over "ambiguity" and thereby overlooks the domain of the political and the ethical. One might have added that Sartre favors "vision" over "touch" or even "praxis," which Merleau-Ponty thinks he understands as just "pure" action.[18] In sum, Merleau-Ponty believes that Sartre has simply translated

14. Sartre, *Anti-Semite*, 148.
15. Merleau-Ponty, *Adventures*, 204–208, 213–214.
16. Sartre, *Entretiens*, 38–39; author's translation, emphasis added.
17. Sartre, *Being and Nothingness*, 512–531, quote on 512. See also Flynn, *Sartre and Marxist Existentialism*, 74–75 and 28–30.
18. See Merleau-Ponty, *Adventures*, 153.

the holistic terms of Marxian dialectic, for example, into the discourse of his Cartesian individualism: "praxis, revolution, history, the proletariat, and the Party, taken in the sense Marx conceived them, are transformed into their Sartrean homonyms."[19] If correct, this does threaten to undermine whatever examples one might cite in support of a Sartrean "dialectic." In his lectures at the *Collège*, Merleau-Ponty levels a similar criticism against anyone who lacks the "dialectical spirit" which, in his view, seems even to include both Hegel and Marx.[20]

This claim too has some validity, especially Merleau-Ponty's added remark that,

> Ultimately, pure action [the "unanimous Party"] is either suicide or murder. Generally, it is an imaginary (and not, as Sartre believes, an ideal) action. When it tries to impose itself on things, it suddenly returns to the unreal [irréel] from which it was born. It becomes . . . theater. From this come both the extraordinary description of the May 28 demonstration as 'street theater' in which the Parisian population plays the part 'Parisian population,' and Sartre's sympathy for the demonstrations in which the proletariat "shows itself."[21]

Merleau-Ponty is certainly on target when he underscores Sartre's penchant for the imaginary; what he says of Kojève could apply to Sartre as well: "But the question is to know whether there is an original [of the permanent revolution], other than in the realm of the imaginary."[22] The challenge is to distinguish the imaginary from the ideal, from the "as if" that Sartre also favors.[23]

Note the fundamentally ambiguous nature of the "imaginary" in Sartre's usage.[24] It relies on the "irrealising" (sometimes, "derealising") power of

19. Ibid.
20. Merleau-Ponty, *La dialectique*, 35, 40.
21. Merleau-Ponty, *Adventures*, 118.
22. Ibid., 207.
23. See Bürger, *Sartre*. An initial response would be to distinguish the theoretical from the practical. If the imaginary is generic and the ideal a species, one might clarify the problem, if not resolve it, for then it would have to face Sartre's claim that "there is only the point of view of committed (engagée) knowledge" (Sartre, *Being and Nothingness*, 308). The role of the ideal increases as Sartre subsumes, if not abandons, consciousness for a philosophy of praxis. On the role of the "as if" in Sartre's thought in the context of the Kantian presence in his work generally, see Flynn, "Kant and Sartre," 62–76.
24. The imaginary returns in Sartre's studies of Jean Genet (*Saint Genet*) and Gustave Flaubert (*The Family Idiot*) not to mention its incarnation in the events of May, 1968, which a pseudonymous professor at the University of Paris (Nanterre) has

the imagining consciousness in relation to the object by means of an "analogon" that at once invites, directs and limits our experience in a relation that Sartre, in *What is Literature?* describes as an action wherein "the reader is conscious of disclosing in creating, and of creating by disclosing."[25] As he explains, "the process of writing implies that of reading as its dialectical correlative and the two connected acts necessitate two distinct agents. It's the combined effort of author and reader that gives rise to the concrete, imaginary object that is the work of the mind. There is no art except for and by others."[26] Reading seems, in fact, to be the synthesis of perception and creation.[27] But Sartre's dialectic might seem to be "a dialectical going-and-coming" understood as a mere reciprocity or mutuality between artist and viewer, as we suggested above—were it not for the reader/viewer's synthesizing role of perception and creation, as we have just seen.[28] Something irreducibly new is being produced: the work of art.[29]

Even more basic, of course, is Sartre's claim in *Being and Nothingness* that "the situation, the common product of the contingency of the in-itself and of freedom, is an *ambiguous phenomenon* in which it is impossible for the for-itself to distinguish the contribution of freedom from that of the brute existent."[30] We might call this the ambiguity of the "given" and the "taken" in each situation. This exhibits what he calls "the paradox of freedom: there is freedom only in a situation, and there is a situation only through freedom."[31] Admittedly, Sartre has not yet acknowledged the insuperable ambiguity of this phenomenon, for he will later add that this "antin-

---

characterized as a "Sartrean" revolution (See Epistémon, *Ces idées,* 78–87). And the imaginary will play a role in Sartre's "resolution" of seemingly antithetical dichotomies such as fact/value, good/evil (*Saint Genet*), socialism /freedom and perhaps even fraternity/terror (*Hope Now*). But the distinction between the imaginary and the ideal is itself ambiguous and its ambiguity appears, for example, in the *utopian* character of Sartre's adoption of the Marxian discourse of a "new man" concomitant with the philosophy of freedom "that we cannot yet conceive of" in our present alienated state (*Search*, 34). And then there is his projected ideal of a "socialism of abundance" in his Flaubert study (*The Family Idiot*, 5:171). Although Merleau-Ponty wrote an appreciative review of Sartre's early *L'Imagination*, he never lived to witness these later expressions of Sartre's penchant for the imaginary. On this point see Flynn, "Sartre as Philosopher of the Imagination," and *Sartre* (where it functions as the general thesis and theme).

25. Sartre, *What is Literature?*, 48 and 52–53.
26. Ibid., 52.
27. Ibid., 51–52.
28. Ibid., 62.
29. Flynn, "The Role of the Image," 431–442.
30. Sartre, *Being and Nothingness*, 488; emphasis added.
31. Ibid., 489.

omy . . . will give to us the exact relation between freedom and facticity."[32] Of course, it does not reveal any exact relation. But it does open the door for various aspects of the "given" to reveal what Sartre will say remains "an unnamable and unthinkable [sic] *residuum*" which belongs to the in-itself under consideration.[33] One senses that the "rationalist" in Sartre is pausing before the door of an insurmountable ambiguity.

Consider two examples that Sartre discusses in *Being and Nothingness* to illustrate this *residuum*: the slave facing the practice of slavery and the alpinist encountering a "rock that is too steep for scaling." The factical dimension of the slave's situation Sartre characterizes as an "obscure constraint" that forms the *residuum* in the "given" of the situation of enslavement; the factical dimension of the would-be alpinist's situation is the physical dimension and formation of the rock.[34] Sartre admits that these "objective qualities" like the resistance of the rock to the alpinist, are given, not directly, but "only as an *indication* . . . of an inapprehensible quid." He leaves us with a question: Is the world telling me about itself or myself? And his answer: I can never know.[35] This ambiguous situation, whether properly "dialectical" or merely inchoately so, does open the door even in the "Cartesian" *Being and Nothingness* to a resolution—if only Sartre can overcome the barrier of his "looking/looked-at" model of interpersonal relations on which the ontology of *Being and Nothingness* depends. But both in the case of slavery and for the "we-subject" analyzed in *Being and Nothingness*, Sartre at best seems incapable of achieving more than appeal to "A purely subjective *Erlebnis* [experience]."[36] In other words, he seems bound to a psychological account of the interpersonal. In this regard, Merleau-Ponty's critique of the social inadequacies of *Being and Nothingness* is correct.

It is in his seminal essay "Materialism and Revolution" that Sartre directs our attention to the concept of "situation" as the vehicle on which his conversion from an individualist to a holist (socialist) social ontology will turn. "It is the elucidation of the new ideas of 'situation' and 'being-in-the-world' that revolutionary behavior specifically calls for."[37] If it is to enter into a dialectical relationship, the concept of situation must be "temporalized," that is, made fluid; it must be socialized by including essential relations to other individuals, and it must be "materialized" in that it will resist any

---

32. Ibid., 490–491.
33. Ibid., 482.
34. Ibid., 550.
35. Ibid., 488–489.
36. Ibid., 420.
37. Sartre, "Materialism and Revolution," 253.

aspects of an idealist reading without descending into a crassly materialist metaphysics. Sartre continues to reject dialectical materialism in this essay as he had done in *Transcendence of the Ego*. In fact, though he will adopt labor as the model of praxis in the *Critique of Dialectical Reason* and will acknowledge the decisive role of what Marx called the forces and relations of production in historical development, as we shall see, he consistently rejected what he called Marxist "economism," as did Althusser and arguably Marx himself.[38] In a 1960s conversation with two Maoist activists, Sartre expounds the rather heretical thesis that morality is not merely a function of the superstructure but "exists at the very level of production." He agrees with his young discussants that "a worker is moral [*moral*] by the sole fact that he is an alienated human who demands freedom for himself and for all."[39] By then, he will have described his years of fellow-traveling with the French Communist Party as a phase of "amoralist realism,"[40] a stance that comes close to what Merleau-Ponty in *La dialectique* calls Marx's "naturalizing" of the dialectic.[41]

(4) The last objection raised by *Adventures of the Dialectic* is that Sartre fails to justify the properly social; that is, "he grounds communist action precisely by refusing any productivity to history and by making history, insofar as it is intelligible, the immediate result of our volitions."[42] Again, Merleau-Ponty has spotted a weakness but has failed to recognize it as an invitation for properly dialectical repair. It is the *lack of mediations* in Sartre's consciousness-oriented ontology that prevents him from achieving a properly "dialectical philosophy." Where one expects process, unintended consequences and the productive negation of negation, one gets spontaneity, voluntarism, and a rationalist drive for transparency.[43]

Merleau-Ponty catches Sartre in a particularly vulnerable position when he quotes him as saying "No one believes any longer in the proletariat fetish, a metaphysical entity from which the workers might alienate themselves. There are humans, animals, and objects."[44] To this Merleau-Ponty responds: "Marx, on the other hand, thought there were relationships be-

38. Althusser, *For Marx*, 108–109 and 213.
39. Gavi, et al., *raison de se révolter*, 45.
40. Ibid., 79.
41. Merleau-Ponty, *La dialectique*, 76 n.122.
42. Merleau-Ponty, *Adventures*, 97–98. Merleau-Ponty also notes, "Sartre founds Communist action precisely by refusing any productivity to history and by making history, insofar as it is intelligible, the immediate result of our volitions. As for the rest, it is an impenetrable opacity" (*Adventures*, 97–98).
43. See Merleau-Ponty, *La dialectique*, 92.
44. Sartre, *Communists and Peace*, 89.

tween persons 'mediated by things,' and for him revolution, like capitalism, like all the realities of history, belong to this mixed order." And he concludes: "Sartre today [in *The Communists and Peace*] is as far away from Marx as when he wrote *Materialism and Revolution*."[45]

Merleau-Ponty has asserted that Sartre transforms Marxist discourse into existentialist meanings. This again is partially true. Whatever label Sartre bears, it will always carry his particular signature. As he said, even his fellow-traveling with the *French Communist Party* will be based on *his* principles, not theirs. But there are remarks in *The Communists and Peace* that, *pace* Merleau-Ponty, show Sartre continuing to move in a Marxian, dialectical direction. The "obscure constraints" of facticity mentioned earlier have now hardened from psychological phenomena into the kind of historical necessity which Lukács defends. Sartre begins to speak of an objective contradiction arising for the workers between the need to survive and the need to be human: the contradiction is not only *in* him; it is imposed on him; mass production requires that he be contradictory. He is simultaneously a man and a piece of machinery. People demand his services whenever it is too difficult or too costly to build an automatically controlled machine; the progress of cybernetics will render him useless."[46] Indeed, Sartre now judges the fortunes of the workers' movement *sub specie totalitatis*: "The historical whole determines our power at any given moment; it prescribes their limits in our field of action and our real future; it conditions our attitude toward the possible and the impossible, the real and the imaginary, what is and what should be, time and space."[47] Now in full possession of the concept of objective possibility, he continues memorably: "It is history which shows some the exits and makes other cool their heels before closed doors."[48] But again, as with the "bases and structures" of the anti-Semite's choices, the details of these relationships have still not been addressed.

The Challenge Renewed and the Response Strengthened

It now remains to discuss the foregoing in terms of Sartre's *Search for a Method* and *Critique of Dialectical Reason*.[49] But first let me consider sev-

45. Merleau-Ponty, *Adventures*, 124.
46. Sartre, *Communists and Peace*, 53.
47. Ibid., 80.
48. Ibid.
49. Merleau-Ponty fails to mention these works by name in his working notes to *Visible and Invisible*. *Search* was originally published in fall 1957 and the *Critique* was

eral traits of a dialectical philosophy that Merleau-Ponty articulates in his *"Notes préparatoires."* Though I shall focus on features that he takes to be ingredient in *any* dialectical philosophy, my chief concern is with conditions for a genuine dialectic that Sartre may be considered not to have met, especially those mentioned in Merleau-Ponty's brief consideration of Sartre toward the end of his preparatory notes.

The Challenge Renewed

Although Merleau-Ponty does not want to give us the "essence" of dialectic or of dialectical philosophy in these lecture notes, he clearly believes that the "necessary" conditions for what he terms the "modern" dialectic can be discerned. He concentrates on four philosophers who do not meet these conditions completely: Hegel, Kierkegaard, Marx and Sartre. It is their inadequacies, he insists, that enable us to sketch the outline for a genuine dialectic. So let us consider these conditions as missed by the others to determine the degree to which Sartre is presumed to fail this test as well.

Hegel. It is curious that this master of the modern dialectic should be considered wanting in its regard. But Merleau-Ponty criticizes his slide into *spéculation* as a betrayal of the dialectic as a philosophy of the concrete in favor of what Kierkegaard criticizes as "The System." It was Kierkegaard, recall, who remarked: "It is perfectly true, as philosophers say, that life must be understood backwards. But they forget the other proposition, that it must be lived forwards."[50] In Merleau-Ponty's view, Hegel has overlooked the fundamental *ambiguity* of the dialectical relationship in favor of an "equivocation" between thesis and antithesis. In effect, he has removed the "risk" of the future for the sake of what Marx called "*post festum*" necessity. Silently waiting at the end of the dialectical process, as both Merleau-Ponty and Foucault agreed, is Hegel's form of identity—the fruit of equivocation having overcome ambiguity.

Kierkegaard. The melancholic Dane also failed Merleau-Ponty's test. He famously denied the philosophy of "mediation" and with it the Hegelian dialectic in favor of an either/or that called for a decisive "leap" in place

---

originally published in May, 1960. Merleau-Ponty's last working note is dated March 1961 (he died on May 3 1961). Given his long-standing interest in the Sartrean dialectic, it is unlikely that he had not read *Search* or was unfamiliar with the *Critique*. In fact an entry for June 1, 1960 does mention Sartre's philosophy of history by name and refers to the concepts of "praxis individuelle" and "la matière ouvrée" [worked matter]. The latter occurs in the *Critique* but not in *Search*. So it seems likely that Merleau-Ponty had some familiarity with that text which had appeared the month before.

50. Kierkegaard, *Journals*, entry for 1843, No. 465.

of a reconciling *Aufhebung*. Kierkegaard takes this as the "individualizing" act *par excellence*, but Merleau-Ponty points out that Kierkegaard "blames the notion of mediation, that is, the dialectic itself for this failure to reach the concrete."[51] Merleau-Ponty describes this joyful leap out of ignorance as "religious atheism"[52]—an expression worthy of Nicholas of Cusa or the Rhineland Mystics in its attempt to reach the concrete with a voluntaristic act.[53]

Marx. Like Hegel, Marx is criticized for reading the fundamental dialectical relation as one of "equivocation" rather than of ambiguity. But in the case of Marx, the equivocation is resolved in terms of "Nature" and not "*Geist*." As the American epistemologist W.V.O. Quine "naturalized" epistemology, so Marx, in Merleau-Ponty's view, has "naturalized" the dialectic against Feuerbach. Engels is commonly seen as the culprit with his three natural "laws" of the dialectic: the transformation of quantity into quality and inversely; the interpenetration of opposites, and the *negation of negation*. It is this third "law" that Merleau-Ponty reads as "mediation" and which he notes Engels finally abandoned.

Sartre. In addition to the criticism devoted to him in *Adventures of the Dialectic*, Merleau-Ponty reserves several additional critical remarks for Sartre at the end of his "Notes préparatoires." After claiming that Sartre's negative is equivocal in principle, he links him with Kojève and Lukács as anthropologizing the dialectic in favor of a "humanism." The proper locus of dialectic is man, they are arguing. There could not be a dialectic of Nature because consciousness is essentially *néantissant* and constitutes the source of whatever negativity one experiences in the world. The analogies between Kojève and Sartre are sufficient to justify applying to the latter what Merleau-Ponty says of the former. Taking the example of a gold ring as an analog for the human being, Merleau-Ponty begins a phenomenological description of a properly dialectical relationship as understood by Kojève/Sartre. Without pursuing Merleau-Ponty's complex and rather obscure argument in *La dialectique*, its upshot is that Sartre's dualistic ontology again makes a dialectical relationship impossible so long as the *en-soi* merely absorbs the nihilating relation of the pour-soi or passively returns its "othering" power.

51. Merleau-Ponty, *La dialectique*, 62.

52. Ibid.

53. Kierkegaard's situation is a bit more complex than is often conceived. Discussing "the aesthetic validity of marriage" with a young aesthete, for example, the writer warns: "If you cannot reach the point of seeing the aesthetic, the ethical, and the religious as three great allies, if you do not know how to preserve the unity of the different expressions everything acquires within these different spheres, then life is without meaning . . ." (Kierkegaard, *Either/Or*, 469).

The "double negation" and thus the dialectic for Sartre will have to be limited to for-itselves.

Merleau-Ponty goes on to show that there exists a "dialectic" that is the polar opposite to that of Marx.[54] Again, the problem is Sartre's insuperable duality and its grounding of the social on the looking/looked-at relation that supports no properly "social" realm, no "*intermonde*," as Merleau-Ponty insists, but only a plurality of individual consciousnesses: "In Sartre, there is a plurality of subjects but no intersubjectivity."[55] He adds perceptively, "On a closer look, the absolute right that the I accords the other is rather a duty. They are not joined in action, in the relative and the probable, but only in principles and on condition that the other stick rigorously to them, that he does credit to his name and to the absolute negation that it promises."[56] This is another challenge that Sartre will meet with his discussion of the "group in fusion" in the *Critique of Dialectical Reason*.

Secondly, Merleau-Ponty presciently contrasts the "terrorist" aspect of Kojève's dialectic and by implication that of Sartre with the "excessively optimistic" one of Marx. According to Kojève, "Marx maintains the themes of struggle and work . . . but neglects the theme of death." In effect, he fails to recognize "the Hegelian theme of terror."[57] But, of course, this anticipates the contrasting pair of "fraternity terror" that will figure prominently in the *Critique*, not to mention in Sartre's sympathy with *Les Maos* in the late sixties and early seventies. This is a duality that Sartre will admit to Benny Lévy in his final interviews that he has never succeeded in resolving.[58]

It is worth noting that a somewhat similar criticism of Hegel, Marx and Sartre is made by Merleau-Ponty's former student, Michel Foucault. Addressing the humanism of Sartre, he remarks:

> Humanism, anthropology and dialectical thought go together. What ignores man is contemporary analytical reason that entered the scene with Russell and which has appeared with Lévy-Strauss and the linguistic philosophers. This analytic reason is incompatible with humanism whereas dialectic itself appeals to humanism if need be.
>
> It does so for several reasons: because it is a philosophy of history, because it is a philosophy of human practice, because it is a philosophy of alienation and reconciliation. For all these

---

54. Merleau-Ponty, *La dialectique*, 92.
55. Merleau-Ponty, *Adventures*, 205
56. Ibid.
57. Merleau-Ponty, *La dialectique*, 92, see also *Adventures*, 216.
58. Sartre and Lévy, *Hope Now*, 93.

reasons and because it is always fundamentally a philosophy of return to oneself, the dialectic promises the human being that in some way he will become authentic and true. It promises man to man and, to that extent, is indissociable from a humanist ethic. In this sense, the ones most answerable for contemporary humanism are obviously Hegel and Marx.[59]

In sum, the necessary condition for achieving a genuine dialectic is the double "internal negation," a negation that is not a return to the *status quo ante* (as is the double negation in analytic reason) but a truly "synthetic" relation, one that, as Hegel said, at once "negates, conserves and raises up"; in other words, *eine Aufhebung*. If this terminology has been too closely associated with German idealism and subsequently with its Marxist inversion, Merleau-Ponty is suggesting and Sartre would seem to agree that what is called for today (at least in the late 1950s) is to abandon the letter of the dialectic for its spirit. And that dialectical "spirit" is one of *perpetual* contestation, "a tension in which alterity (even and especially within ourselves) is ever sublimated. This spirit is open, not closed. If it is haunted by the evil spirit of identity, it should be resisted as Kant advised one to avoid the sorcerers of transcendent metaphysics."[60]

The Response Strengthened

As before, I would like to discuss Sartre's response to Merleau-Ponty's critique of his so-called *dialectique ratée*, but this time stressing his consequential response as distinct from his "preemptive" response given earlier.

In *Search for a Method*, it is almost as if Sartre had the text of *Adventures of the Dialectic* at hand when he addressed the issues of relations and mediation. Regarding the first, he could not have been more explicit: he agrees with Marx that "there are only men and *real relations* between men."[61] The entire social ontology that he will articulate in the *Critique* hangs on this principle. So too does the "dialectical nominalism," whether consistent or not, that he invents to support it.

As for the matter of mediation, Sartre devotes an entire chapter of *Search for a Method* to the topic. In doing so, he has an eye on the biography of Flaubert on which he had been laboring for years. In fact, though *Search for a Method* is attached to the *Critique* as a kind of Introduction, it was not written for that purpose and, in several respects is more relevant to *The*

59. Foucault, *Dits,* 541. See Merleau-Ponty, *La dialectique,* 41.
60. See Merleau-Ponty, *La dialectique,* 15.
61. Sartre, *Search,* 76.

Family Idiot than to the *Critique*. The function of mediation for Sartre as for the others is to enable us to understand the individual. There is no "science of the singular," Aristotle insisted, but Hegel, the German Aristotle, as he has been called, argued the contrary (reconceiving Aristotle's concepts of science and of dialectic in the process). In brief, Sartre repeats the gesture, this time arguing against the "economism" of Marxist "scholastics of the 1950s": "Valéry is a petit bourgeois intellectual, no doubt about it. [. . .] But not every petit bourgeois intellectual is Valéry. The heuristic inadequacy of contemporary Marxism," Sartre urges "is contained in these two sentences. Marxism lacks any hierarchy of mediations . . ."[62] This is what *Search for a Method* will supply with its progressive-regressive method and both the *Critique* and *The Family Idiot* will exhibit in detail. So pervasive does the concept become in Sartre's subsequent work that Louis Althusser can call him, "The philosopher of mediations *par excellence*."[63]

Turning to the *Critique*, which can be read as a lengthy and verbose response to *Les Aventures*, I shall concentrate on three issues that form the heart of the controversy and of Sartre's position in view of Merleau-Ponty's pointed critique: (1) the conceptual elements of Sartre's social ontology, specifically praxis and the practico-inert; (2) the particular genius of *le tiers médiateur* (the mediating third) and (3) what he calls a "dialectical nominalism" that is fashioned to bring these elements into play so that Raymond Aron's challenge of 1946 which is echoed by Merleau-Ponty ten years later can be answered, namely, the possibility of uniting Kierkegaard and Marx into a complete and coherent social theory.[64]

(1) Praxis and the practico-inert

Sartre defines "praxis" in several places at increasing length. Although praxis (purposive human activity in its sociohistorical context) had already entered Sartre's vocabulary in *What is Literature?* (1947), where it is defined as "action in history and on history; that is, a synthesis of historical relativity and moral and metaphysical absolute, with this hostile and friendly, terrible and derisive world which it reveals to us,"[65] as well as in his posthumously published *Notebooks for an Ethics*, composed in 1947–1948[66], praxis assumes

---

62. Ibid., 56.
63. Althusser and Balibar, *Reading Capital*, 136.
64. "A follower of Kierkegaard cannot at the same time be a follower of Marx" (Aron, *Marxism and the Existentialists*, 30).
65. Sartre, *What is Literature?*, 194.
66. Sartre, *Notebooks*.

a threefold primacy in the *Critique* and, I would argue, in Sartre's later philosophy in general. It inherits the intentionality and the self-transparency of the for-itself. Like consciousness, praxis is ontologically free, for it is the unifying and reorganizing transcendence (*dépassement*) of existing circumstances toward the practical field.[67] But Sartre has come to realize that this transcendence is *dialectical*; that is, it is simultaneously negation, conservation and spiraling advance. In other words, praxis is *totalizing*. Still, every totalization of which free organic praxis is a part, is *eo ipso* de-totalizing as well. Like "human reality" in *Being and Nothingness*, "free organic praxis" in the *Critique* is non-coincidental with itself. In both cases, we are dealing with a "being of distances," as Merleau-Ponty and Heidegger would say.

I spoke of a *threefold primacy of praxis* in the *Critique*: Epistemic and methodological, Ontological, and Ethical. I have developed each of these at length elsewhere [68] But the point here is that, *pace* Lévy-Strauss, analytic rationality is grounded in the dialectical comprehension of "free organic praxis," whether alone or in mediated relations; secondly, ontologically praxis is the existential foundation of social efficacy via mediated reciprocities in the group or via the alienating power of practico-inert mediation in series and institutions; and, finally, the same free organic praxis is the locus of moral responsibility for even the most impersonal social structures and systems. If Sartre can write of colonialism or capitalism that "the meanness is in the system,"[69] referring to practico-inert structures and processes, the moral primacy of praxis demands that we qualify that statement: the meanness is "not entirely" in the system. As Marx stated famously, the capitalist is both the beneficiary and the victim of the capitalist system. So with Sartre, in principle, one can always find morally responsible agents amidst the most "necessary" social structures and processes when one moves from the abstract to the concrete. In response to Merleau-Ponty's question: Who/what bears the dialectic? Sartre can point to free organic praxes in their real relations.

The practico-inert is a major Sartrean contribution to social thought. It accounts for the kind of "social" causality that other, more analytic thinkers ascribe to "iron laws" or "impersonal systems." Sartre is not denying the value of analytic reason, which deals with structures and processes. But we should understand that the practico-inert is *practico*-inert. That is, it is the sedimentation of previous praxes. The dialectical ambiguity of Sartre's earlier ontology of the in-itself and the for-itself is being played out here

---

67. Sartre, *Critique*, 1:310n.
68. Flynn, *Sartre and Marxist Existentialism*, 105–112.
69. Sartre, *Communists and Peace*, 183.

as well. But now in a chastened manner. The practico-inert is not only a major historical player in terms of its counter-finality, but it figures in what thinkers like Althusser would call "structural" causality. Even though Sartre will speak of the practico-inert as "anti-dialectical" since it supports analytical reasoning, its status again as "practico"-inert confers on it a dialectical ambiguity as well.[70]

(2) *The particular genius of the mediating third*

Dialectical reason with its stress on the concrete requires the mediation of a third. Simply stated, where the practico-inert mediates (as with the television-viewing audience), the resultant human relations are "serial," they are "othering"; where praxis mediates, Sartre insists, the relations are free. He refers to relations where praxis mediates as constituting "a free interindividual reality."[71] There are third parties that objectify (usually taken to mean "alienate") others as Sartre explained in detail when discussing the "us-objet" in *Being and Nothingness*. But, thanks to praxis, the ontological obstacle of the looking/looked-at model of social relations has been removed and a genuinely ontological "we-subject" has emerged. Such is the group-in-fusion as well as the group *simpliciter* and the group-member as such. The group is a new and ontologically "higher" ordered set of relations (Husserl) endowed with qualities distinct from those of individual nonmembers. First of these qualities is *power* (a typical example from methodological holism). But Sartre speaks of other "common qualities such as "adopted inertia [e.g., the oath] . . . rights and duties, structure, violence and fraternity" as well. The member "actualizes all these reciprocal relations as his new being, his sociality."[72] If Merleau-Ponty could justifiably claim that the properly social, the "interworld" was missing in *Being and Nothingness*, he could scarcely say that of the *Critique*.

What I'm calling the "genius" of the third refers to its capacity to *mediate without objectifying* the plurality of praxes in its circle. The objectifying third is operative in serial relations mediated by the practico-inert, where the unity takes the form either of an organic identity among individuals (as in the totalitarian State) or as the merely extrinsic denomination of serialized individuals (as in the crowd at a football match). The mediating third, on the contrary, constitutes a relation of "sameness," not "identity" among the members. The union is one of common interest and practice as in the

---

70. See Sartre, *Critique*, 1:310n.
71. Ibid., 367.
72. Ibid., 510.

football team or the Party cell (Sartre's examples). As a group member, the organic individual can accomplish things impossible alone. In fact, the later Sartre acknowledges to his Maoist interlocutors: "I think that an individual in the group, even if he is a little bit terrorized [sic], is much better than an individual alone and thinking separation. I do not believe that the individual alone can accomplish anything."[73]

Though I can only sketch that relationship and its particular function here, I am especially concerned to locate the mediating third in the inner life of the group in light of what Merleau-Ponty in *La dialectique* points out is Plato's concept of the same ("*le même*" as *l'autre que l'autre*), since both mediating third and *the same* are properly dialectical concepts, it seems to me. They both are doubly negating in a positive manner that resists return to simple identity. The mediation of the group cannot be that of some organic whole. Sartre introduces two technical terms, "the same" and "ubiquity," to maintain the nonsubstantial character of the group's unity and mediation—since the group as a relational entity mediates the unity as does the praxis of each mediating third. Their function is to account for that practical unity which reflects multiplicity as transformed from serial impotence to power. "Ubiquity" refers to the circularity proper to the group, where each is doing what I as member would do were I over there. In other words every "over there" is a "here" in terms of my practical identity and active concern. This contrasts with "serial" unity, which Sartre calls a "unity of flight," a pseudo unity, a unity in otherness, where each is other to the other (consider, for example, the trading floor on Wall Street or the initial hour of a major sale at a department store).

(3) *The paradox of a dialectical nominalism*

I would argue that this is Sartre's paradoxical and possible dialectical answer to the various objections that Merleau-Ponty has marshaled against his would-be dialectical thought. The theory is paradoxical because it is a strange kind of nominalism that speaks of "real" relations among individuals. And yet, it would be an equally curious dialectic that did not because the "negations" and "negations of negations" on which the modern dialectic turns, are chiefly, though not exclusively (*pace* F.H. Bradley) "internal." To put it briefly, what makes Sartre's position dialectical is the *ambiguity* inherited from the existential "situation" but now rendered negating, conserving and uplifting by *totalizing praxis*. What keeps it "nominalistic" is the threefold primacy of free organic praxis. This too is what guards its properly

---

73. Gavi, et al., *raison de se révolter*, 171.

"existentialist" character: One can always make something out of what one has been made into and, correspondingly, one should always seek responsible individuals in the midst of the most impersonal processes (again the meanness is not entirely in the system). For this reason, Sartre can speak of a "decapitated dialectic" in the sense that every totality is a detotalized totality because of the inner distance of organic praxis and likewise refer to "a dialectic with holes."[74] These holes are the tiny slivers of freedom that define the existential individual, whether as for-itself (*Being and Nothingness*) or as organic praxis (*Critique of Dialectical Reason*).

Concluding Remarks

Early in his preparatory lecture notes, we observed Merleau-Ponty reflect: "We are leaving the letter of the dialectic for its spirit."[75] Does this gesture toward another misadventure? A matter of getting "beyond" Marx and perhaps beyond the dialectic itself? Was not this Merleau-Ponty's undertaking at the time of his death? He seemed to be heading away from a philosophy of consciousness to one of language and beyond.[76] And does this not portend Sartre's own move as well? In an interview he gave to Michel Contat as he turned seventy, Sartre remarked how it was Marxism as a philosophy of power that he rejected, not several of its tenets such as the class struggle, surplus value and the rest, that he continued to find valid. But he added: "We must develop a way of thinking which takes Marxism into account *in order to go beyond it*, to reject it and take it up again, to absorb it. This is the condition for arriving at a *true socialism*."[77] In the famous exchange of letters between the two erstwhile friends, Sartre accused Merleau-Ponty of having abandoned politics to pursue philosophy in his work on *Le Visible et l'invisible* whereas we know that Sartre himself was in the process of moving in the other direction, bidding his adieu to imaginative literature with *Les Mots* and joining the youthful enthusiasts of truth and violence under the banner of "Maoism"—though, to repeat, he never was a Maoist. Whatever the direction that politics or *La Pensée* would subsequently take, the writing, the example and the spirit of Merleau-Ponty and Sartre, whether intertwined or in creatively mutual opposition have continued to be felt by succeeding generations.

74. Sartre, *Notebooks*, 459.
75. Merleau-Ponty, *La dialectique*, 15.
76. See Lefort, "Editor's Forward," xviii–xx.
77. Sartre, *Life/Situations*, 61; emphasis added.

Bibliography

Althusser, Louis. *For Marx*. Translated by Ben Brewster. London: Verso, 1969.
Althusser, Louis, and Étienne Balibar. *Reading Capital*. Translated by Ben Brewster. London: Verso, 1970.
Aron, Raymond. *Marxism and the Existentialists*. New York: Harper & Row, 1969.
Beauvoir, Simone. "Merleau-Ponty and Pseudo-Sartreanism." Translated by Veronique Zaytzeff. In *The Debate between Sartre and Merleau-Ponty*, edited by Jon Stewart, 448–91. Evanston: Northwestern University Press, 1998.
Bürger, Peter. *Sartre. Ein Philosophie des Als-ob*. Frankfurt: Suhrkamp, 2007.
Epistémon (Didier Anzieu). *Ces idées qui ont ébranlé la France*. Paris: Feyard, 1968.
Flynn, Thomas. "Kant and Sartre: Psychology and Metaphysics: The Quiet Power of the Imaginary." In *Comparing Kant and Sartre*, edited by Sorin Baiasu, 62–76. London: Palgrave Macmillan, 2016.
———. "Praxis and Vision: Elements of a Sartrean Epistemology." *The Philosophical Forum* 8 (1976) 21–43.
———. "The Role of the Image in Sartre's Aesthetic." *The Journal of Aesthetics and Art Criticism* 33 (1975) 431–42.
———. *Sartre: A Philosophical Biography*. Cambridge: Cambridge University Press, 2014.
———. *Sartre and Marxist Existentialism: The Test Case of Collective Responsibility*. Chicago University Press, 1984.
———. "Sartre as Philosopher of the Imagination." *Philosophy Today* 50 (2006) 106–12.
Foucault, Michel. *Dits et écrits 1954–1988*. Vol. 1, *1954–1969*. Edited by Daniel Defert et. al. Paris: Gallimard, 1994.
Gavi, Philippe et. al. *On a Raison de se Révolter: Discussions*. Paris: Gallimard, 1974.
Kierkegaard, Søren. *Either/Or. A Fragment of Life*. Abridged and translated by Alistair Hannay. London: Penguin, 1992.
———. *The Journals of Søren Kiekegaard*. Translated by Alexander Dru. Oxford University Press, 1951.
Lefort, Claude. "Editor's Foreword." In Maurice Merleau-Ponty, *The Visible and the Invisible*, edited by Claude Lefort, xi–xxxiii. Translated by Alphonso Lingis. Evanston, IL: Northwestern University Press, 1968.
Merleau-Ponty, Maurice. *Adventures of the Dialectic*. Translated by Joseph Bien. Evanston, IL: Northwestern University Press, 1973.
———. *La dialectique: Notes de Cours du Collège de France (1955–1956)*. Transcribed and annotated by David Belot and Jean-Philippe Narboux. Paris: Seuil, forthcoming.
———. *Themes from the Lectures at the Collège de France. 1952–1960*. Translated by John O'Neill. Evanston, IL: Northwestern University Press, 1970.
———. *The Visible and the Invisible*. Edited by Claude Lefort. Translated by Alphonso Lingis. Evanston, IL: Northwestern University Press, 1968.
Sartre, Jean-Paul. *Anti-Semite and Jew*. Translated by George J. Becker. Schocken, 1976.
———. *Being and Nothingness*. Translated by Hazel E. Barnes. Philosophical Library, 1956.
———. *The Communists and Peace, with A Reply to Claude Lefort*. Translated by Marthe H. Fletcher and Philip R. Berk. New York: Braziller, 1968.
———. "Consciousness of Self and Knowledge of Self." Translated by Mary Ellen Lawrence and Nathaniel Lawrence. In *Readings in Existential Phenomenology*,

edited by Nathaniel Lawrence and Daniel O'Connor, 113–42. Englewood Cliffs, NJ: Prentice- Hall, 1967.

———. *Critique of Dialectical Reason*, 2 vols. Translated by Alan Sheridan Smith and Quentin Hoare. London: New Left Books, 1976.

———. *Entretiens sur la politique*. Paris: Gallimard, 1949.

———. *The Family Idiot*. 5 vols. Translated by Carol Cosman. Chicago: University of Chicago Press, 1981–1993.

———. "The Itinerary of a Thought." Translated by John Matthews. In *Between Existentialism and Marxism*, 33–64. New York: Verso, 2008.

———. *Life/Situations: Essays Written and Spoken*. Translated by Paul Auster and Lydia Davis. New York: Pantheon, 1977.

———. "Materialism and Revolution." Translated by Annette Michelson. In *Literary and Philosophical Essays*, 198–256. New York: Collier, 1962.

———. *Notebooks for a Ethics*. Translated by David Pellauer. Chicago: University of Chicago Press, 1992.

———. *Saint Genet: Actor and Martyr*. Translated by Bernard Frechtman. New York: Pantheon, 1983.

———. *Search for a Method*. Translated by Hazel E. Barnes. New York: Vintage, 1968.

———. *The Transcendence of the Ego: An Existentialist Theory of Consciousness.*. Translated by Forest Williams and Robert Kirkpatrick. New York: Noonday, 1957.

———. *"What Is Literature?" and Other Essays*. Introduction by Steven Ungar. Cambridge: Harvard University Press, 1988.

Sartre, Jean-Paul, and Benny Levy. *Hope Now: The 1980 Interviews*. Translated by Adrian van den Hoven. Chicago: University of Chicago Press, 1996.

6

The End of the Gaze

—Shaun Gallagher

At the end of your gaze, there I am; at the end of my gaze, there you are. Neither you nor I, however, are frozen in place. Sartre famously thinks of the gaze as freezing or reifying the other as an object. But the gaze does something different. It calls for a response. Levinas conceives this response as a response to the transcendence of the other, the otherness of the other that makes this an asymmetrical relation. I will argue, even if these two philosophers are quite different in their emphases, they agree on the formal asymmetrical nature of the gaze. I'll further argue that their analyses capture only derivative phenomena, and that the primary phenomenon that they fail to grasp concerns the interactive aspect of intersubjectivity. In this regard, I'll argue, the gaze primarily serves interaction, and that the notion of transcendence should be understood in that context.

Sartre

Sartre's concept of the gaze is well known. It's a dramatic part of his analysis of bad faith. The gaze is objectifying in that context, but as Thomas Busch points out, it also opens up the possibility of encountering the other as a subject, and the possibility of an authentic relationship.

> The Other as subjectivity cannot, by definition, be given to me as an appearance, for this would cast the Other into objectivity. The other side of the coin, of course, is that the Other can look

at me, fixing me into the mode of the in-itself. It is through my experience of my objectivity for the Other that I encounter the Other as a subject.[1]

Sartre works out his position in this regard by consulting Hegel, Husserl, and Heidegger. He quickly dismisses Husserl's analysis; one could say that Sartre's critique of the transcendence of the ego was also a critique of the transcendence of the alter-ego. As he notes, however, this doesn't help to solve the problem of intersubjectivity.[2] Sartre finds more inspiration in Hegel. For Hegel, self-consciousness must become a consciousness of self as object. The other is the mediator of this process.

> The mediator is the Other. The Other appears along with myself since self-consciousness is identical with itself by means of the exclusion of every Other. Thus the primary fact is the plurality of consciousnesses, and this plurality is realized in the form of a double, reciprocal relation of exclusion . . . it is by the very fact of being me that I exclude the Other. The Other is the one who excludes me by being himself, the one whom I exclude by being myself.[3]

This reciprocal exclusion sets the stage for an oppositional relation. The other, a self-conscious being, appears to me as an ordinary object immersed in the being of life. I appear to the other in the same way: "as a concrete, sensible, immediate existence." In the Hegelian analysis, this is the negative part of the dialectic. My existence (being-for-itself) is conditioned by the recognition of the Other. This involves a mutual recognition, which only comes about if I recognize the other as another self-consciousness. This is sometimes problematic, as we learn from Hegel's master-slave dialectic.

> To the extent that the Other apprehends me as bound to a body and immersed in life, I am myself only an Other. In order to make myself recognized by the Other, I must risk my own life. To risk one's life, in fact, is to reveal oneself as not-bound to the objective form or to any determined existence-as not-bound to life.[4]

Accordingly, my being-for-others turns out to be a necessary condition for my being-for-self. According to Sartre, however, there is still a problem since this relation remains a relation of mere formal knowledge—as if my life or

1. Busch, *The Power of Consciousness*, 34.
2. Sartre, *Being and Nothingness*, 235.
3. Ibid., 236.
4. Ibid., 237.

existence were simply being-an-object of the other's consciousness. Sartre famously favors the idea that one's existence (being-for-itself) excludes all objectivity. In effect, relations where there is a simple knowing of the other as object, or a knowing by the other of me as object, fail as genuine encounters. With Hegel, on Sartre's reading, we end up with two objects when we really need two subjects.

Sartre thus turns to Heidegger's notion of "being-with" (*Mitsein*), which is already part of the structure of human existence. But after the excitement of opposition in Hegel, Sartre finds Heidegger's analysis too tame. It lacks the frontal relation of recognition and the implicit conflict found therein. Being-with one another suggests the solidarity of "the they" (*Das Man*), or an "oblique interdependence" as we work through our pragmatic tasks. Indeed, there is good reason to question Heidegger's analysis on just this ground, i.e., that he characterizes human intersubjective relations overwhelmingly in terms of encountering others in and through our involvement in pragmatic relations with one another.[5] Heidegger improves on Hegel only in characterizing this relation, not in terms of knowledge, but in terms of being. The problem, for Sartre, is that Heidegger doesn't explain how the coexistence of *Mitsein* comes about or how opposition comes about.

According to Sartre's own analysis, we perceive the other as an object, but not as a mere object—we experience a relation to the other—a "being-in-a-pair-with-the-Other" which involves experiencing the other as a subject. "This relation, in which the Other must be given to me directly as a subject although in connection with me, is the fundamental relation, the very type of my being-for-others."[6] He gives the example of another person entering into a park in which I have been sitting alone. This other person is not just an object; indeed, his subjectivity has an effect on me, and on my perception of the surroundings: "an element of disintegration in that universe is what I mean by the appearance of a man in my universe."[7] There is a rearrangement of the world that I cannot fully grasp since I cannot fully take up his perspective as a subject.

The effect of the other person on me is best described in Sartre's analysis of the gaze. He gives us the famous example of the peeping tom who is caught in the act.[8] As someone caught in the act, I become an object for the other. This means, first, that the other is not an object for me, since only a subject has this power to gaze at me as an object. It is just here, as

---

5. See Gallagher and Jacobson, "Heidegger and Social Cognition."
6. Sartre, *Being and Nothingness*, 253.
7. Ibid., 254.
8. Ibid., 259–260.

Busch indicates, that I encounter the other as a subject. But again, there is something here I cannot grasp; although I am an object for the other, I can never experience this from the other's perspective – my existence as an object in the other's perspective escapes me. At the same time I become this object and experience it through my own perspective, in the form of shame. "It is shame or pride which reveals to me the other's gaze and myself at the end of that gaze. It is the shame or pride which makes me *live*, [rather than] *know* the situation of being looked at."[9] Through the gaze of the other I am set up within a world that is made alien to me, "for the Other's gaze embraces my being and correlatively the walls, the door, the keyhole. All these instrumental-things in the midst of which I am, now turn toward the Other a face which on principle escapes me."[10]

More than one Heideggerian aspect enters into this analysis. Not only is it the *living* (rather than the knowing) that Sartre want's to highlight, and not only is there a modulation of my way of being-in-the-word that the other brings about, but also, it is a break down that involves the pragmatic situation that, for Heidegger, best characterizes being-in-the-world and *Mitsein*. Sartre adds to this the idea that our relations (at least in bad faith) amount to a set of external observations. The other is "looking at and judging" me. For me to be what I am (something in-itself), "it suffices merely that the Other look at me."[11]

> The shock of the encounter with the Other is for me a revelation in emptiness of the existence of my body outside as an in-itself for the Other. Thus my body is not given merely as that which is purely and simply lived . . . [it becomes] extended outside in a dimension of flight which escapes me.[12]

A different and more positive conception of the gaze is possible, however. Infants focus on their caregiver's eyes very early and although an infant may start to follow the other's gaze, usually the caregiver is looking at the infant. What is experienced in such cases, or more generally, when the other looks at you? In intersubjective contexts, visual perception of the face of the other is not equivalent to either glancing at or a prolonged observation of an object. It's not a matter of me seeing the other's face, *simpliciter*, but of seeing that the other sees me (or quiet literally, seeing the other seeing me). The other's gaze is precisely not something that can be subsumed into a strictly

---

9. Ibid., 261. Translation revised.
10. Ibid.
11. Ibid., 262.
12. Ibid., 352.

visual representation of eye direction since it has an affective impact on my own system that sets me up for further response. Perhaps, then, we would require the kind of analysis offered by Levinas.

Levinas

For Levinas, what I see in the other's face is irreducible to its objective properties, its physiognomy, shape, color or morphological features. Rather, I see significance that transcends any such properties. The other person, resists being simply a physical object, and at the same time resists being simply an epistemological subject. The other transcends this subject-object categorization. This also means that the transcendence of the other is not equivalent to an invisible mind, a set of mental states that we might be able to reach through processes of inference. The other is not composed of a set of mental states that are like mine, analogically displaced in another body. Rather, according to Levinas, the other, in her alterity, makes an ethical demand on me, to which I am obligated to respond. The face-to-face relation is primarily an ethical order; I perceive the other as an obligation to respond.

I experience the transcendence of the other "when the face has turned to me, in its very nakedness. It is by itself, and not by reference to a system."[13] In contrast to Heidegger who might speak about a system of involvements that constitute the pragmatic world, Levinas describes a direct embodied encounter with the other. In contrast to Hegel, the face-to-face is not oppositional; complete oppositional arrangements are disrupted by the transcendence of the other. Levinas associates opposition (war, control or manipulation) with the concept of totality (a complete system, the opposite of a never complete infinity). "War renders morality derisory."[14] It involves an objectification (or de-subjectification) of the other in practices that include covering or ignoring the other's face.[15] This kind of denial of the face reduces the other to a component of a complete system which excludes the possibility of further interaction. Competitive or instrumental systems can only be derivative, secondary disorders of the primary ethical relationship.

In the circumstance of gazing at the other's face the other's vulnerability shines through, independent of context, and elicits a response from me. The other, in such circumstances, is characterized by both proximity

13. Levinas, *Totality and Infinity*, 75.
14. Ibid., 21.
15. Seeing the face of the other in battle has profound inhibitory effects on violent behavior directed towards the other. See Grossman, *On Killing*, and Protevi, "Affect, Agency, and Responsibility."

and distance at the same time. When the other is close to me, she is so not merely in physical geographical terms, the way an object, artifact, or instrument might be. This closeness demands a response "that could range from a passionate kiss to a punch, or some less extreme and more polite behavior of moving away or asking for space."[16] Even in the other's closeness, however, there is a distance in so far as I cannot fully grasp the other. This is specifically the transcendence that is most apparent in the other's face. As we find in Sartre, there is always something that escapes our grasp. Something irreducible in the other always escapes my gaze. It is something that is "beyond understanding" (*déborde la compréhension*).[17] The face (or more generally, the body) is never the totality of the other.

For Levinas, as for Sartre, my encounter with the other has an effect on me; but it is not, as in Sartre's analysis of bad faith relations with others, a circumstance that robs me of my subjectivity or reduces me to an object; it's a call, or a demand or obligation for me to respond; it pulls me out of myself towards something that I cannot completely grasp. If for Sartre the gaze is judgmental, for Levinas it is imperative. It makes the demand: "do not kill me." For both thinkers, however, the intersubjective relation is a non-reciprocal, asymmetrical relation. The gaze of the other comes at me; it makes demands on me. This doesn't mean that it cannot be part of a dialectic (as in Hegel and Sartre) or the start of a response and conversation (as in Levinas).

Interaction

There is much more in Sartre and Levinas relevant to these considerations that I cannot explicate here; there are, in fact, pointers to the point I now want to make. In effect, I propose to reframe or reorder considerations about the gaze and the face-to-face to establish a context in which we can make more sense out of them. The context involves the primacy of interaction.

Here's the point I want to make. There is neither the possibility of transcendence nor the possibility of reification without interaction. Transcendence is not an objective feature of the other person, something that belongs to the person as an essential feature. Nor is it some object that can be observed. Not only is its perception dependent on someone perceiving it, its very existence depends on the interaction involved in such instances of perception. The transcendence of the other—the transcendence that I can see in the other's face—just is the other's ability (or possibility) to gaze

16. Gallagher, "In Your Face."
17. Levinas, *Entre Nous*, 18.

at me and to see the same transcendence in my face. Transcendence is not an absolute fact; it's a relational contingency. Likewise, the failure to see that transcendence, as when we simply objectify or reify the other person, is a possibility of relational contingency.

It's clear that we perceive affordances for possible responsive actions in the face of the other. Face perception presents not just objective patterns that we might recognize as emotions. It involves complex interactive behavioral and response patterns arising out of an active engagement with the other's face—not a simple recognition of facial features—but an interactive perception that constitutes the recognition of emotions. This is consistent with the Levinasian view. Faced with the other's face subjects make eye contact with very subtle eye movements. The fact that the other returns the gaze, and that this strongly registers in our perception (as Sartre makes clear), provides part of the basis for regarding the other not as mere object but as a perceiving subject.

Recent analyses of intersubjectivity have emphasized this subject-encountering-subject with references to both Levinas and the type of I-thou encounter found in Buber.[18] I want to suggest, however, that encountering the other as a subject (on certain definitions) can be just as much a case of bad faith as encountering her as an object; but also that when the other is "given to me as an appearance" this does not necessarily mean that the other is cast into objectivity.

Any sighted person who holds an infant whose eyes are open likely experiences a gaze that takes nothing as subject or object, in the sense that we have been considering here (setting aside objective descriptions that would stipulate that if the infant sees X, and X is some object, then the infant sees an object, and also setting aside any psychoanalytic definitions of 'object'). This gaze of the infant escapes description in terms of perceiving subject or object. The infant encounters the other, but in a non-conceptual, pre-epistemic way. She sees the other's face, but not as a body (or body part) in-itself. In the following I'll focus on face perception, but one can generalize to the perception of other non-facial aspects of social encounters.

We know that infants respond differently to "things" that are agents (persons) and those that are non-agents (objects). Although it's likely impossible to find a positive phenomenological description of the infant's experience, we can consider our own experience of the infant. In some very basic sense, the infant's gaze is taken as a response to which we offer our own response. The gaze, in such instances, is neither a passive observation nor a disorganized glance; it appears, at the very least, as an active,

---

18. For example Stawarska, *Between You and I*.

interested questioning—and we experience it as something to which we need to respond.

I'll refer to this aspect of the gaze as a form of *elementary responsiveness*. I prefer this term to the term "recognition," because it reflects the fact that it is more akin to emotive or agentive processes than to cognitive ones. Elementary responsiveness can be found at the very ontogenetic beginning of interaction (in infant-caregiver interaction); it's the kind of embodied interactive relation that we find in primary intersubjectivity, and importantly we can find it throughout the lifespan, because we can find primary intersubjectivity throughout the lifespan.[19] That is, this kind of gaze as a form of elementary responsiveness can also happen between adults.

When I look at the face of another person who happens to be looking at me, I see neither an object nor a subject, per se, that is, understood as an epistemological (or Cartesian) subject who is a bearer of mental states. Rather, I see meaning and emotion in the other's face. In elementary responsiveness, visual perception of the face of the other is not equivalent to glancing at an object. As I've indicated, it's not a matter of me seeing the other's face, *simpliciter*, but of *seeing the other seeing me*. I see a transcendence in the other (rather than the other as an object) only when the direction of that transcendence is towards me or towards some other person. My perception of the other's gaze is precisely not something that can be subsumed into a strictly visual representation of eye direction since it has an affective impact on my own system that sets me up for further response.

Scientific evidence reinforces this phenomenological description. Perception of another's face activates not just the face recognition area and ventral visual pathway (which correlates to visual recognition of an object or person), but also the dorsal visual pathway (which is known to connect directly with the motor system and to inform motor control with respect to intentional action). This suggests that we perceive the other in the mode of the "I can" (or "I cannot")—that is, we perceive affordances for possible responsive actions in the face of the other.[20] The perception of the other's face, then, is not a simple recognition of facial features; it presents not just objective patterns that we might recognize as emotions, for example. In more positive terms, my perception of the other's face calls forth a complex interactive behavioural and response pattern; it constitutes an interactive perception. I perceive the other person as a social affordance—as someone with whom I can interact, or with whom I must interact.

19. Trevarthen, "Communication and Cooperation."
20. Debruille et al., "N300 and Social Affordances."

My perception of the other and the other's perception of me, are, in fact, whole body activities. I don't mean merely that we perceive one another's postures, movements, gestures, vocal intonations, prosodies, as well as communicative and narrative practices, place-related and contextual factors and so on (we do perceive such things, of course), but, in addition, that our perception activates our own bodily processes in response to what we see. In this regard, we can also say that some of what is true of perception in general also applies to perception of the other person. For example, recent research shows that even neuronal activity in the earliest of perceptual processing areas of the brain reflects more than simple feature detection; neurons in V1 anticipate reward if they have been relevantly attuned by prior experience.[21] What we see in the present, including faces, incorporates an affective sense of relevant past experiences, so that reportable visual perception is already informed with affective value from the start.

Barrett and Bar, for example, show that "responses signaling an object's salience, relevance or value do not occur as a separate step after the object is identified. Instead, affective responses support vision from the very moment that visual stimulation begins."[22] Simultaneous with the very earliest part of visual perception the perceiving organism initiates a host of muscular and hormonal changes. The activated sensory-motor patterns include involvement of organs, muscles, and joints associated with prior experience, and are integrated with current exteroceptive sensory information helping to guide response and subsequent actions. Changes in the perceiver's breathing, muscle tension or stomach motility have an effect on perceptual experience even if they are recessive to what the perceiver experiences.[23] Visual and affective processes modify the body of the perceiver to re-create the somatic context associated with previous experiences. As a result, we literally see objects and persons through the affective response that they generate in us.

Because facial expressions play a large role in intersubjective interaction, we anticipate facial responses and when they do not occur interaction can be disrupted in terms of its dynamics and affectivity, leading to confusion or feelings of social discomfort. This occurs, for example, in cases of Möbius Syndrome (MS), a form of congenital bilateral facial paralysis resulting from developmental problems with the sixth and seventh cranial nerves.[24] Indeed, part of the problem for subjects with MS is not *in* MS itself,

---

21. Shuler and Bear, "Reward Timing."
22. Barrett and Bar, "See it with Feeling," 1325.
23. Ibid., 1326.
24. On MS see Briegel, "Neuropsychiatric Findings"; Cole, "On 'Being Faceless'";

but in the way others regard the person with MS. Specifically, others often fail to respond because they see no facial response in the subject with MS.[25]

Jonathan Cole gives an excellent account of MS and other conditions, and he also indicates the relevance of Levinas's analysis. In the kind of moral or ethical responsibility described by Levinas, "the face of the other requires me to respond and enter into a relationship, but a relationship that I cannot fully control, that neither of us can fully control. It involves a risk so evident for many of those with facial problems that they avoid it."[26]

It is perhaps Merleau-Ponty, rather than Levinas or Sartre, who finds the right angle on these issues in his appeal to Valéry, whom he quotes:

> As soon as gazes meet, we are no longer wholly two, and it is hard to remain alone. This exchange (the term is exact) realizes in a very short time a transposition or metathesis—a chiasma of two "destinies," two points of view. Thereby a sort of simultaneous reciprocal limitation occurs. You capture my image, my appearance; I capture yours. You are not me, since you see me and I do not see myself. What I lack is this me that you see. And what you lack is the you I see. And no matter how far we advance in our mutual understanding, as much as we reflect, so much will we be different . . .[27]

Merleau-Ponty, I suggest, could easily accept a revision to his statement that "to see a face . . . is to have a certain hold on it"[28], which, as Thomas Busch suggests, would be resisted by Levinas.[29] One could rather say: "for me to see a face is for it to have a hold on me." Merleau-Ponty and Valéry highlight the inadequacy of any non-reciprocal relation. I'm suggesting that the experience of transcendence, in the other and in myself, depends on some degree of reciprocal interaction, although this does not mean an absolutely symmetrical relation or a complete reversibility—certainly not a reduction of the other to the same.[30] On the one hand, Sartre might say that at the end

---

and Cole and Spalding, *The Invisible Smile*.

25. Gallagher, "In Your Face"; Krueger and Michael, "Gestural Coupling."
26. Cole, *About Face*, 196.
27. Merleau-Ponty, "Man and Adversity," 196.
28. Merleau-Ponty, *Phenomenology of Perception*, 264.
29. Busch, *Circulating Being*, 95; For a general discussion of Merleau-Ponty's relation to Levinas, see 91–97.
30. Levinas takes reversibility as more of a closed relation than Merleau-Ponty. "The reversibility of a relation where the terms are indifferently read from left to right and from right to left would couple them *one* to the *other* . . . The intended transcendence would thus be absorbed into the unity of the system, destroying the radical alterity of the Other" (cited in Busch *Circulating Being*, 95–96). But for Merleau-Ponty reversibility

of the gaze there is nothing, that is, pure subjectivity or transcendence. On the other hand, Levinas might say that at the end of the gaze, there is no end—the gaze veers off towards infinity. The conception of transcendence based on relational contingencies and elementary responsiveness, however, is one that remains closer to our existential lifeworld encounters—a transcendence that is not nothing, but also not everything.

Bibliography

Barrett L. F., and Moshe Bar. "See It With Feeling: Affective Predictions During Object Perception." *Philosophical Transactions of the Royal Society B: Biological Sciences* 364 (2009) 1325–34.
Briegel, Wolfgang. "Neuropsychiatric Findings of Möbius Sequence: A Review." *Clinical Genetics* 70 (2006) 91–97.
Busch, Thomas W. *Circulating Being: From Embodiment to Incorporation: Essays on Late Existentialism*. New York: Fordham University Press, 1999.
———. *The Power of Consciousness and The Force of Circumstances in Sartre's Philosophy*. Bloomington: Indiana University Press, 1989.
Cole, Jonathan. *About Face*. Cambridge, MA: MIT Press, 1999.
———. "On 'Being Faceless': Selfhood and Facial Embodiment." In *Models of the Self*, edited by Shaun Gallagher and Jonathan Shear, 301–18. Exeter: Imprint Academic, 1999.
Cole, Jonathan, and Henrietta J. Spalding. *The Invisible Smile: Living without Facial Expression*. Oxford: Oxford University Press, 2009.
Debruille, J. Bruno et al. "N300 and Social Affordances: A Study with a Real Person and a Dummy as Stimuli." *PLOS One* 7 (2012). http://journals.plos.org/plosone/article?id=10.1371/journal.pone.0047922
Gallagher Shaun. "In Your Face: Transcendence in Embodied Interaction." *Frontiers in Human Neuroscience* 8 (2014) 495. http://journal.frontiersin.org/article/10.3389/fnhum.2014.00495/full
Gallagher, Shaun, and Rebecca S. Jacobson. "Heidegger and Social Cognition." In *Heidegger and Cognitive Science*, edited by Julian Kiverstein and Michael Wheeler, 213–45. London: Palgrave Macmillan, 2012.
Grossman, Dave. *On Killing: The Psychological Costs of Learning to Kill in War and Society*. New York: Back Bay, 1996.
Krueger, Joel, and John Michael. "Gestural Coupling and Social Cognition: Möbius Syndrome as a Case Study. *Frontiers in Human Neuroscience* 6 (2012) 81. http://journal.frontiersin.org/article/10.3389/fnhum.2012.00081/full
Levinas, Emanuel. *Entre nous: Essais sur le Penser-à-l'Autre*. Paris: Poche, 1991.
———. *Totality and Infinity: An Essay on Exteriority*. Translated by Alphonso Lingis. Duquesne Studies. Philosophical Series 24. Pittsburgh: Duquesne University Press, 1969.

---

is never complete and never collapses into coincidence or sameness. As Busch puts it, "Merleau-Ponty's ontology resists absorbing differences . . . [H]is understanding of reversibility is not reductive" (ibid., 96).

Merleau-Ponty, Maurice. "Man and Adversity." In *The Merleau-Ponty Reader*, edited by Ted Toadvine and Leonard Lawlor, 189–240. Evanston, IL: Northwestern University Press, 2007.

———. *Phenomenology of Perception*. Translated by Donald Landes. London: Routledge, 2013.

Protevi, John. "Affect, Agency and Responsibility: The Act of Killing in the Age of Cyborgs." *Phenomenology and the Cognitive Sciences* 7 (2008) 405–13.

Sartre, Jean Paul. *Being and Nothingness*. Translated by Hazel E. Barnes. New York: Philosophical Library, 1956.

Shuler, Marshall G., and Mark F. Bear. "Reward Timing in the Primary Visual Cortex." *Science* 311 (2006) 1606–9.

Stawarska, Beata. *Between You and I: Dialogical Phenomenology*. Athens: Ohio University Press, 2009.

Trevarthen, Colwin B. "Communication and Cooperation in Early Infancy: A Description of Primary Intersubjectivity." In *Before Speech: The Beginning of Interpersonal Communication*, edited by Margaret Bullowa, 321–47. Cambridge: Cambridge University Press, 1979.

7

Sartre in Dialogue with Husserl and Beauvoir

The Evolution of Existential Freedom

—Shannon M. Mussett

In his essay, "Beyond the Cogito: The Question of the Continuity of Sartre's Thought," Thomas W. Busch opens by noting the following admission by Sartre: "When pressed to identify an overriding philosophical unity of his corpus, he claims that it is freedom."[1] Busch agrees that Sartre maintains the centrality of freedom throughout his work, but adds that "Sartre radically changed his mind about several important philosophical issues which affect the understanding of freedom itself."[2] Still, in his own writings on the matter, Busch emphasizes that Sartre upholds a devotion to the idea of freedom at the core of his philosophical oeuvre. Despite the (sometimes radical) modifications that Sartre made on the notion of freedom, he consistently requires that the existent be free on some basic ontological level.

Given the length and success of their philosophical careers, it is no surprise that both Sartre's and Beauvoir's conceptions of freedom evolved and deepened over time. In Sartre's case, many read his later works as a rejection of the naïve ontology of his earlier writings, particularly, of *Being and Nothingness*. Busch himself admits that the tension in Sartrean

---

1. In Busch, "Beyond the Cogito," 189. This admission comes from the script of *Sartre By Himself* (28).
2. Busch, ibid.

ontology is pushed to the point of breaking altogether when comparing the early and later Sartre. In his article, "Simone de Beauvoir on Achieving Subjectivity," Busch concludes that Sartre's later shift towards *praxis* in the *Critique of Dialectical Reason* "put enormous (I would say fatal) strain upon the ontological categories of *Being and Nothingness*" insofar as subjectivity conceived as *praxis* "has serious repercussions on the ontological claim of incommensurability between body as subject and body as object."[3] He moves on to conclude that Sartre's reorientation toward concrete subjectivity in the *Critique* and *Saint Genet: Actor and Martyr*,[4] brings him closer to Beauvoir's own philosophical position in works such as *The Second Sex* and *The Mandarins*. While I wholeheartedly agree that the adoption of the more nuanced formulation of situated freedom in both thinkers is closer to lived experience, this essay highlights the notion of radical freedom, in its multiple configurations, particularly in the philosophy of Sartre. To accomplish this task, I begin with the connection between Husserlian phenomenology and Sartre in order to illustrate the emergence of freedom in Sartre's philosophy out of Husserl's intentionality of consciousness. Following this, I show how Beauvoir's philosophy communicates with Sartre on this idea of freedom. Beauvoir scholars have always been more attuned to a continuity, rather than a disjunction, in Beauvoir's works, and I believe that such a continuity is evident in Sartre's philosophy as well. With the help of Busch's writings, I show how freedom—whether conceived as non-positional self-awareness, the nihilating action of being-for-self, or the ambiguous action of disclosing being—remains central to the existentialist project of authenticity and liberation.

Part One: Husserl, Sartre, and Freedom

Busch consistently argues throughout his corpus that the intentionality of consciousness (along with the Cartesian *cogito* and radical doubt) form the key elements of Sartre's own burgeoning philosophy of consciousness and freedom. Throughout Busch's early essays, this connection is central as, for example, when he writes: "I believe that a strong case can be made that Sartre's philosophy is, in its essential thrust, the most faithful to Husserl's program of those thinkers influenced by Husserl."[5] Husserl's phenomenological reduction, in which the actual existence of phenomena are brack-

---

3. Busch, "Achieving Subjectivity," 182.

4. Busch sometimes includes *The Words* in this category as well (see Busch, "Beyond the Cogito," 195).

5. Busch, "Phenomenology as Humanism," 128.

eted through the *epoché*, is meant finally to overcome the Kantian dualism between phenomena and noumena.[6] Husserl's reduction opens up the possibility of things to be given to a consciousness that, by its very nature, intends them: "this is not to say that the things once more exist in themselves and 'send their representatives into consciousness.' This sort of thing cannot occur to us within the sphere of phenomenological reduction. Instead, the things are and are given in appearance and in virtue of the appearance itself."[7] We must no longer concern ourselves with the existence of things apart from their appearances, instead, we must bracket their existence—be they objects in the world, the ego, or other people.[8]

Husserl's answer to the problems surrounding objectivism and positivism focuses on consciousness in the act of constituting its world. What comes under investigation is the very meeting of consciousness intending its object in experience. In order to concern himself with the "pure Ego" or "reduced" consciousness, Husserl first employs a bracketing off of things as they exist in themselves. Rather than closing us off from the truth, the *epoché* therefore "does not leave us confronting nothing. On the contrary we gain possession of something by it; and what we . . . acquire by it is my pure living . . . the universe of 'phenomena' in the . . . phenomenological sense."[9] Husserl's method allows us to describe experience without proving the world's existence. No longer weighed down by an unthinkable, yet necessary shadow realm of the Kantian *noumenal*, Husserl is able to philosophize human experience as it is lived. Freed from the presuppositions of an individual Ego with a specific personality or an object existing independently of consciousness, Husserl discovers universal concepts in appearances that will serve as the building blocks of a new scientific method.[10]

   6. In a move away from Kantian dualism, Husserl emphasizes that *"I must exclude all that is transcendentally posited"* because, as Kant has shown us, that which transcends human cognition is veiled in illusion and what Husserl seeks is *"clarity"* (*Idea of Phenomenology*, 4). As Busch notes, *Ideas* was the most influential Husserlian text on Sartre's philosophical development (*Power of Consciousness*, 4).

   7. Husserl, *Idea of Phenomenology*, 10.

   8. Ibid. 34.

   9. Husserl, *Cartesian Meditations*, 20–21.

   10. As is well known, this method had profound influence on his student, Martin Heidegger, whose impact on French Existentialism is enormously important but which lies beyond the scope of this paper. Heidegger's early phenomenology in *Being and Time* is a radical break from the Husserlian purified consciousness intending and constituting its world. This method of studying *Da-sein* (or human being) in its everydayness reveals that "the *'substance'* of human being is not the spirit as the synthesis of body and soul, but *existence*" (Heidegger, *Being and Time*, 110). The emphasis on the lived experience of human being in its everyday life can be seen in Beauvoir's own emphasis on the philosophical importance of *la réalité humaine* in *The Second Sex*.

In Sartre's study of Husserlian phenomenology, he is taken by the notion of the intentionality inherent in cognition's meeting with the world. This activity, the *intentionality of consciousness*, sparks the young Sartre's own adoption of the new existential philosophy. For Husserl, the intentionality of consciousness is such that "cognitive mental processes (and this belongs to their essence) have an *intentio*, they refer to something, they are related in this or that way to an object. This activity of relating itself to an object belongs to them even if the object itself does not."[11] In other words, what is emblematic of cognition is that it *relates* to an object in the world regardless of whether or not that object exists (making that object's existence inconsequential to phenomenological study). But this intentional character of consciousness still aims at a world and this world still appears to it—i.e., is given to it in appearance. Defining consciousness in this way opens up a whole new horizon of investigation of appearances, or phenomena, of every kind. This is part of what was so appealing to Sartre in his study of Husserl, *The Transcendence of the Ego*. Guided by Husserl, Sartre's project begins with intentionality and moves to purify the reflective act of consciousness in order to break from the natural attitude (our naïve and uncritical immersion in the world). As Busch explains, "Purifying reflection in the early Sartre was his version of the phenomenological reduction whereby consciousness could extricate itself from submersion in a world of supposedly pregiven meaning and value and grasp itself as the constitutive origin of its world."[12]

Yet, Sartre quickly breaks with Husserl when the question of the freedom of the existent comes to the foreground of the discussion. As Busch explains, "*The Transcendence of the Ego* also marks, after his initial enthusiasm, Sartre's first criticism of Husserl, for he now accuses Husserl of betraying phenomenology's fecund view of consciousness by failing to subject the ego to phenomenological reduction."[13] In particular, Sartre calls into question the substantiality of the transcendental ego revealed by Husserl's reduction. For his part, Husserl asserts that, "through the *epoché* I have penetrated into the sphere of being which is prior in principle to everything which conceivably has being for me . . . I, the ego performing the *epoché*, am the only thing that is absolutely indubitable."[14] In fact, the most significant insight of all of phenomenology is the "discovery" of the transcendental ego.[15] This indubitable entity, containing and capable of multitudes, turns

---

11. Husserl, *Idea of Phenomenology*, 43.
12. Busch, "Beyond the Cogito," 201.
13. Busch, *Power of Consciousness*, 5.
14. Husserl, *Crisis*, 78.
15. Husserl notes that this ego, purified of its concreteness through the act of

out to be deeply problematic for Sartre. As he opens his analysis in *The Transcendence of the Ego*, he writes, "we should like to show here that the ego is neither formally nor materially *in* consciousness: it is outside, *in the world*. It is a being of the world, like the ego of another."[16] Husserl's ego, it turns out, is simply too *substantial* for Sartre—the activity of intentionality is subordinated to the substantiality of the transcendental ego. But Sartre asserts that freedom—what makes us human—must necessarily be an *activity* rather than a content in or a quality of an ego.

Returning to Husserl so as to grasp Sartre's critique, we find Husserl claiming that the ego splits into a natural ego and a phenomenological ego such that the former is naïvely interested in the world and the latter is a disinterested observer.[17] Thus the ego can be both interested in the natural, naïve world as well as a disinterested and unbiased phenomenological observer. Sartre argues against Husserl that the transcendental ego although "disinterested" and "unprejudiced," is a kind of thing intending, rather than the activity of intention itself. For Sartre, the consciousness that does what the transcendental ego does for Husserl, is no kind of thing, but is instead *nothing at all*. According to Sartre, the persistent ego that stands behind Husserl's formulation of consciousness is unnecessary and in fact, contrary to the essence of Husserl's project. In truth, as Busch aptly notes, "the *ego* is seen to arise only with reflection and is not identified as an immanent structure of transcendental consciousness, but as a transcendent object. Husserl is accused of not extending his phenomenological reduction far enough, of himself being a victim of the natural attitude, confusing a product of consciousness with consciousness itself."[18]

Despite his criticisms of the solidity of the transcendental ego, Sartre finds a philosophical gold mine in Husserl's intentionality of consciousness. According to Sartre, "it is certain that phenomenology does not need to appeal to any such unifying and individualizing *I*. Indeed, consciousness is defined by intentionality" as Husserl defines it.[19] Because consciousness always intends an object—consciousness is always consciousness *of* something—Sartre will have a great deal of difficulty accepting this first order consciousness (or the naïve ego) as being anything more than a spontaneous act of constitution and therefore in itself, nothing at all. The first order

---

bracketing, "*has an enormous inborn a priori*" and all of phenomenology "is revelation of this inborn *a priori* in its infinite multiplicity of facets" (Husserl, *Introduction*, 25).

16. Sartre, *Transcendence*, 31.
17. Husserl, *Cartesian Meditations*, 35.
18. Busch, "Senses of Alienation," 151.
19. Sartre, *Transcendence*, 38.

of consciousness, because it is always that which spontaneously constitutes its world, can never itself be objectified and thematized. This first order of consciousness (what Sartre defines as a non-thetic awareness of self) is defined as nothingness, which is, for Sartre, human freedom.[20]

Using the intentionality of consciousness, Sartre brings to light the difference between the ego as the solidified, unified, and concrete object of thought and the non-thetic consciousness which spontaneously reflects on this ego. The two will never meet and are as different from each other as being and nothingness. The first order of consciousness, which is the spontaneous impulse that thinks this ego, is "quite simply an empty concept which is destined to remain empty" and "in a sense, it is a *nothing*."[21] As Sartre further develops in *Being and Nothingness*, because consciousness is always consciousness of something, it can never be a thing but only the negating action by which Being comes to be revealed.[22]

In *Being and Nothingness*, Sartre struggles both with and against the phenomenology of Husserl and Heidegger in trying to give voice to how we can philosophize experience. Busch captures it succinctly: "It became apparent in *Being and Nothingness*, that Husserl was relied upon to defend the autonomy of consciousness and Heidegger to defend the implantation of consciousness in the world."[23] In this work, Sartre undertakes the phenomenological task of exploring the relationship of human being (or human consciousness) and the world in experience passed on from Hegel, Husserl, and Heidegger. Using the terms, "being-in-itself" (*l'être-en-soi*)

---

20. In order to show how the first order of consciousness is absolute spontaneity, Sartre maintains a Husserlian split where there are two different orders of consciousness—the one non-thetic or non-positional and the other thetic or positional. In philosophizing, we have a tendency to conflate the former with the latter. Take for example, Sartre's famous example of the streetcar in *Transcendence*. When I am running after a streetcar, there is no substantial *I*, no ego per se. There is only "consciousness *of the streetcar-having-to-be-overtaken*, etc., and non-positional consciousness of consciousness. In fact, I am then plunged into the world of objects . . . but *me*, I have disappeared; I have annihilated myself" (*Transcendence*, 49). Accordingly, non-positional self-awareness (which exists at both the pre-reflective level of consciousness intending objects and the reflective level of consciousness intending itself) is a consciousness which can never be thematized or concretized. This example is clear because it is easy for us to see the difference between being caught up in the moment and consciously reflecting on our actions. But regardless on what level consciousness engages its world, non-positional awareness of self (or freedom) underlies all activity and can never be made explicit to any order of consciousness.

21. Sartre, *Transcendence*, 89, 93.

22. This is largely the theme of the subchapter, "The Origin of Nothingness" in the first chapter of Part One, *The Origin of Negation* in *Being and Nothingness*.

23. "Beyond the Cogito," 193.

and "being-for-itself" (*l'être-pour-soi*) to describe the plenum of the world over against the negativity that is introduced by human freedom, Sartre builds a dichotomy between human subjectivity and the rest of the world. He describes being-for-itself as "a being such that in its being, its being is in question in so far as this being is essentially a certain way of *not being* a being which it posits simultaneously as other than itself."[24] Being-for-itself is opposed to being-in-itself which, as Busch explains, is "a mode of objectified being whose sense is constituted in contrast with the temporal self-surpassing of the for-itself. The in-itself is not a particular object, but the modality of object-being."[25] In Sartrean terms, the for-itself is not a being but a nothingness. As nothingness, the for-itself is that which negates the given conditions and relates itself to the in-itself. The in-itself is the opaque given or that which "can encompass no negation. It is full positivity."[26] Put simply, being-for-itself is transcendent human freedom—the ability to negatively rupture the solidity of the given—whereas being-in-itself is the brute existence of the world and the things which reside in it—be they objects, other people, or even our own static egos.

Human being is freedom, but this essence is also nothingness or the negating of the world. This world is pure being and because the existent can "stand back" from it, put distance between itself and the given through thinking and acting, the existent is in its essence, nothingness. Continuing the insights from *The Transcendence of the Ego*, we see that freedom is not a concrete "thing" or something that one *has*; it is an active movement of negativity, or the introduction of nothingness into the world. Sartre is therefore able to conclude that "as soon as one attributes to consciousness this negative power with respect to the world and itself, as soon as the nihilation forms an integral part of the *positing* of an end, we must recognize that the indispensable and fundamental constitution of all action is the freedom of the acting being."[27] This understanding of freedom as a negating activity of rupturing the given clearly builds from his early understanding of Husserl's intentionality of consciousness.

Busch elaborates at great length the change undergone by Sartre as he moves away from the early Husserlian understanding of the intentionality of consciousness and the tacit freedom that underlies all actions. As Busch notes, the reliance on the Cartesian-inspired dualism between being-for-self and being-in-itself results in an unbridgeable ontological gap between

24. Sartre, *Being and Nothingness*, 174.
25. Busch, *Power of Consciousness*, 24.
26. Sartre, *Being and Nothingness*, lxvi.
27. Ibid. 436.

freedom and the world. It is only in his later treatments of Genet and Marxism, where Sartre realizes that the situation is far more entangled than the notion of a free nothingness rupturing the given can possibly account for. In this light, he comes much closer to the insights of Beauvoir's own analyses of freedom in situation.

Part Two: Beauvoir in Communication with Sartre

Busch is certainly correct that the early Sartre backs himself into a corner; while attempting to rescue consciousness from *determinism*, he ends up asserting that the for-itself is wholly *unconditioned*. This gives consciousness really only two choices: the acceptance of radical freedom in authenticity, or a life of bad faith. It might be tempting to think that Sartre's later focus on the study of childhood and the material conditions of the situation are a rejection of the notion of freedom born in his earlier works. But I think this is a misguided interpretation. Because of Busch's teaching and writings, I have always been profoundly affected by the strain of radical freedom that runs through both Sartre and Beauvoir's works. I have previously studied how Beauvoir's understanding of freedom emerges directly as an adoption of and a challenge to Hegelian freedom understood as negativity.[28] In that earlier paper, I argue that there are both productive forms of freedom (expressed by Beauvoir as revolt and creativity) and more or less impotent forms (expressed as complaint and resignation). I maintain that no matter how much material and cultural situations can work to oppress existents, ontological freedom remains, even if only implicitly, ever ready to be made explicit through action. Furthermore, with certain changes to circumstances, this freedom can erupt into acts of revolution and creativity on the individual and cultural level. This insight is what guides Beauvoir's study into the situation and emancipation of woman in *The Second Sex*, for example. According to Beauvoir, even the act of resigning to the most degraded situations (which is the most impotent expression of ontological freedom)—such as women living under the constraints of extreme mystification, Jews struggling for survival in concentration camps, or Algerians suffering in torture chambers—implicit freedom persists and calls for liberation. This is what both gives hope to revolutionary and emancipatory efforts, as well as what frightens oppressors. In sum, "taking into account the excesses of oppression, Beauvoir forces us to admit that even in resignation there is still freedom. Freedom, in other words, can never be destroyed in human

---

28. Mussett, "Expressions of Negativity."

beings, even if it is completely ineffectual in its diffusion."[29] She shares this dedication to the centrality of freedom with Sartre.[30] Thus one can say that freedom forms a continuous thread throughout both thinkers' works as they develop, metamorphose, and evolve.

Busch is not the only commentator who notes Sartre's allegiance to freedom throughout his writings. Beauvoir maintains the centrality of freedom in Sartre's work as well. In her autobiography, *After the War: Force of Circumstance Vol. 1*, she writes that despite their evolving appreciation of Communism, Sartre never wholeheartedly adopted Marxism. Beauvoir explains that Sartre's fierce individualism allowed him to take what he needed from Marxism, without causing him to abandon the heart of his existentialist project. She explains that Sartre,

> [B]elieved in the phenomenological intuition which affords objects immediately "in flesh and blood." Although he adhered to the idea of *praxis*, he had not given up his old, persisting project of writing an *ethics*. He still aspired to *being*; to live morally was, according to him, to attain an absolutely meaningful mode of existence. He did not wish to abandon—and indeed, never has abandoned—the concepts of negativity, of interiority, of existence and of freedom elaborated in *Being and Nothingness*. In opposition to the brand of Marxism professed by the Communist Party, he was determined to preserve man's human dimension.[31]

As Beauvoir here makes clear, when Sartre's philosophy came into contact with Marxism and Communism, he shifted his focus to *praxis, without ever abandoning his concern for freedom, ethics, meaning, and the thickness of lived experience*. Sartre's early affirmation of the lack of deep identity that results from the *néant* in being-for-itself later changes to an idea of "achieved subjectivity" and the construction of "character" from social conditioning. Yet, as both Sartre and Beauvoir elucidate, there is much to be said about preserving the freedom at the heart of transcendence for the purposes of liberating ourselves and others from alienation, social destination, and oppression. As Beauvoir shows in *The Ethics of Ambiguity* and *The Second Sex* (as does Sartre in his later works), freedom and autonomous choice are deeply complicated when studying existents who have been raised and conditioned in circumstances that enforce a kind of identity that is neither

---

29. Ibid. 10.

30. Unlike, for example, Camus and Merleau-Ponty who largely eschew the emphasis on radical freedom.

31. Beauvoir, *After the War*, 7.

chosen nor fully present to self. If we were to express this in Husserlian terms, the idea of fully extricating the ego from the natural attitude is a herculean feat in light of the material conditions that seek to limit, curtail, and extinguish this move.

As explored in detail above, Sartre's initial revelation about human freedom is deeply immersed in Husserlian phenomenology. Beauvoirian freedom emerges from a similar orientation but is, I find, much more deeply connected to the Hegelian dialectic than any other phenomenologist. Freedom as negativity forms the cornerstone of Hegelian consciousness and is one that Beauvoir adopts in her earliest formulations of freedom in all of its engagements and prohibitions. As Hegelian negativity is a *process* rather than a *thing*, Beauvoir finds common ground as early as *Pyrrhus and Cineas* (1944) where she writes, "I am not first a thing, but a spontaneity that desires, that loves, that wants, that acts" and consequently, "what is mine is therefore first what I do."[32] In *The Ethics of Ambiguity*, she writes succinctly that "man is originally a negativity."[33] Yet, the focus on freedom as action brings her into confrontation with the limitations on the effectual expression of freedom sooner than Sartre.

As Busch notes, the early Sartre maintains a tension between "immersion in the world and a purifying distance from the world."[34] Or, put differently, there is a tension between the nihilating activity and the pure being that is negated by it. This kind of tension appears in Beauvoir's *Ethics* as a tension between the desire to *be* and the desire to *disclose being*. There she argues that the authentic attitude is not one wherein we choose the side of authentic subjectivity over against the objective world, but rather one where the failure to unify being-in-itself and being-for-itself (to use Sartrean language) is *assumed*: "to attain his truth, man must not attempt to dispel the ambiguity of his being but, on the contrary, accept the task of realizing it. He rejoins himself only to the extent that he agrees to remain at a distance from himself."[35] Thus, to be free is to reside in the ambiguous movement between being (essence, identity, engulfment in the being of the world) and the disclosure of being (distance, negation, freedom from engulfment in the world). Although she does not use the language of "purification" to describe this, she does note the ethical dimensions of disclosure. However, there is no absolute breaking from this ambiguous movement for Beauvoir. Negation,

---

32. Beauvoir, *Pyrrhus and Cineas*, 93.
33. Beauvoir, *Ethics of Ambiguity*, 118.
34. Busch, "Beyond the Cogito," 193.
35. Beauvoir, *Ethics of Ambiguity*, 13.

nihilation, freedom—all of these moves remain profoundly entangled in the world that involves these actions.

Based on Beauvoir's review of Merleau-Ponty's *Phenomenology of Perception* (1945), Sonia Kruks argues that Beauvoir "implies that there are degrees, or gradations, of freedom—and that social situations modify freedom itself and not merely its facticity or exteriority."[36] This idea—that ontological freedom is paramount, but that it must be understood along a kind of continuum between immanence and transcendence—is at the heart of Beauvoir's philosophy almost from the beginning. Beauvoir is aware that:

> [A]lthough everyone is ontologically free, not everyone shares the same concrete *possibilities* for expressing this freedom. Some individuals may be in a favorable situation conducive to the expression of their freedom, and others may simply suffer a loss of their transcendence so much so that it takes on the appearance of immanence, i.e., the appearance of givenness. Therefore, one's situation can in some cases serve not merely as a limitation to be surmounted in an upsurge of freedom, but as an intractable and oftentimes unknown constraint on action.[37]

Pyrrhus and Cineas, her earliest philosophical essay, notes that possibilities can vary between people depending upon their circumstances, but she has not yet become fully cognizant of the extent that the situation can be a barrier to freedom's expression. Very soon thereafter, however, this realization becomes a kind of underlying narrative to the ethical analysis she offers in *The Ethics of Ambiguity*. Here, we find that one can be condemned to a kind of immanence wherein one merely lives without the possibility to project meaning into an open future. This is what Beauvoir calls the situation of oppression.[38] As Busch notes, race and gender are not aspects of one's concrete situation that are taken seriously by Sartre until his later work. Beauvoir, however, takes up these intersections of human existence very seriously in the *Ethics*. Like Sartre, there is a great deal of bad faith evident in human choice in the attitude of seriousness. Serious people flee from the vertiginous sense of freedom as nothingness and turn toward an identification with their egos, much like Sartre describes in *The Transcendence of the Ego*. Nodding to Sartre, Beauvoir explains that "*Being and Nothingness* is in large part a description of the serious man and his universe. The serious man gets rid of his freedom by claiming to subordinate it to values which would be

---

36. Kruks, "Teaching Sartre," 84.
37. Mussett, "Expressions of Negativity," 6.
38. Beauvoir, *Ethics of Ambiguity*, 81.

unconditioned."[39] And although Beauvoir agrees that the attitude of seriousness is by far the most prevalent inauthentic attitude that human beings adopt, it is not fair to place individuals along the diametrically opposed poles of bad faith or inauthenticity as we find in Sartre's early existentialism. As she observes, of all the disingenuous attitudes detailed in the *Ethics*, the reason that seriousness "is the most widespread [is] because every man was first a child."[40] Simply put, because almost every person grows up in a world of pregiven, absolute, and unquestioned values, we have a strong inclination to cling to that world into adulthood. What took Sartre the intensive study of Genet to fully understand, Beauvoir is attuned to even before writing *The Second Sex*. And yet, it is fair to say that the ontological freedom of negativity, negation, and nihilation shared by both thinkers at the beginning of their careers, undergo similar transformations as their meditations on history, power, and the material conditions which effect freedom deepen. To illustrate these transformations, I now turn briefly to key examples in both thinkers.

Busch zeroes in on the profound difference between Sartre's treatment of the young bride terrified at her vertiginous freedom in *The Transcendence of the Ego* and the oppressed Dop shampoo worker from *The Critique of Dialectical Reason* whose life is totally dominated by the material conditions in which she lives. This transition illustrates Sartre's intensifying awareness of the forces that shape freedom. The former, on her bourgeois perch, has the time and ability to contemplate the radical freedom to solicit passersby as a prostitute and the consequent anxiety that pervades her when she realizes there is nothing to stop her from doing what her ego identity cannot abide. She has the leisure and material wherewithal to enact a kind of simple phenomenological reduction whereby the act of the constituting the ego appears as categorically different than the ego constituted. This awareness of her freedom fills her with terror. As Busch summarizes, "She was shocked out of this 'natural attitude' regarding herself with the apprehension that consciousness as spontaneous freedom creates and sustains the 'ego'" rather than the ego supporting her acts and decisions.[41] But certainly, not all existents have the luxury of being able to affect this "shock" to the natural attitude and to study the ensuing vertigo when all that is left is the monstrous activity of consciousness.

When we place the young bride beside the example from Sartre's *Critique*, we are confronted by the stark realities of class and material

39. Ibid. 46.
40. Ibid.
41. Busch, "Phenomenological Reduction," 56.

deprivation. The woman who works in a factory under brutal physical pressures for a pittance does not have the same luxury of "standing back" and enacting a Husserlian *epoché*. Rather, she lives in an oppressed totality wherein choice (even the choice about the object of fantasy) is wholly external, residing in the *practico-inert*. "The existentialist position that one 'makes oneself' must be reunderstood," writes Busch, such that we now understand that "the existent makes itself but within a given encompassing situation which defines the existent."[42] Even and despite the fact that the possible is defined in terms of a situation that marks out a field (some fields opening possibilities while others foreclose them), Busch acknowledges that throughout his analysis of situations of extreme oppression, "Sartre continues to maintain that the human existent is a projection toward ends, toward possibility."[43] Despite the fact that the woman in the Dop shampoo factory exists as a "transcendence transcended," such that her choices are so limited as to necessitate that we understand her situation as one of oppression, she still remains free to choose within those confines—she is, in other words, never wholly determined. Despite the misery of the manipulated conditions in which she lives, she can choose or not choose to have an abortion, for example, even though this notion of choice challenges the radical freedom lauded by the early Sartre. But as with Beauvoir, choice requires freedom, even if freedom is dramatically constrained from expressing itself in positive, affirmative, or creative acts.

In order to help us come to terms with the seemingly bizarre understanding of choice that Sartre maintains even in the *Critique of Dialectical Reason* (after all, what kind of choice are we talking about when an oppressed working class woman must "choose" whether or not to have an abortion) Busch asks that we understand Sartre's use of freedom not *literally*, as total independence from the conditions of one's circumstances, but *hyperbolically*. The latter idea allows us to see that no matter how brutally restrictive our conditions are they do not fully determine our actions. As Busch explains, "one must understand the hyperbolic use of 'total independence' to describe the relation of free subjectivity to social structures. The expression is meant to convey that 'no factual state can determine consciousness.'" In other words, no matter what one's situation, there are always options."[44] In short, Sartre, much like Beauvoir, maintains that freedom is at the heart of the existent, but is acutely aware of how this freedom can

---

42. Busch, "Beyond the Cogito," 198.

43. Ibid. 199.

44. Busch, "Sartre's Hyperbolic Ontology," 199; quotation is from Sartre, *Being and Nothingness*, 435–436.

be degraded and manipulated by upbringing, language, class, race, and the general circumstances of one's situation into a frighteningly limited field of possibilities.[45] This is why Busch asks that we think of the development of Sartrean freedom in terms of a "spiral," insofar as it evolves over time to move from the more abstract sense of ontological freedom to the more concrete sense, one that requires that the realities of the situation be taken into account in the *expression* or enactment of that freedom.[46] This spiraling development allows Sartre to take seriously the forces of concrete alienation in living, laboring, and choosing one's profession, as well as the effects of one's upbringing in the projection of future possibilities.

As soon as she turned her full attention to ethics, Beauvoir became acutely aware of how these kinds of forces shape situations in ways that make it very difficult (if not *almost* impossible) for freedom to be realized in action. Not only is Beauvoir sensitive to the effects of the childhood on one's situation, she is also mindful of the fact that not everyone can be held accountable for ontological freedom once adulthood is reached:

> Certain adults can live in the universe of the serious in all honesty, for example, those who are denied all instruments of escape, those who are enslaved or who are mystified. The less economic and social circumstances allow an individual to act upon the world, the more this world appears to him as given. This is the case of women who inherit a long tradition of submission and of those who are called 'the humble.'[47]

As is clear, Beauvoir thinks it is possible for certain adults, *in all honesty*, to live in the infantile world of the serious person. Such people are "mystified" into being unaware of their ontological freedom through the concrete barriers of the infantile world constructed around and through them: "having been kept in a state of servitude and ignorance, they have no means of breaking the ceiling which is stretched over their heads. Like the child, they can exercise their freedom, but only within the universe which has been set up before them, without them."[48] Examples of such people are American slaves and women in many civilizations. Of course, this insight forms the

---

45. It would actually be helpful to expand on Busch's own treatment of childhood and class in Sartre's formation of the subject, by looking at issues of colonialism and race as we find in Sartre's Preface to Frantz Fanon's *The Wretched of the Earth*. There he does not affirm absolute freedom but writes, "I do not say that it is impossible to change a man into an animal: I simply say that you won't get there without weakening him considerably" (Sartre, "Preface," 15).

46. Busch, "Sartre's Hyperbolic Ontology," 200.

47. Beauvoir, *Ethics of Ambiguity*, 47–48.

48. Ibid. 37.

foundation of her world-changing work *The Second Sex*, where she explores all of the ways that woman is made, not born. Beauvoir finds that for woman, ontological freedom is cast into a world that, much like the world of the child, is not a world where she recognizes herself. Rather,

> [S]he discovers and chooses herself in a world where men force her to assume herself as Other: an attempt is made to freeze her as an object and doom her to immanence, since her transcendence will be forever transcended by another essential and sovereign consciousness. Woman's drama lies in this conflict between the fundamental claim of every subject, which always posits itself as essential, and the demands of a situation that constitutes her as inessential.[49]

Just as Busch highlights Sartre's realization concerning the Dop shampoo factory worker, whose life is dominated by a situation of doomed immanence (of transcendence transcended), Beauvoir notes that this reality is the reality of most women in western civilization.

And yet, for both Beauvoir (as with Sartre above) even in oppressive circumstances, one is never totally denied the possibility of freedom. I call this "the paradox of immanent freedom" insofar as one is free, but only in the abstract sense (similar to what Busch calls the ontological sense of freedom in the early Sartre). For Beauvoir, this manifests in the empty expenditures of freedom in complaint (which changes nothing) or resignation (where one's freedom merely dissipates but does not get eradicated).[50] But even in empty expenditures, positive liberation is always possible for Beauvoir, just as it is for Sartre. What is more, if one is in a situation where one has greater possibilities and a more open futural horizon for action, then the onus is *to help others do the same*. The two expressions of "transcendent" freedom, revolt and creation, are what the "authentic" person engages in, both for themselves and for those who do not have similar material possibilities for concrete action. Thus Beauvoir focuses on how we live within an ambiguous situation where we both form and are formed by circumstances. From this position, at the crossroads of determination and freedom, we can distance ourselves from circumstances through revolt (particularly against oppressive structures) and actively change them through creation. This possibility of revolt against oppression is key to the ethical call to help others who are in situations of oppression. But such a call is only meaningful if one believes that ontological freedom, even if only in its implicit or trapped form, underlies all revolutionary movements.

49. Beauvoir, *Second Sex*, 17.
50. Mussett, "Expressions of Negativity," 8.

As the work of Thomas Busch helps us to see, the evolution of Sartrean freedom can be viewed through the bookends of Husserlian phenomenology and Beauvoirian existentialism. The intentionality of consciousness revealed to Sartre the existence of a kind of radical freedom that cannot be captured by the reflective actions of the transcendental Ego. This non-positional awareness of self became the radical nothingness capable of rupturing Being in the act of nihilating the given. The ability to stand back from the world in order to thematize it, question it, and shape it, undergoes profound transformations as Sartre's thought evolves. As he becomes more aware of the effects of language, class, childhood, and material circumstances, he backs off from his earlier belief in the radical split between human freedom and the world. Rather than being-for-itself standing on the one side and everything else standing squarely on the other, he becomes sensitive to the deep entanglements in which embodied subjects find themselves. These entanglements are clear to Beauvoir almost from the beginning of her works on ethics and cultural criticism. As such, Sartre's later works bring him into a closer connection to Beauvoir's philosophy of ambiguity. But to claim that Sartre or Beauvoir ever jettisoned their commitments to freedom would be clearly wrongheaded. Their own philosophical and political orientations prevent them from going in the direction of post-modern tendencies to see the subject as simply produced by the situation. Rather, maintaining the deep conviction that all of us, so long as we live and strive, are ontologically free on some level, allows existentialism to remain one of the most powerful philosophies of liberation and transformation in the western tradition.

Bibliography

Astur, Alexandre and Contat, Michel. *Sartre by Himself: A film directed by Alexandre Astruc and Michel Contat with the participation of Simone de Beauvoir, Jacques-Larent Bost, Andre Gorz, Jean Pouillon.* Translated by Richard Seaver. New York: Urizon, 1978.

Beauvoir, Simone de. *After the War: Force of Circumstance.* Vol. 1. Translated by Richard Howard. New York: Paragon House, 1992.

———. *The Ethics of Ambiguity.* Translated by Bernard Frechtman. Secaucus, NJ: Philosophical Library, 1997.

———. *Pyrrhus and Cineas.* In *Simone de Beauvoir: Philosophical Writings.* Edited by Margaret A. Simons with Marybeth Timmermann and Mary Beth Mader, 77–150. Translated by Marybeth Timmermann. Chicago: University of Illinois Press, 2004.

———. *The Second Sex.* Translated by Constance Borde and Sheila Malovany-Chevallier. New York: Knopf, 2010.

Busch, Thomas. "Beyond the Cogito: The Question of the Continuity of Sartre's Thought." *Modern Schoolman* 60 (1983) 189–204.

———. "Phenomenology as Humanism: The Case of Husserl and Sartre." *Research in Phenomenology* 9 (1979) 127–43.
———. *The Power of Consciousness and the Force of Circumstances in Sartre's Philosophy*. Bloomington: Indiana University Press, 1990.
———. "Sartre's Hyperbolic Ontology: *Being and Nothingness* Revisited." *Symposium: Canadian Journal of Continental Philosophy* 15 (2011) 191–200.
———. "Sartre: The Phenomenological Reduction and Human Relationships." *Journal of the British Society for Phenomenology* 6 (1975) 55–61.
———. "Sartre and the Senses of Alienation." *The Southern Journal of Philosophy* 15 (1977) 151–60.
———. "Simone de Beauvoir on Achieving Subjectivity." In *The Contradictions of Freedom*, edited by Sally J. Scholz and Shannon M. Mussett, 177–88. Albany: SUNY Press, 2005.
Heidegger, Martin. *Being and Time*. Translated by Joan Stambaugh. Albany: SUNY Press, 1996.
Husserl, Edmund. *Cartesian Meditations: An Introduction to Phenomenology*. Translated by Dorion Cairns. Dordrecht: Kluwer, 1993.
———. *The Crisis of European Sciences and Transcendental Phenomenology*. Translated by David Carr. Evanston, IL: Northwestern University Press, 1970.
———. *The Idea of Phenomenology*. Translated by William P. Alston and George Nakhnikian. Dordrecht: Kluwer, 1990.
———. *Ideas Pertaining to a Pure Phenomenology and to a Phenomenological Philosophy, First Book*. Translated by Frederick Kersten. Dordrecht: Kluwer, 1998.
———. *Introduction to Transcendental Phenomenology*. Translated by Cyril Welch. New Brunswick, NJ: Atcost, 2003.
Kruks, Sonia. "Simone de Beauvoir: Teaching Sartre About Freedom." In *Feminist Interpretations of Simone de Beauvoir*, edited by Margaret A. Simons, 79–96. University Park: Pennsylvania State University Press, 1995.
Mussett, Shannon M. "Expressions of Negativity: Simone de Beauvoir's Response to Hegelian Freedom." In *Essays in Celebration of the Founding of the Organization of Phenomenological Organizations*. Edited by Cheung Chan-Fai et. al, 2003. *Indo-Pacific Journal of Philosophy*, pdf e-book, http://www.ipjp.org/images/e-books/OPO%20Essay%2034%20-%20Expressions%20of%20Negativity%20-%20Simone%20de%20Beauvoir%E2%80%99s%20Response%20to%20Hegelian%20Freedom%20-%20By%20Shannon%20M.%20Mussett.pdf.
Sartre, Jean-Paul. *Being and Nothingness*. Translated by Hazel Barnes. New York: Random House, 1956.
———. *The Transcendence of the Ego: An Existentialist Theory of Consciousness*. Translated by Forrest Williams and Robert Kirkpatrick. New York: Noonday, 1957.
———. "Preface." In *The Wretched of the Earth* by Frantz Fanon. Translated by Constance Farrington. New York: Grove Weidenfeld, 1963.

8

"Bad Faith" in *Being and Nothingness*

Unambiguously Epistemological as well as Ontological

—Ronald E. Santoni

In a recent article entitled "The Misplaced Chapter on Bad Faith, or Reading *Being and Nothingness* in Reverse,"[1] Matthew Eshleman—in my judgment one of the most astute and promising of the rising and challenging Sartre scholars—says repeatedly that the "primary function" of Sartre's probing analysis of "bad faith" in his *Being and Nothingness* (1943) chapter entitled "Bad Faith" is not to analyze bad faith but to discover what peculiarity of human reality allows the possibility of bad faith to take place. For Eshleman, reading *Being and Nothingness* in reverse makes this regressive conclusion a conclusive one. And in both this article and his rejoinder[2] to my critique[3] of it, he contends that this reversive reading also makes clear a shortcoming in my scholarship (which he has studied assiduously and even labels "Herculean") to recognize sufficiently the social aspects of bad faith. Moreover he contends strongly that bad faith is "essentially" and "ineluctably" (I take this to mean "necessarily") an "intersubjective social phenomenon."[4]

In my aforementioned reply to him, I have already taken issue with Eshleman's critique, so I shall not repeat it here. Instead, my primary intent

1. Eshleman, "The Misplaced Chapter."
2. Eshleman, "Necessarily Social," 40–47.
3. Santoni, "Necessarily Social?," 23–39.
4. Eshleman, "The Misplaced Chapter," 17.

here will be to give a concise reformulation of the key aspects of Sartre's concept and analysis of "bad faith," and show the critical importance of the epistemological form of it, too often ignored by many of Sartre's commentators and readers. In my judgment—and this will not likely surprise those who are familiar with my work on Sartre—the phenomenon of "bad faith" pervades Sartre's thoughts, concerns, socio-political positions, psychoanalysis, and—dare I say it—ethics, from the beginning to the end of his philosophical/literary oeuvre. Please note, however, that I am not contending that bad faith is the most fundamental concept in Sartre's ontology or philosophy: freedom[5]—specially freedom as human reality—or perhaps even contingency—may justifiably make a stronger claim to that. Rather, I am trying again to emphasize bad faith's multidimensionality in Sartre's thought. And, by so doing, I shall at least be suggesting how bad faith often serves as a kind of criterion by which Sartre evaluates not only the actions and views of others but also our individual and collective praxes, mindsets, movements, and socio-political positions, for example.

Over fifty years after the publication of *Being and Nothingness*, I need not offer another highly detailed analysis of either the puzzle that leads Sartre to offer a meticulous analysis of bad faith or Sartre's analysis of the mechanisms of bad faith. I, for one, have already attempted this in earlier works.[6] Yet I must provide at least a summary of the most salient points in that analysis.

Early in *Being and Nothingness*, Sartre, employing Nietzsche's precise characterization of it, allows that bad faith is "a lie to oneself."[7] However, insisting against Freud, that consciousness is translucent, he struggles to understand how bad faith can be possible, for unlike the "strict lie" or "falsehood," the translucent bad faith consciousness cannot have the ontological duality between the "deceiver" and the "deceived," between "myself and myself before the Other."[8] If bad faith is lying to oneself, if the one who lies and the one to whom the lie is told are one and the same, and if all consciousness is conscious of itself, how can I lie to myself, or, in other words, how can I conceal the truth from myself? The psychoanalytic notion of "a lie without a liar" violates the psychic unity and translucency of consciousness.[9]

---

5. For my most recent analysis of Sartre's view of freedom, see Santoni, "Camus on Sartre," 785–813.

6. See e.g., Santoni, *Bad Faith, Good Faith*, and "Unaufrichtigkeit."

7. Sartre, *Being and Nothingness*, 48.

8. Ibid., 49; translation amended.

9. Ibid., 51.

Perplexed by this puzzle but persuaded by what he regards as clear evidence of people living in bad faith (he offers a number of controversial examples), he attempts a conceptual and epistemological solution (note!) to this epistemological paradox. But this must not ignore the ontological questions that may be at the core of the puzzle. Sartre's analysis of bad faith is preceded by his recognition that the human being is not only the one by whom concrete negations (*négatités* such as absences or lacks) come into the world, but also the one who can adopt "negative attitudes with respect to [oneself]" (*des attitudes négatives vis-à-vis de soi*).[10] So, initially, it is in order to illustrate this self-differentiating possibility of self-negation that Sartre chooses to examine bad faith as "one determined attitude ... essential [note!] to human reality" that "direct[s] its negation" towards itself.[11] And, of course, unambiguous evidence of Sartre's ontological concern with bad faith lies in his related question, "What must be the being of a man if he is to be capable of bad faith?"[12] This question is, without doubt, the basis for Eshleman's more recent, and, I've contended, highly questionable contention that the "primary function" of Sartre's probing analysis of bad faith is to establish the paradoxical "nature" of human reality.[13]

I repeat this background not simply to exhibit the "problematic" of bad faith, but also to show that although the core of Sartre's analysis of bad faith is ontological, in our practical life it is frequently epistemological in its structure. This will allow the reader to understand why Sartre treats bad faith as both a problem of *being* and a problem of *belief*—not to mention morality for the moment—and why, albeit with reservations, I have made and continue to make a distinction between *ontological* bad faith and *epistemological* bad faith, even though the two are intimately interrelated. The gist of this distinction may be summarized in the following way.

Ontological bad faith relates to the "spontaneous determination of our being,"[14] to our coming into the world, to our original or primitive project, to the primitive "negative attitude" that human reality adopts in its upsurge towards its own being in the world. Our primitive project of Being may be said to constitute our original bad faith. Abandoned or condemned to freedom, human reality as Nothingness wants to "incorporate the in-itself as its true mode of being."[15] It tries perpetually to refuse to recognize its

10. Ibid., 47.
11. Ibid., 48.
12. Ibid, 55; see also 45.
13. Eshleman, "The Misplaced Chapter."
14. Sartre, *Being and Nothingness*, 68.
15. Ibid., 440.

freedom. Empty and lacking being—it is not what it is—it seeks Being; it desires to be, "it can aim only at its being."[16] Always in question, then, my freedom, which "is identical with my existence,"[17] attempts in *bad faith* to escape its inescapable condition and the anguish of that condition by tying itself down as fixed, stable, self-coincident, identifiable—all attributes of *being-in-itself* (i.e., object or thing). In Sartre's words, we flee the *anguish* of becoming aware of our unstable condition "by attempting to apprehend ourselves from without as an other or as *a thing*". This primitive, "immediate," original, "natural" attitude or "disposition," which "tends" or is inclined towards bad faith, and is freedom's original or "natural" pursuit of Being in order to flee the angst of Nothingness, is the primitive ontological pattern of bad faith. This "pursuit of being," this *quête de l'être* can never be suppressed: for this reason, in *Notebooks for an Ethics*, he refers to it as "hell".[18] In my judgment, this attitude is at the root of all analyses and judgments that Sartre offers to elucidate, illustrate, or indict bad faith.[19]

To bring this to a head, from the point of view of ontology, any project or behavioral pattern that attempts to escape the inescapable, metastable freedom, or free consciousness, that we *are*, constitutes bad faith. What follows radically from this—if I may invoke Sartre's key distinction between *being-for-itself* (*l'être-pour-soi*) and *being-in-itself* (*l'être-en-soi*)—is that any attempt on the part of being-for-itself to treat being-for-itself as being-in-itself, whether by treating oneself or Others as objects, by giving oneself or Others a fixed identity, by holding human beings in bondage, or by treating human reality (in any way) as less than freedom, is in *bad faith*. In one way or another, any such conduct violates the freedom that human reality *is*, and is directly or indirectly related to free consciousness's original or primitive (bad faith) refusal of its anguished, non-substantial freedom, and its consequent pursuit of solidity, self-coincidence, and identity. Thus, as Sartre puts it, bad faith is a type of *being in the world* which is like that of objects.[20] (In passing, let me just say that much, but not all, of Sartre's analysis of "Concrete Relations with Others" in Chapter 3 of *Being and Nothingness* would testify to this contention.)

Now, let me highlight a few distinguishing marks of what I have called *epistemological bad faith*, acknowledging from the start that I do not regard

16. Ibid., 564.
17. Ibid., 444.
18. Sartre, *Notebooks*, 37.
19. For a detailed discussion of ontological bad faith as our "natural attitude" and "primitive project" of Being (our "original fall"), see Santoni, "Necessarily Social?," 23–47.
20. Sartre, *Being and Nothingness*, 68.

it as totally dichotomous with ontological bad faith. I view it, rather, as a method or contrived technique by which we can "lie to ourselves:" a way by which, given the translucency of consciousness, we can attempt to turn away from our freedom, take refuge in either facticity or transcendence, identities or possibilities, and come to believe what our self-conscious consciousness recognizes as not worthy of complete belief or acceptance as truth. One must first understand that, viewed epistemologically, bad faith is, for Sartre, a matter of faith, not certainty. Sartre contends that the primitive project of bad faith is itself in bad faith; it is a decision in bad faith about the nature of faith.[21] "Conscious of its structure," bad faith consciousness begins with an awareness that human reality (i.e., free consciousness) is not what it is and is what it is not; that it is always *in question* and at a distance from itself. With this awareness, bad faith assumes that all belief, like all consciousness, questions its own being, that all believing includes non-believing, and, hence, that there is no "perfect" or "pure" belief, for perfect belief would contradict the metastable, evanescent, nature of consciousness and "self-destruct." So if all belief falls short of belief (*n'est pas assez croyance*) there is room for imperfect belief.[22] On this intuition and assumption, bad faith consciousness "resigns" itself in advance to not being fulfilled by evidence, and prepares itself to accept "non-persuasive evidence" as "persuasive" even when it is not fully persuaded. By exploiting the nature of "faith" and the elusiveness of consciousness, by deciding on weak evidential requirements for belief, persuasion, and truth, bad faith consciousness can bring itself to believe what it does not fully believe, or not believe what it believes in the translucency of consciousness.[23] Hence, the person in epistemological bad faith, having met the incomplete and selective criteria of persuasion he has contrived, can count himself *persuaded*, even when, in the translucency of consciousness, he is *not* fully persuaded. To illustrate by reference to one of Sartre's oft-criticized examples, the bad faith of the coquette involves precisely her acceptance of her believing that she is engaged intellectually, not bodily, with her companion, even though, given the translucency of her consciousness, she is not fully persuaded. As I have shown in past works, she deceptively plays "see-saw" with the believing/not believing dynamic, the facticity/transcendence double-property of human consciousness or reality. By exploiting the ambiguity of all belief (to believe involves not believing and not believing involves some believing), she is persuaded only in the sense of what we may call "half-persuasion."

21. Ibid., 67–68.
22. Ibid., 69.
23. Ibid., 70.

A critic may justifiably ask, "Why make a distinction between ontological bad faith and epistemological bad faith? Isn't the latter simply an elucidation of the mechanism by which bad faith or lying to oneself takes place?" This is an arguable and very complex issue which has merited, and will continue to merit considerable attention at another time. But I believe that my distinction helps to clarify Sartre's analysis of bad faith and elucidates the pervasiveness of his concern and discussions of the phenomenon of bad faith. *Ontological* bad faith is an attitude to our human reality, to our upsurge as freedom, rather than to specific beliefs and evidence. While in *ontological* bad faith we try to flee the distinctive freedom we *are* and the "anguish" we experience in knowing from what we are fleeing,[24] in *epistemological* bad faith we exploit the ambiguity of our consciousness and belief by allowing the non-coincidence and evanescence of our belief to become an excuse for believing what we don't fully believe (or for not believing what we don't fully disbelieve, in the translucency of consciousness). In each case, the bad faith "attitude" takes advantage of the elusive structure of human reality that makes it possible—namely, that we are non-substantial, metastable, free beings who are not what we are and are what we are not. Moreover, we can better understand Sartre's over-all discussion of bad faith if we distinguish carefully between the bad faith of our "primitive project" or "coming into the world,"[25] and the bad faith of our everyday attitudes, actions, choices, beliefs, behaviors, decisions, which Sartre illustrates in his discussion of the flirt, the homosexual, the waiter, and the frigid woman. Although these may be derivative from or secondary to our "immediate" or "primitive attitude" of bad faith (flight from freedom and responsibility), they are expressions or manifestations of it, and their mechanisms can be explained via the epistemological analysis that Sartre has provided. That the two concepts are mutually supportive does *not* vitiate the need to distinguish them. Yet I would not quarrel strongly with a critic who might contend that epistemological bad faith is derivative from Sartre's ontology of bad faith.

This summary of Sartre's analysis of bad faith in *Being and Nothingness* may now serve as the background from which both the reader and I may proceed. In another work, I hope to provide extensive detailed evidence for contending that Sartre's notion of bad faith pervades, and often dominates, the corpus of his philosophical and literary œuvre. A consequence of my thesis will be my strong suggestion, for which I shall provide representative

---

24. Ibid., 43.
25. Most recently, in "Necessarily Social?", I have tried to elucidate the details of a troublesome issue in Sartre's account of our primitive project or our original "coming into the world." I have argued against the view that this original bad faith is "ineluctably" or "essentially" "social."

illustrations, that Sartre's meticulous analysis of and continuous appeal to the notion of bad faith have generated ongoing discussion since Sartre first introduced them, and have had an important impact on twentieth century, and, thus far, twenty-first century, considerations of issues related to authentic living and the moral life. For, one may reasonably argue that an "authenticity" and "bad faith" are, for Sartre, alternate version of the traditional distinction between "good," and "bad," "moral," and "immoral."[26]

Bibliography

Eshleman, Matthew. "Bad Faith Is Necessarily Social." *Sartre Studies International* 14 (2008) 40–47.
———. "The Misplaced Chapter on Bad Faith, or Reading *Being and Nothingness* in Reverse." *Sartre Studies International* 14 (2008) 1–22.
Santoni, Ronald. *Bad Faith, Good Faith, and Authenticity in Sartre's Early Philosophy.* Philadelphia: Temple University Press, 1995.
———. "Camus on Sartre's 'Freedom'—Another 'Misunderstanding.'" *Review of Metaphysics* 61 (2008) 785–813.
———. "Die Unaufrichtigkeit der Gewalt—und ist Sartre hinsichtlich der Gewalt unaufrichtig?" Translated by Erik M. Vogt. In *Über Sartre: Perspektiven und Kritiken*, edited by Thomas Flynn et. al. 217–38. Vienna: Turia & Kant, 2005.
———. "Is Bad Faith Necessarily Social?" *Sartre Studies International* 14 (2008) 23–39.
Jean-Paul Sartre, *Being Nothingness*. Translated by Hazel Barnes. New York: Philosophical Library, 1956.
———. *Notebook for an Ethics*. Translated by David Pellauer. Chicago: University of Chicago Press, 1992.

---

26. I offer this short piece to join in honoring Tom Busch's retirement from the Philosophy Department of Villanova University. I personally wish to honor his scholarship, done at a time when too much philosophy was given to rather dry analytic problems or puzzle-solving. Tom has devoted himself to the issues of existentialism and phenomenology—that is to say, issues directly related to our lives and being-in-the-world. And his scholarship has been broad, focusing primarily on Sartre and Merleau-Ponty, but including Husserl, Marcel, Gadamer, and Levinas, for example. As a Sartre scholar myself, I wish, in particular, to thank him for his book, *The Power of Consciousness and the Force of Circumstance in Sartre's Philosophy*, a book from which I learned and to which I am indebted.

Thus, on this occasion, I pay tribute to Tom Busch, a valued teacher, a fine and prolific scholar, a reflective and concerned human being, and a friend whom I have not seen or engaged philosophically frequently enough.

9

Beauvoir on Communication and Incorporation in *The Mandarins*

Building on Insights from Thomas Busch

—Sally Scholz

Introduction

At one crucial moment in *The Mandarins*, Simone de Beauvoir's award-winning novel, Henri, a well-known leftist newspaper editor and author of a moving book about the resistance as well as one of the narrative voices, struggles with whether or not to publish news of the Soviet work camps. He knows that publishing the news will likely destroy the leftwing political party, the SRL, founded by famed writer Robert Dubreuilh in part out of the fellowship of the resistance. One of the questions that emerges from this scene pertains to the obligations to a political party: do individuals have some responsibility not just to maintain their loyalty to a group but to also avoid actions that might jeopardize the loyalty of others to the group? Certainly groups are not all the same and some groups ought to be challenged and dissolved from within. But there are some groups whose existence is vital for struggles against oppressive regimes and systematic injustice. Although here framed as a moral question pertaining to the conflict of obligations, this question might also be framed as an ontological question about the existence and nature of the group: how does the group exist? And does writing, especially political or politicized writing, carry the power of incorporation? In this paper, I explore these latter questions first and then offer some suggestions for how Beauvoir approaches the former question of responsibility and loyalty. Although I draw from a variety of Beauvoir's philosophical works, my primary focus is *The Mandarins* because it illustrates the pull of allegiance to a politically motivated group in tension with individual projects. This is the pull of *incorporation,* or solidarity.

Thomas Busch writes eloquently about a public embodiment, politically or ethically motivated, that he calls "incorporation:"

> Many fine studies of Camus, Marcel, Sartre, and Merleau-Ponty have traced out and definitively established the centrality of embodiment and lived experience in their works. What is far less established and publicized is how their works, particularly their late works, move beyond, without denying, embodiment to what I call 'incorporation,' the transcendence of individual experience in the discursive circulation of Being, a circulation which, while admitting individual differences, calls discussants together ethically and politically.[1]

Busch sees incorporation as an ethical and political category. To transcend "individual experience in the discursive circulation of Being" transforms embodiment to incorporation. To incorporate is to become more than the being of each of the existents taken individually. Incorporation is experienced by each both similarly and differently. In other words, incorporation is a collective embodiment, a group that acts and feels together even while each existent simultaneously acts and feels individually.

In this article, I extend Busch's project by examining incorporation in one of Simone de Beauvoir's most famous novels. The main characters continually turn to the power of literature or writing to bring people together, but they also see in writing a personal escape from political and ethical responsibility. Literature, according to Beauvoir, can facilitate incorporation because it establishes and relies on communication between the author and the reader. In her defense of the "metaphysical novel," Beauvoir transforms metaphysics into a subjective experience of the world; rather than an abstract philosophical system about the nature of being, she proffers the messy but communicable involvement in the world that literature presents. The metaphysical novel speaks to, or of, the ambiguity of experience.[2] This speaking is for others, and it is only because others exist that the novel lives.

1. Busch, *Circulating Being,* x.
2. See Beauvoir, "Literature and Metaphysics"; and Merleau-Ponty, "Metaphysics and the Novel."

According to Merleau-Ponty, the value of the metaphysical novel "consists of actively being what we are by chance, of establishing that communication with others and with ourselves for which our temporal structure gives us the opportunity and of which our liberty is only the rough outline."[3] Presenting experience with all of its contradictions and tensions, without a moral or moralizing message, evokes embodied feeling in readers and creates a new "body." Incorporated thusly, the collective acts. Individual acts are not always elements of incorporation, but all individual acts take on new significance in light of the embodied collective. In other words, literature can be understood as a tool in the transcendence of individual experience toward incorporation.

In his important book *Circulating Being*, Busch appeals to "solidarity" as the Camusian contribution to the discourse of incorporation in late existentialism.[4] A similar move is possible for Beauvoir, but, as I will show, her conception of solidarity or incorporation offers something unique to the mix, making her contributions to late existentialism profoundly important to philosophical thinking about social movements.

The Mandarins

The Mandarins is set in the immediate post-World War II period. A group of intellectuals struggles with their memories of the Occupation while trying to maintain the purpose and collective engagement of the Resistance in France.[5] The book has two narrators: speaking in the first-person, Anne is a psychoanalyst married to Robert Dubreuihl. Their daughter, Nadine, was an adolescent during the war and lost her lover in the death camps. The second narrator, Henri, is presented in the third-person. Henri was a leader in the resistance. His newspaper, *L'Espoir*, played an important role in not only communicating with fellow resisters but in providing a home or common ground for activists. In the post-war period, however, he struggles to keep the newspaper afloat while the younger reporters and writers seek to maintain the collective, to recover from the horrors of war—including those horrors they perpetrated—and to rediscover meaning in the world.

3. Merleau-Ponty, "Metaphysics and the Novel," 40.
4. Busch, *Circulating Being*, chapter 1.
5. A number of scholars highlight the novel for philosophical work on collective engagement or political praxis. See especially Kruks, "Living on Rails"; McBride, "The Conflict of Ideologies"; and Scholz, "Sustained Praxis." See also, Suleiman, "Memory Troubles."

The storyline of the novel vacillates between private struggles and world politics as the Cold War gains a foothold. One scene interweaves a bicycle holiday with news of the US bombing of Hiroshima and Nagasaki; the scene evokes the bucolic countryside and a leisurely breakfast at a café punctuated with newspaper headlines. The reality of the atomic bomb places the very question of existence on the forefront of the characters' minds, and, in doing so, offers the same to the reader.[6] Both feel the pleasant sense of a holiday after a long period of deprivation, the crushing feeling of futility against world powers and politics outside of one's control, and the absolute necessity to take one's place in the distribution of moral and political responsibility. In her review, Iris Murdoch describes *The Mandarins* using the compelling phrase "the contradictions of freedom."[7] Having survived the Nazi Occupation, the characters in Beauvoir's novel, like their real-life counterparts in the post-war era, grapple with the question of how to deal with collaborationists, how to sustain leftist politics against the rising power of the United States, how to respond to new instances of oppressive dictatorships, and whether love—or any deep connection with others—is possible given the variety of experiences and compromises endured during the war.

Although numerous elements of the story and suggestive passages lend themselves to developing a Beauvoirian account of incorporation, I will concentrate on one particular passage, focusing in on Henri, because it neatly brings together so many elements of late existentialist concerns regarding embodiment and solidarity that Busch describes as incorporation. Shortly after the end of the war, Henri, said to be loosely modeled on Camus, publishes a book about his time in the resistance. His secretary hands him a folder marked "Correspondence—Novel." The folder contains both published reviews and informal letters from readers. The following lengthy passage captures this moment for Henri:

> He had written the novel during the war without ever having given any thought to what the future might hold for him; he hadn't even been sure that the future would hold anything at all for him. And now the book had been published, people had already read it. All at once, Henri found himself judged, discussed, classified, as he himself had so often judged and discussed others. He spread out the clippings and began going through them one at a time. 'A sensation,' Paula had said, and he had thought she was exaggerating. But, as a matter of fact, the critics also used some mighty impressive words. Lambert, of course, was

---

6. See also McBride, "The Conflict of Ideologies."
7. Murdoch, "At One Remove from Tragedy."

prejudiced; Lachaume, too. And all those young critics who had just come into their own had a natural predisposition for the writers of the Resistance. But it was the admiring letters sent by both friends and strangers that confirmed the verdict of the press. Really, without getting a swelled head about it, it was certainly enough to make any man happy. His pages, written with deep feeling, had actually stirred people! Henri stretched happily. In a way, it was sort of miraculous, what had just happened. Two years earlier, thick curtains had veiled blue-painted windows: he had been completely shut off from the black city, from the whole earth; his pen would pause hesitantly over the paper. Now those unformed sounds in his throat had become a living voice in the world; the secret stirrings in his heart had been transformed into truths for other hearts. 'I should have tried explaining it to Nadine,' he said to himself. 'If others don't count, it's meaningless to write. But if they do count, it's wonderful to gain their friendship and their confidence with words; it's magnificent to hear your own thoughts echoed in them.'[8]

In what follows, I unpack this passage in order to reveal and connect Beauvoir's thoughts on historicity, communication through literature, embodied feeling, politics, and most importantly, incorporation.

Historicity

"He had written the novel during the war without ever having given any thought to what the future might hold for him."

For Henri, literature occurs in a particular historical moment and social context. For both his novel and Beauvoir's novel in which we read about it, the moment is both too raw for fiction and too important to be forgotten. Henri's novel appeared in the immediate period after the war, while Beauvoir's was not published until 1954, when the risk of memories fading issued a new historical moment. Beauvoir's fiction encouraged a revisiting of the war years, at a time when Cold War tensions seemed on the verge of erupting into yet another world war. Henri's fiction chronicles the lost fellowship of Resistance, the contradictions of collaborators, and the looming threat of new dictatorships in post war Europe. Moreover, by using the technique of a novel within a novel, Beauvoir both foreshadows the reception of her own novel and offers a suggestive account for how literature acts on the

8. Beauvoir, *Mandarins*, 112.

world. Henri "hadn't even been sure that the future would hold anything at all for him." His book does not record history; it participates in it. His novel, written with deep feeling, was not meant to determine a future or prescribe meaning for the past or present in light of a particular future. It opened the future by disclosing the present.[9]

Beauvoir uses the mechanism of a novel within a novel to discuss the power of literature, not to advocate or theorize but to communicate among and between subjects in a particular historical moment or sharing a particular social context. Such communication does not preclude a communicative potential with readers who do not share the same historical moment and social context; instead, they too read from their particularity, and they experience the novel from that moment. As Busch describes, Sartre referred to this latter as a virtual audience: "the virtual audience is composed of all who can possibly read and respond to the work"; this is distinct from the actual audience consisting "of those who, under specific historical conditions, know how to read, have access to books, and so forth."[10] The reaction to Henri's book is the reaction of the actual audience; it might be argued that Beauvoir employs a third distinction by placing his book within her own. Present-day readers of Beauvoir's novel are spectators to Henri's book, removing us from the historical circumstances of his book as well as Beauvoir's but opening communication nonetheless. Readers of Beauvoir's novel today are virtual readers of her book and spectators to Henri's. But we are nonetheless brought together with all actual and virtual readers insofar as we allow literature to speak, to open the future, and to present the ambiguity of personal and political choice.

"Thick curtains had veiled blue-painted windows."

Henri's book is remarkable both because it is the first book published to address the situation of Occupation and Resistance, and because it functions in the way Busch describes incorporation: it takes the embodied and lived experience of individuals and transforms it into a "discursive circulation of Being, a circulation which, while admitting individual differences, calls discussants together ethically and politically."[11] "Two years earlier" Henri, like other intellectuals in occupied France, was isolated behind "thick curtains" and "blue-painted windows." The individuals' embodied experience of the war and Occupation, of being walled in behind curtains and cut off from

---

9. Beauvoir, *Ethics of Ambiguity*, 70–71.
10. Busch, *Circulating Being*, 67.
11. Ibid., x.

their previous existence by blue painted window, creates a shared context. Each individual, in his or her own way experiences the particular historical moment,[12] but taken together they transcend their own experience in a "discursive circulation of Being" that is both individuated and collective. This collective is understood without being specified, it is the embodied feeling of isolation transcended to a shared experience of political oppression or violence.[13]

Second, the contrasting isolation of the blue painted windows with the post-war reception of Henri's book highlights the temporal subject. Drawing on Beauvoir's discussion of time and the individual subject in *The Ethics of Ambiguity* reveals that Henri's notion, mentioned in the epigraph of this section—that he had written without a thought toward the future—is a deliberate refusal to succumb to the serious, to fall in with the line of thought that explains the present in reference to a promised future. Just as the promise of a heaven after earthly suffering creates a complacency that denies freedom in the here and now, investing in a future at the expense of confronting the horrors of the present moment denies freedom. Beauvoir explains, "Those who project themselves toward a Future-Thing and submerge their freedom in it find the tranquility of the serious."[14] That tranquility reduces the individual to a thing, it is a flight from freedom. Beauvoir describes the serious man: "He forgets that every goal is at the same time a point of departure and that human freedom is the ultimate, the unique end to which man should destine himself."[15]

A similar renunciation of freedom transpires for those who live in the past. Perhaps the most compelling discussion of living in the past is Beauvoir's account of the "woman in love" in *The Second Sex*. The woman in love devotes herself to the beloved in a way that reifies the initial moments of love; she tries to always be what the beloved loved and, barring that, to always be the love object of the beloved. Beauvoir explains, "She first sought in love a confirmation of what she was, her past, her personage; but she also commits her future: to justify it, she destines it to the one who possesses all values; she thus gives up her transcendence: she subordinates it to that of the essential other whose vassal and slave she makes herself."[16] Within *The Mandarins*, Henri's lover Paula plays the role of the woman in love. Paula

12. See also Tidd, "For the Time Being."

13. Duran notes how Beauvoir explores this transformation from solipsistic thinking to political being in her novels; the former is the heart of *L'Invitee*, while the latter is the force behind *The Mandarins* (Duran, "Wartime Philosophy").

14. Beauvoir, *Ethics of Ambiguity*, 117.

15. Ibid., 48–49.

16. Beauvoir, *The Second Sex*, 691.

lives in the past when her love for Henri appeared to save and sustain him. She has given up a career as a successful singer in order to be the lover of a successful man. Renouncing her freedom, Paula attempts to be Henri's timeless lover.

The temporal subject grapples with the contradictions of life in the particularity of a historical moment. This grappling with ambiguity, rather than a display of a consistency in character, marks the novel. A temporal subject acts in the moment with no thought of an expected or promised future, as Henri does in writing his book. This is not to deny the significance of the future or the past but rather to affirm one's freedom in the present situation which will, of course, take on its own significance when looked at from any of the possible futures that open up. As Busch describes, Beauvoir's novel "evoke[s] richly a specific historical situation and characters struggling to make sense of their lives in that situation."[17] Henri's novel does the same for others within his milieu.

Paula's reaction to Henri's writing is important for our purposes here. Although she calls the war-time book a "sensation," she laments Henri's dedication to the paper as well as his subsequent decision to write a light novel, both of which draw him away from what she considers true writing. Her expectations for Henri posit a fixed future wherein his greatness as a literary voice is secured. Paula badgers him because he will not let her read his new work. His refusal to let her read his writing (even going so far as to lock it into his desk) is a rejection of her account of the future or a rejection of a determined future project that shapes the present moment. Although Henri might be criticized for attempting to dwell in the security of a "light novel," Paula is the character who most clearly disavows her subjectivity.

Henri's rejection of Paula also an explicit attempt to close communication with her as a reader of his work. One way to look at this interaction is as an affirmation of the communicative potential of literature but only with or for readers who share historicity and accept their status as temporal subjects, the relationship between reader and writer is severed if history is denied. In addition, however, Beauvoir seems to posit something more in this relation. Paula has renounced her freedom in her attempt to be Henri's timeless lover.

Others have written more extensively on the topic of historicity and the temporal subject,[18] but it is evident that the present moment must not be dictated by some hoped-for future. That is the flaw of the serious person

---

17. Busch, "Achieving Subjectivity," 177.

18. Tidd, "For the Time Being"; Bjørsnøs, "Representing Time"; and Tidd, "Testimony, *Historicité*, and the Intellectual."

described in *The Ethics of Ambiguity*. The present moment, informed by but not determined by a past, opens the future. Beauvoir's discussion of the future in the *Ethics of Ambiguity* emphasizes freedom but, of course, her conception of freedom for the individual is bound up with the freedom of others. This is why "incorporation" is such an important idea for Beauvoir in *The Mandarins*: Henri's project carries the potential to fall back on the past or open the future. Readers and writers participate in communication that discloses freedom. Paula is unable to read the new book in part because she is unable to participate in the communication of writer and reader as a temporal subject, but also in part because she refuses her own freedom. Consider, too, Beauvoir's description of the liberation of Paris in *The Ethics of Ambiguity*, the very celebration that invites readers of *The Mandarins* into the project:

> Existence must be asserted in the present if one does not want all life to be defined as an escape toward nothingness. That is the reason societies institute festivals whose role is to stop the movement of transcendence, to set up the end as an end. The hours following the liberation of Paris, for example, were an immense collective festival exalting the happy and absolute end of that particular history which was precisely the occupation of Paris.[19]

Compare this to Beauvoir's description of the metaphysical novel: "the novel will permit us to evoke the original upspringing [*jaillissement*] of existence in its complete, singular, and temporal truth."[20] The metaphysical novel reveals the particularity of the characters, but, in doing so, invites the reader to enter into a collective existence wherein one's own freedom is bound up with that of so many others.[21] The novel and the world are an interconnected singularity: "For, after all, there is only one reality; it is in the midst of the world that we think the world through."[22] In other words, Beauvoir's account of literature in her philosophical essays as well as in *The Mandarins* prompts an examination of the "upspringing of existence." Like the festival, literature tries to capture or stop the "movement of transcendence" but the very acts of writing and reading belie that possibility. Instead, the embodied

---

19. Beauvoir, *Ethics of Ambiguity*, 125.

20. Beauvoir, "Literature and Metaphysics," 274.

21. In addition to Beauvoir's own essay on the topic, "Literature and Metaphysics," see Simons, "Introduction"; Bogaerts, "Beauvoir's Lecture"; and Scholz "The Power of Literature."

22. Beauvoir, "Literature and Metaphysics," 269.

experience of the individual is transcended toward, at least momentarily, incorporation with others.

Communication through Literature

"Those unformed sounds in his throat had become a living voice in the world."

Henri's embodied existence is evoked through the "unformed sounds in his throat." Incorporation is at least suggested via the "living voice in the world." If there are no others for whom one writes, then there can be no transcendence, no incorporation. The folder full of letters is a telling element of the reaction to Henri's novel, but it is also an indication of the collective. The letters serve as a tangible mark of the participation of readers with the writer in the project of the novel. They express deep feeling and connection. Henri feels connected and even obligated to these readers.

Beauvoir described her commitment to the metaphysical novel in a lecture and subsequent essay in 1945 and 1946 respectively.[23] Although the traditional conception of the metaphysical novel propounds a metaphysical truth, the existentialists of the 20th century reconceptualized it as a literary method that evokes being in the world: "it is to realize in oneself the metaphysical attitude, which consists in positing oneself in one's totality before the totality of the world." She includes such experiences as "presence in the world," "abandonment," "freedom," "opacity of things," and "the resistance of foreign consciousnesses."[24] Beauvoir was particularly interested in the disclosure of ambiguous, contradictory, or challenging aspects of existence. The reader must enter into communication with the author and find lived experience within the text as "an authentic adventure of the mind."[25] A metaphysical novel cannot have an established conclusion or message; the author must allow the facets of experience to unfold, presenting a reality that is full of unanswerable questions. The author writes without controlling the unfolding of reality in the novel: "the imagination of the writer runs away with her."[26] Margaret Simons argues that *The Mandarins* aptly fits Beauvoir's description.[27]

23. Simons, "Introduction," 266.
24. Beauvoir, "Literature and Metaphysics," 273.
25. Ibid., 272.
26. Holveck, "Can a Woman Be a Philosopher?," 72; see also Bogaerts, "Beauvoir's lecture," 23.
27. Simons, "Introduction"; see also, Scholz, "The Power of Literature."

In his insightful essay, "Sartre on Language and Politics," Busch argues that the Sartre of "What is Literature?" and the Merleau-Ponty of *Signs* offer somewhat opposing understandings of the relation between the writer and the reader in literature. Busch explains Sartre's position:

> Literature, as communicative, is a dialectic between writer and reader wherein each recognizes the freedom of the other, affording a glimpse into a positive reciprocity in human relationships ... The expressive and communicative nature of literature implies an ideal community, a collaborative use of freedoms.[28]

Two key features of literature thus emerge: literature has the power to reveal the world unfolding as both the writer and the reader experience it. Literature assumes "an ethics of mutual respect and recognition" between writer and reader. The disclosure of the world is full of ambiguity and doubt. That is why literature, more than philosophy, has the power to disclose. It makes no claims to truth but requires a commitment that entails participation with others.

Beauvoir makes explicit the claim of incorporation via literature in the passage from *The Mandarins*, she writes: "the secret stirrings in his heart had been transformed into truths for other hearts." Through writing, Henri had transcended his embodied experience of the war and moved to what Busch calls the "discursive circulation of Being." The "truths for other hearts" cannot be articulated or quantified but they unite all participants in an embodied communicative whole. Elsewhere, she describes literature as "a mode of communication irreducible to any other."[29] Literature reveals the complexity and ambiguity of the individual's existence; it simultaneously discloses the freedom of the author and the reader: "In revealing the lived world, the prose writer raises it to the thematic level where it is presented to others for their response. Literature, as communicative, is a dialectic between writer and reader wherein each recognizes the freedom of the other, affording a glimpse into a positive reciprocity in human relationships."[30] The early Sartre posits an idealized notion of the transparency of literature whereas Merleau-Ponty suggests that "'language is much more like a sort of being than a means.'"[31] Beauvoir might be seen as offering a third view which emphasizes the power of literature not solely to convey meaning, although

---

28. Busch, "Sartre on Language and Politics," 66.
29. Beauvoir, "Literature and Metaphysics," 270.
30. Busch, "Sartre on Language and Politics," 66.
31. Merleau-Ponty, "Indirect Language," 43, cited in Busch, "Sartre on Language and Politics," 70.

that is not excluded, but rather as a means through which relationships are formed and reformed.

"His pages, written with deep feeling, had actually stirred people!"

Literature, more than any other form of writing, evokes feelings in both reader and writer. This communicative affect could be seen as one facet of incorporation: shared embodied feeling, as when individuals are stirred by the words Henri had written. According to Beauvoir, literature evokes a reaction from readers, "the reader ponders, doubts, and takes sides."[32] Readers who feel with the characters will also make connections to their own lived reality, as Alexandra Morrison and Laura Zebuhr argue, "Beauvoir recognizes that the literary writer's task is subtle because she must negotiate a delicate balance between enacting a concrete experience in readers—provoking them to feel—and getting them to think."[33]

An accomplished author and storied member of the resistance, Henri's post-war life is taken up with the more mundane aspects of running a newspaper. Readership drops off and the paper must find a financial backer in order to stay afloat. This contrast highlights the contrast between writing for newspapers, including editorials, and writing literature. The former serves a designated audience and conveys information or opinion. Certainly communication is important to the task of newspaper editing but the communication is of a very different sort than literature. Literature communicates feelings. That is important to understanding Beauvoir's account of incorporation or solidarity; it is the tension, turmoil, joy, or despair of human existence evoked in a novel, more than anything else, that allows individuals to transcend their own embodied existence to enter into relations with others.

In an essay recognized by the editors as one of the top essays published in the history of the *Journal of the British Society for Phenomenology*, Busch explains the communicative potential of literature by drawing on Sartre's *What is Literature?* In Busch's words, "In thus transcending the real, the act of writing is a free act. Reading, as well, is a free act, since the reader must re-create the aesthetic object. The reader, as it were, loans his freedom to the writer, who through the analogon (the paper and print, etc.) projects the consciousness of the reader into the aesthetic world."[34] The writer and the reader create a cooperative relationship. Writing, for both Beauvoir and

---

32. Beauvoir, "Literature and Metaphysics," 270.
33. Morrison and Zebuhr, "The Voice of Ambiguity," 425.
34. Busch, "The Phenomenological Reduction," 60.

Sartre, is the prototypical form of communicating for incorporation because it relies on and affirms the freedom of participants.

Politics

Sharing a historical moment and communicating are not, of course, sufficient for incorporation. There must be some project, in Beauvoir's terms, that unites subjects into the incorporated Being or solidarity. Henri's book captures the solidarity of the Resistance. Beauvoir's account of it and of the lives of intellectuals in the post-war period in *The Mandarins* reveals both the possibilities and the obstacles to solidarity. Elsewhere, I argue that Beauvoir's novel explores an ethics of solidarity through four pivotal scenes; in each scene, one of the main characters confronts an impossible choice.[35] One of the most central elements of lived experience communicated in *The Mandarins* is the often fraught ambiguity of political obligation. Henri's trip to Portugal with Nadine, Robert and Anne's daughter, vividly captures the ambiguity as well as the conflicting sense of existence as an individual subject pulled by the collective. It exemplifies a choice that reverberates throughout the novel: whether to engage in the risk of political action or succumb to the lure of a private life of writing. Beauvoir is here drawing a contrast between types of writing. The writing that communicates—or requires the engagement of the author and the reader—is a political action. Beauvoir is contrasting it with what might be thought of as formulaic writing or writing for commercial purposes. Anne punctuates this point in thinking about Robert's future: "Well, all he would have to do is resign himself to writing to order. Others do it. Others, but not Robert. If I had to, I could imagine him working actively for a cause halfheartedly. But writing is something else again; if he were no longer able to express himself freely, the pen would fall from his hand."[36] Writing is not the only to participate in politics, but it is the most authentic way for these characters to act on their freedom and recognize the freedom of others.

Although many other moments in the unfolding of the novel display the ambiguity of political life and the fraught choices one must confront, two important decisions in the novel pertain to the newspaper's political obligations. In one instance, Henri must decide whether to take money from a backer with a particular political agenda and also give him a position on the editorial staff. He feels the obligation to stay true to the ideals of the Resistance and the men and women who fought for freedom, but the

---

35. Scholz, "Sustained Praxis."
36. Beauvoir, *Mandarins*, 56.

financial reality of the situation calls into question the continued existence of the paper. Considering the paper as the linchpin or heart that maintains the embodied collectivity of the Resistance means that to sell out a share of the editorial decision-making is nothing short of announcing the end of the collective. Through the character of Henri, Beauvoir grapples with the obligations of loyalty to a group and the responsibility to sustain the group. Without providing guidance or judgment, she reveals how burdened and burdening such obligations appear. Every decision carries the weight of the future and potential passing away of the collective.

The second was alluded to in the opening paragraph of this article. Henri must decide whether to publish news of the existence of work camps in the Soviet Union. The question is not merely whether the news is true or not, although that too is at issue, but rather what publishing it will do to leftist politics in France. On one hand, publishing the news appears to align the paper (and hence the SRL) with the capitalist (and imperialist) politics of United States. On the other hand, not publishing the news seems like a betrayal of the liberatory politics that inspired the Resistance and subsequent commitments to leftist ideology to begin with. Wrapped up with these are numerous personal relationships, each with their own expectations of loyalty and role-fulfillment. Henri struggles mightily with the decision, but in the end he realizes that freedom does not ask for party loyalty or role-fulfillment: "For a freedom wills itself genuinely only by willing itself as an indefinite movement through the freedom of others."[37]

Incorporation

"'If others don't count, it's meaningless to write. But if they do count, it's wonderful to gain their friendship and their confidence with words; it's magnificent to hear your own thoughts echoed in them.'"

In her literature as well as her philosophical essays, Simone de Beauvoir frequently explored the effects of social movements or political parties on individual freedom. To be sure, both carried the potential of allowing individuals to bury their freedom within the movement's cause like the "serious man" described in the *Ethics of Ambiguity*. An individual who cedes freedom to the movement "refuses to recognize that he [sic] is freely establishing the value of the end he [sic] sets up" and becomes "the slave of that end."[38] But there is an alternate path as well. Movements and political parties need not

37. Beauvoir, *Ethics of Ambiguity*, 90.
38. Ibid., 48–49.

subsume the individual but can instead provide an avenue for transcending individual experience through communication with others. I turn briefly to Beauvoir's discussion of solidarity in *The Second Sex*. Although she appeals to the concept multiple times, even drawing on Emile Durkheim's well-known distinction between organic solidarity and mechanical solidarity,[39] her discussion of the lack of solidarity among women is most revealing for this account of incorporation. Moreover, Busch's concept of incorporation invites the examination of the relation between a group engaged in political movement and the subjectivity of individual participants. In the case of women as an oppressed group, political movement for liberation requires mutual recognition, as Beauvoir explains in *The Second Sex*.

In the introduction to *The Second Sex*, Beauvoir compares women to other oppressed groups. Drawing on Hegel, she asserts the role of oppositional consciousness for the claim of subjectivity. Each individual and each group is other to all others: "whether one likes it or not, individuals and groups have no choice but to recognize the reciprocity of their relations." Yet, as she goes on to argue, this is not the case for women: the reciprocity between the sexes does not exist: "one of the terms has been asserted as the only essential one, denying any relativity in regard to its correlative, defining the latter as pure alterity." Beauvoir compares women to other oppressed groups, noting that women do not say "we," they do not assert their subjectivity or see themselves as a group: "They lack the concrete means to organize themselves into a unit that could posit itself in opposition" and are usually in solidarity with men of their class rather than with other women.[40] Women lack an embodied connection as well as a sense of political obligation to other women.

According to Beauvoir, then, solidarity is based on a subjectivity asserted against an opposition. Abstract notions of liberation or freedom are not enough to unite individuals. *The Mandarins* brings this aspect of her philosophy to light. The Resistance exists and thrives because each individual transcendences him or herself to incorporate with others in opposition to the Nazi occupiers. Similarly, the SRL is sustained not by commitment to abstract leftist ideas but in opposition to capitalist forces. That is why the publication of the information about the Soviet Union is so traumatic: it marks a disruption in the standard understanding of the opposition which is necessary for the constitution of the solidary group. Similarly, Henri's false testimony to save a collaborator is an overt action that destroys the "discursive circulation of Being" of the Resistance. In a very moving scene,

39. Beauvoir, *Second Sex*, 571.
40. Ibid., 7–8.

Henri offers testimony that contradicts the testimony of two members of the Resistance. The doubt and disbelief that scrolls across their face is not just directed at Henri but at themselves. They come to wonder about their own experience of the collective; the word of Henri Perron cannot possibly be contrary to what they all experienced and so they must call into question their own experience. Henri's false testimony is not only a refusal to participate in incorporation; it is an act that destroys the embodied collective.

In short, Beauvoir's account of solidarity or incorporation entails reciprocity in the assertion of subjectivity of the group in opposition to some Other. All three elements—opposition to another, assertion of subjectivity, and reciprocity—come into being and pass away. For those moments when it exists, the individual recognizes that freedom requires the freedom of others; as Beauvoir explains, her ethics is not solipsistic, "since the individual is defined only by his relationship to the world and to other individuals; he exists only by transcending himself, and his freedom can be achieved only through the freedom of others."[41] The movement in which an individual assumes freedom is both a positive assumption of a project and a negative rejection of oppression. Beauvoir's account of incorporation, then, speaks not just of fellowship or embodied collectivity, but of liberation.

Bibliography

Beauvoir, Simone de. *The Ethics of Ambiguity*. Translated by Bernard Frechtman. Secaucus, NJ: Citadel, 1948.

———. "Literature and Metaphysics." In *Simone de Beauvoir: Philosophical Writings*, edited by Margaret Simons, with MaryBeth Timmerman and Mary Beth Mader, 269–78. Urbana: University of Illinois Press, 2004.

———. *The Mandarins*. Translated by Leonard M. Friedman. New York: Meridian, 1960.

———. *The Second Sex*. Translated by Constance Borde and Shiela Malovany-Chevallier. New York: Knopf, 2010.

Bjørsnøs, Annlaug. "Representing Time: On the Experience of Temporality in *The Mandarins* by Simone de Beauvoir." In *Simone de Beauvoir: A Humanist Thinker*, edited by Tove Petterson and Annlaug Bjørsnøs, 147–68. Studies in Existentialism. Leiden: Brill Rodopi, 2015.

Bogaerts, Jo. "Beauvoir's Lecture on the Metaphysical Novel and Its Contemporary Critiques." *Simone de Beauvoir Studies* 29 (2013) 20–32.

Busch, Thomas. *Circulating Being: From Embodiment to Incorporation, Essays on Late Existentialism*. New York: Fordham University Press, 1999.

———. "Sartre on Language and Politics (with Reference to Particularity)." In *Circulating Being: From Embodiment to Incorporation, Essays on Late Existentialism*, 62–79. New York: Fordham University Press, 1999.

---

41. Beauvoir, *Ethics of Ambiguity*, 156.

———. "Sartre: The Phenomenological Reduction and Human Relationships." *Journal of the British Society for Phenomenology* 6 (1975) 55–61.

———. "Simone de Beauvoir on Achieving Subjectivity." In *The Contradictions of Freedom*, edited by Sally J. Scholz and Shannon M. Mussett, 177–88. Albany: SUNY Press, 2005.

Duran, Jane. "Wartime Philosophy: Camus, Beauvoir and the French Resistance." *Journal of the British Society for Phenomenology* 43 (2012) 326–36.

Holveck, Eleanore. "Can a Woman Be a Philosopher? Reflection of a Beauvoirian Housemade." In *Feminist Interpretations of Simone de Beauvoir*, edited by Margaret A. Simons, 67–78. University Park: Pennsylvania State University Press, 1995.

Kruks, Sonia. "Living on Rails: Freedom, Constraint, and Political Judgment in Beauvoir's 'Moral' Essays and *The Mandarins*." In *The Contradictions of Freedom*, edited by Sally J. Scholz and Shannon M. Mussett, 67–86. Albany: SUNY Press, 2005.

McBride, William. "The Conflict of Ideologies in *The Mandarins*: Communism and Democracy, Then and Now." In *The Contradictions of Freedom*, edited by Sally J. Scholz and Shannon M. Mussett, 33–46. Albany: SUNY Press, 2005.

———. *Sartre's Political Theory*. Bloomington: Indiana University Press, 1991.

Merleau-Ponty, Maurice. "Indirect Language and the Voices of Silence." In *Signs*, translated by Richard McCleary, 39–83. Evanston, IL: Northwestern University Press, 1964.

———. "Metaphysics and the Novel." In *Sense and Non-Sense*, translated by Hubert Dreyfus and Patricia Allen Dreyfus, 26–40. Evanston, IL: Northwestern University Press, 1964.

Morrison, Alexandra and Laura Zebuhr. "The Voice of Ambiguity: Simone de Beauvoir's Literary and Phenomenological Echoes." *Hypatia: A Journal of Feminist Philosophy* 30 (2015) 418–33.

Murdoch, Iris. "At One Remove from Tragedy. Review of *The Mandarins*, by Simone de Beauvoir." *Nation* 182 (1956) 493–94.

Scholz, Sally. "The Power of Literature: Simone de Beauvoir's *Les Mandarins* and the Metaphysical Novel." In *Blackwell Companion to Simone de Beauvoir*, edited by Laura Hengehold and Nancy Bauer. Malden, MA: Blackwell, forthcoming.

———. "Sustained Praxis: The Challenge of Solidarity in *The Mandarins* and Beyond." In *The Contradictions of Freedom*, edited by Sally J. Scholz and Shannon M. Mussett, 47–66. Albany: SUNY Press, 2005.

Simons, Margaret A. "Introduction to 'Literature and Metaphysics.'" In *Simone de Beauvoir: Philosophical Writings*, edited by Margaret A. Simons with Marybeth Timmermann and Mary Beth Mader, 263–68. Urbana: University of Illinois Press, 2004.

Suleiman, Susan Rubin. "Memory Troubles: Remembering the Occupation in Simone de Beauvoir's *Les Mandarins*." *French Politics, Culture, and Society* 28 (2010) 4–17.

Tidd, Ursula. "For the Time Being: Simone de Beauvoir's Representation of Temporality." In *The Existential Phenomenology of Simone de Beauvoir*, edited by Wendy O'Brien and Lester Embree, 107–26. Dordrecht: Kluwer Academic, 2001.

———. "Testimony, *Historicité*, and the Intellectual in Simone de Beauvoir." In *The Contradictions of Freedom*, edited by Sally J. Scholz and Shannon M. Mussett, 87–104. Albany: SUNY Press, 2005.

10

The Devil and the Good Lord

Demystifying Feudalism, God, and the Devil

—Adrian van den Hoven

In a 1959 interview published in *Sartre on Theater*, the author declared "that there is no personal drama which is not wholly conditioned by the historical situation and at the same time no personal drama which does not react to the social situation and is conditioned by it."[1] And he added that he "wanted the audience to see the world from the outside, as something alien, as a witness. And at the same time participate in it."[2] In addition, he insisted "that the theater has no need of psychology" and that he was "always looking for subjects so sublimated that they [would be] recognizable to anyone, without recourse to minute psychological details."[3] Finally he declared that he saw "the meaning of theater" in the following terms: "its essential value is the representation of something which does not exist" and he viewed the dramatist's function to allow the public to "participate in this other-worldly drama" and in that way to be demystified and to divest itself of certain illusions.[4] In his biography *Saint Genet: Actor and Martyr* Sartre attempted to come to grips with the outcast Jean Genet, analyze what society had made of him and then, in turn, show how Genet himself made "something" of that. But in a play every act and gesture is deliberately selected by the dra-

---

1. Sartre, *Theater*, 70; translation amended.
2. Ibid., 76.
3. Ibid., 114, 132.
4. Ibid., 143.

matist in order that he may present to the spectators' mind questions and situations that should force them to reflect on contemporary issues. Hence, theater differs from other genres such as biography; even though "in *Saint Genet* the analyses of Good and Evil are quite similar," Sartre's approach is different.[5] In this play he is *not* analyzing a real human being because unlike Jean Genet, Goetz and the others are invented stage characters, straw men and women, if you will, and Sartre can exploit all of their characteristics to suit his own purposes.

Significantly, since this play deals with the "God delusion," Sartre concluded his autobiography *The Words* as follows: "atheism is a cruel and long-range undertaking and I think I've carried it through to the end."[6] But obviously he continued to be preoccupied with this theme, and Sartre the playwright was certainly no stranger to Christian themes. He treated the birth of Christ in his first play *Bariona*, focused on hell in *No Exit* and took up the life of Christ again in the outline of *Le Pari*. In it a destitute couple who have led a terrible life are allowed to foresee the horrible fate that awaits their unborn son, yet the pregnant wife accepts his birth with joy because she is persuaded that he will "transform" his existence into something "joyful" and he will die as "a revolutionary."[7]

In this context John Ireland stresses that all Sartre's plays "reveal in a veiled way a profoundly messianic structure."[8] And this certainly applies to *The Devil and the Good Lord*. So, given his apparent obsession with Christian themes, how should we understand Sartre's messianic proclivities? A revelatory comment Sartre made in 1943 about the death of God in his article entitled "A New Mystic," sheds light on the question. There he says of Georges Bataille that he

> [I]s a survivor of the death of God. And, when one thinks about it, it would seem that our entire age is surviving that death, which [Bataille] experienced, suffered, and survived. God is dead. We should not understand by that that he does not exist, nor even that he now no longer exists. He is dead: he used to speak to us and he has fallen silent, we now touch only his corpse . . . God is dead, but men have not, for all that, become atheists.[9]

Sartre stresses two elements here: God has fallen silent but, yet, people have not given up believing in His existence. These comments, together with

5. Noudelmann and Phillippe, *Dictionnaire*, 135.
6. Sartre, *Writings*, 158; translation amended.
7. Sartre, *Théâtre*, 1214–1217.
8. Ireland, *Sartre*, 95.
9. Sartre, *We Have*, 54–55.

Sartre's claim that atheism has been a life-long struggle for him, allows us to better grasp his interest in Christian themes and the topic of the God's existence. As a "messianic" playwright he clearly saw it as his enduring task to raise the question of man's role in relationship to God and to demonstrate in dramatic terms that man is free and can dispense with His existence. The very Christian ending of *Bariona* may appear ambivalent but, even so, the play's conclusion stresses that Bariona is "free and that he "hold[s his] destiny in his own hands."[10] In *The Flies*, Orestes also stresses the importance of freedom and rejects Jupiter's authority. As he remarks: "I am neither master nor slave, Jupiter. I am my freedom! You had barely created me and already I didn't belong to you anymore."[11] In *No Exit* it is not the initial concerns of Garcin with the conventional Christian conception of hell - that of physical torture - that ultimately matter but the fact that modern hell is made up of "other people" who continuously torture each other.[12] Hence, as Sartre explained in a 1960 interview in *Sartre on Theater*, he exploits ready-made sources from Antiquity, Christianity or past history, in order to demystify contemporary notions that preoccupy society.[13]

And of this *The Devil and the Good Lord* is a perfect example. Inspired by Cervantes's play *El Rufian dichoso* (1615) and, according to Yaffa Wolfman, also by Goethe's *Faust* the action takes place during the German Peasants Wars in 1550-51.[14] The play is set in a far-away place and time because Sartre envisioned the stage as representing "a totally closed world [that] we cannot enter" and his goal was to draw the interest of the contemporary audience by providing specific historical contexts for questions, themes and topics that should resonate with the public.[15] Amongst these are Goetz's struggle to behave ethically in the absence of a divine sanction as well as his attempt to outdo God and the devil in order to show his own superiority while, ultimately, he realizes that he can best play his role by using his talents in the service of other people's struggles. But we cannot forget that in theatrical terms, the relationship between the action, the actors' gestures and the stage setting and the resultant audience's awareness of these elements is always metonymic. Just as in a Shakespeare play, a few trees can stand for an entire forest and a handful of soldiers for an army, what we see and hear

---

10. Sartre, *Théâtre*, 1178.
11. Ibid., 64.
12. Ibid., 128.
13. Sartre, *Theater*, 77–120.
14. Wolfman, "Goethe's Faust," 182-194.
15. Sartre, *Theater*, 11.

on stage should direct us beyond that to a better grasp of the dramatist's ultimate goals.

To illustrate, let us have a close look at the major characters who, in fact, form two distinct groups whose attitudes differ in their relationship to God, the Devil, and to each other. The first group is composed of Goetz, Heinrich and Catherine. Goetz may seem similar to Genet in that he is a bastard and an outsider but he is first of all a resentful and traitorous member of a feudal society who "has nothing and therefore is nothing."[16] He also resembles Camus's Caligula and Goethe's Faust in his quest to reach for the stars and equal God. Heinrich, the priest, is also a traitor and as such Goetz's counterpart, but he is torn between his allegiance to the Church and his love of the poor. Both outsiders betray their fellows but, if Goetz finally realizes that God does not exist, Heinrich desperately clings to his belief in God and prefers to go to his death rather than renounce his beliefs. Nasti shares Heinrich's love of the poor as well as his belief in God but his strategy is to create by all means necessary a future earthly paradise. Catherine, Goetz's mistress, has been sorely abused by him and, in that respect, resembles Garcin's wife in *No Exit*. Both are victims who have been blinded by love and allowed themselves to be exploited. Catherine does attempt to betray Goetz when he refuses to keep her but at the last moment she changes her mind and betrays Hermann, the man who was going to stab Goetz to death. As punishment, Goetz makes her a sexual prey for the soldiers. When Goetz turns "saintly," he abandons Catherine, and she falls into despair and finally dies comforted by the illusion that Goetz's fake stigmata have saved her soul. Hilda resembles Nasti in that she also loves the poor but she loves them over and above God. Because she has taken care of the dying Catherine, the latter has infected her with her love for Goetz; however, Goetz cannot victimize her: his image may fill her dreams but, when awake, she can see him for what he really is.

In other words, these six characters share characteristics amongst each other but as groups they also differ significantly. And, as the dramatic action unfolds, the initial group composed of Goetz, Heinrich and Catherine is replaced by the second group composed of Goetz, Hilda and Nasti. The first group's relationships proved to be unsustainable because two of its members stubbornly stuck to their obsessions. Nevertheless, we should not see the behavior of these characters in terms of bad faith. As a bastard in a feudal society, Goetz, who has nothing and is nothing, feels compelled to take Catherine by force and, as a result, she becomes affectively enslaved by him. When Goetz, having decided to become "saintly," abandons her, he

---

16. Sartre, *The Devil*, 33. Translation amended.

makes matters worse. When they were together, she could identify with him but now, having become a sexual object to all men, she feels utterly cast out. Heinrich is the Church's victim, having been raised by the Church, he feels compelled to do Bishop's bidding and his total dependency on the institution makes him go so far as to make the false claim that he had "been paid to betray the city" in order to exonerate the Church and give it "a pretext to repudiate [him]."[17] Finally, his total reliance on God and his inability to view his fellow human beings as equals becomes his undoing.

It is actually Catherine who clarifies the extent to which the feudal system has victimized Goetz. When, after Conrad's death, Goetz wants to party and "drink to his [newly gained] land and his castle," she reminds him of his have-not status; "you won't stop being a bastard because you killed your brother . . . Landed property is inherited." Goetz agrees but quickly justifies his rapacious behavior: "Things are mine only when I take them by force."[18] As a nobody, deprived by the feudal system of owning property, he must take forcefully what he cannot have and, hence, his maltreatment of Catherine reveals that he too is completely "caught up in the wheels of the system."

The second group, composed of Goetz, Hilda, and Nasti creates a new relationship. When Goetz realizes that God does not exist and dispenses with his alter-ego Heinrich, he can finally embrace Hilda and love her as a fellow human being, especially since she is a person who has always loved other people over God and is willing to accept him completely. Similarly, it is only when Goetz realizes that Nasti is as lonely as he is that he can identify with him and accept his command to serve under him as the general who will lead the peasants in their struggle against the barons.

The opening scene of the play indicates that Sartre very deliberately chose a religious setting in order to situate the action in a purely Christian environment: as if to say, "Let us do as if God exists and then see how He should behave in various circumstances." And, indeed, the first thing the Archbishop does is invoke the Lord and ask Him to make sure Goetz defeats his half-brother Conrad. But it turns out that God's henchman is capricious when called upon! Goetz succeeds; but then he turns on the Archbishop and decides to destroy the city of Worms. And, even if the archbishop's motto is, "In God we trust," in this play no one, including God, can be trusted and treachery and cheating are threads that run through the entire plot. The archbishop helps Goetz betray his half-brother by promising him his lands and Goetz cheats at least twice. First he deliberately loses the dice game

17. Ibid., 85.
18. Ibid., 38–40.

because he wants to prove that he can be good against all odds and, then, he inflicts stigmata on himself and uses this fakery to console the dying Catherine. Then again Heinrich betrays the citizens of Worms in order to protect the city's priesthood. When Goetz refuses to take Catherine with him, she attempts to betray Goetz with Hermann's help and, in turn, betrays Hermann because she cannot bear to see Goetz killed.[19] Finally, Nasti claims that God has betrayed him after the peasants' revolt is crushed by the barons. This is how he responds when Karl accuses him of having allowed his army to "hemorrhage" to death and "being a false prophet:" Nasti replies, "I am a man [whom t]he Lord has betrayed."[20]

And, of course, Sartre's own preoccupations also feature in the play. The fact that Sartre's grandfather was a Schweitzer from a Lutheran family in Alsace helps to understand his interest in The Peasants' War, Luther and German history; he comes back to the latter two subjects in *The Condemned of Altona*. Also, he had already dealt with sadomasochism and victimization in *No Exit*. When alive, Inès had tortured her partner and in hell she continues to torture Garcin and Estelle. In turn, Garcin, who claimed he had picked his wife out of the gutter, victimized her. In this play Goetz threatened to have the soldiers gang rape Catherine, while in 1946 in *The Victors* Lucie is actually gang raped by the French *milice* but she turns this humiliating treatment into a vehement outburst of defiance against her captors.[21]

Sartre also situates the play in the context of the ongoing debate about the use of violence and the role of God in human affairs and makes use of other French writers to make his own specific case. First of all, Goetz employs Pascal's famous wager on the existence of God but turns it on its head because, as Catherine points out, Goetz cheats in order to lose his bet so that he may reverse roles and change from a diabolical figure into a saintly one. All this to prove that Heinrich is wrong when he claims that evil is common-place but no one can do good. Pascal in his famous wager stresses that "one must" bet that God exists and that one has "no choice" because we are "embarked."[22] Ironically, Goetz does not bet to win but cheats in order to lose so that he can be good but since, unlike Pascal's gambler, Goetz is "absolutely" free in his choice, he can manipulate the game of good and evil and his decision to do only good originates totally from within himself!

Secondly, there are also certain obvious similarities between the play and Camus's *Caligula* and *The Plague* which allowed Sartre to situate himself

---

19. Ibid., 49.
20. Ibid., 144–150.
21. Sartre, *Théâtre*, 194.
22. Pascal, *Pensées*, 93.

in the midst of the debate about good, evil, and the use of violence in order to go beyond Camus' pacifist stance and dramatize publicly his differences with his soon to be erstwhile friend. The "bad" Goetz's behavior resembles that of Caligula while the priest Heinrich shares his ambivalent religious attitude with *The Plague*'s Father Paneloux while, incidentally, it should also be noted that in Goetz's camp the plague also rages when it is stationed outside Worms.

Like Caligula, the early Goetz also finds himself in a "position of limitless power" but there is an essential difference between them. Even though Goetz is like the emperor in that he wants to reach for the moon, Nasti quickly makes very clear to him that: "The moon is not yours, my poor misguided friend, and you've been fighting all your life so that the nobles may enjoy it."[23] As well, Goetz is no emperor but a resentful outcast, the bastard son of a noble woman and a peasant, and, unlike in Camus's play, we are not dealing with a somewhat sterile debate between Roman senators and a Caligula more or less willingly going to his death but with a real and violent historical event.

With respect to *The Plague*'s Father Paneloux and Heinrich, the Jesuit priest's behavior can be summarized as follows: "[d]uring the first stage of the plague, [h]e preaches a sermon [in which] he insists that the plague is a scourge sent by God . . . [And] after Othon's son's . . . death, Paneloux tells Rieux that although the death of an innocent child in a world ruled by a loving God cannot be rationally explained, it should nonetheless be accepted."[24] This is also Heinrich's attitude when he explains to the woman whose child has died that "nothing happens except by the will of the God" and he exclaims: "I believe, O God, I believe that nothing occurs except by Your laws, even to the death of a little child, and that all is Good. I believe because it is absurd! Absurd! Absurd!"[25] However, the two come to very different ends: "A few days after preaching the sermon, Paneloux is taken ill . . . Since his symptoms did not seem to resemble those of the plague, Rieux records his death as a 'doubtful case.'"[26] Heinrich wants to serve the poor and simultaneously remain faithful to the Church and therefore hands Goetz the key to Worms in order to save his fellow priests. Ultimately, at the end of the period during which Goetz had been "good," he encounters Heinrich again, and tells him God does not exist. Because Heinrich only wants to be judged by a superior Being and not his fellow men, he attempts to murder

---

23. Sartre, *The Devil*, 55.
24. Camus, *Théâtre*, 1294–1394.
25. Sartre, *The Devil*, 12–13. Translation amended.
26. Camus, *Théâtre*, 1410.

Goetz and the latter is forced to kill him in self-defence. In *The Plague* Camus treats Paneloux "sympathetically" and he is viewed as a doubtful case; clearly, Heinrich is not to be considered such, not only does he turn traitor he dies as Goetz's mortal enemy.[27]

What distinguishes Goetz from Heinrich and Nasti is his military prowess, which makes him uniquely powerful, and being omnipotent means he can do as he pleases. Therefore, when he appears before his troops with Catherine, he declares that he is not going to wait and is "taking the city tonight" and he adds, echoing Oscar Wilde's "The Ballad of Reading Gaol": "after all we must kill the thing we love."[28] As an aside, this comment may have its origin in Count Orsini's remark in *Twelfth Night* where he proclaims to Viola: "Why should I not . . . kill what I love."[29]

When Goetz is told that a priest, Heinrich, has arrived and is willing to betray the city, he exclaims: "I adore traitors."[30] But, of course, Heinrich is not the only traitor and, when they are alone and stare each other in the face, Goetz remarks that he recognizes that "hypocritical look as his own. I am looking at and I feel sorry for myself; we belong to the same race."[31] Heinrich claims to be "unable to avoid the horrors of war [because he is] only a humble priest powerless to avoid them." But Goetz insists that he is a "[h]ypocrite" and that "[t]onight he has the power of life and death over twenty thousand lives." Heinrich wishes to "reject this power [because] it derives from the Devil" but, according to Goetz, he is "cornered like a rat."[32] At that moment Heinrich is still hoping against all hope that he is only playing in a comedy and that "all is a game" but Goetz tells him to wake up because [Worms] "is a real city with real inhabitants and [Heinrich] is a real traitor."[33] In the ensuing dialogue Goetz insists that he too is a traitor and that, in fact, he is "a double agent by birth: his mother gave herself to a peasant and hence he is composed of two halves that don't fit together; each half is horrified by the other." And he continues: "Do you believe you're better off? You are one half priest and one half poverty stricken; the result will never be a whole man. We are nothing and we have nothing. All legitimate children can enjoy the world without paying. But that is not the case for you or me." And now he makes a remark that harks back to *Being*

27. Sprintzen, *Camus*, 94.
28. Sartre, *The Devil*, 26.
29. Shakespeare, *Twelfth Night*, V, i, 117.
30. Sartre, *The Devil*, 27.
31. Ibid., 28.
32. Ibid., 29.
33. Ibid., 32.

and Nothingness: "Since my childhood, I have been looking at the world through a keyhole: it is a beautiful small egg . . . and in it everybody occupies his assigned place, but I can affirm to you that we are not in it."[34] But in *Being and Nothingness* the person observing the world through the keyhole is surprised by a third and, as a being-for-others, feels objectified and ashamed.[35] In the case of Goetz and Heinrich, neither is viewed as part of society and they will remain perennial outsiders.

When Goetz hears that his brother Conrad has been killed and that he "died without being able to confess and had his face gnawed away by wolves"; Heinrich enquires: "why did you betray him?" And Goetz proclaims: "I desire things to be final. Priest, I am a self-made man, by birth I was made a bastard but the beautiful title of fratricide is due to me only thanks to my own merits . . . From now on, it is mine only."[36] Sartre will take up the theme of the self-made man again in 1953 in his adaptation of Dumas's comedy *Kean* and he will do so once more in the 1956 farce *Nekrassov*. Kean is a comic genius who has made his own career unlike the English aristocrats who inherited their name, while Nekrassov is an impostor who nearly succeeds in making the French press believe he is indeed a Soviet defector. On the other hand, Goetz's behavior is purely destructive and he views his fratricide as an act that is in direct defiance of God. As he proclaims: "Yes, God, I killed him. And what can you do to me. I committed the worst of all crimes and the God of justice is unable to punish me: it has been more than fifteen years that he has damned me."[37] Conrad's murder parallels that of Abel by Cain but while Cain is banished after he murdered his brother, Goetz remains unscathed and inherits his half-brother's property. Goetz's defiant tone may have been inspired by Baudelaire's poem "Abel and Cain." Sartre wrote the preface to Baudelaire's *Ecrits intimes*, published as *Baudelaire*, and most likely knew Baudelaire's poem. Goetz's conclusion contains echoes of that poem: "Race of Cain, assault the skies/ And drag him earthward—bring down God!"[38]

Conrad's death gives Goetz a reason to celebrate and, at that very moment, Heinrich offers him the key to the city and explains how he can find the entrance. Goetz insists that "[i]f he takes the key he will burn everything down" and on an ironic tone he adds: "How the poor are going to love you! How they are going to bless you!" Now Goetz wants to know if his face still

34. Ibid., 33.
35. Sartre, *Being and Nothingness*, 259.
36. Sartre, *The Devil*, 34.
37. Ibid., 34.
38. Baudelaire, *Les Fleurs*, 102–103.

instills horror in Heinrich and he answers: "I see in it that you are horrified by yourself." And Goetz agrees: "It's true but don't put your trust in that. I have been horrified by myself for fifteen years. And so what? Don't you understand that Evil is my reason for being?" And in a further twist, he sees Heinrich as his alter-ego and confuses Heinrich with himself: "But to finish, you are [also] a traitor . . . You have delivered Conrad." Heinrich is surprised: "Conrad?" But Goetz explains: "you resemble me to such a degree that I took you for myself."[39] Ultimately, of course, he will be forced to kill off his alter-ego and when that happens it could be said that he is committing a form of symbolic suicide and sloughing off his former treacherous self. The fact that Goetz confuses Heinrich with himself and momentarily identifies with him as a fellow traitor is seemingly insignificant but, of course, it is not an isolated event but, as has been already indicated, is a thread that runs through the plot. Sartre's purpose is obviously to allow the characters' traits to overlap with one another in order to show how closely they are allied but, at the same time, he needs to differentiate them and this often requires that they make giant acrobatic leaps so that eventually they can uncover the shortfalls of this behavior.

One such leap is made by Goetz when Catherine wants to know if he is suffering and he makes the claim to be so unique that he is even superior to God: "Evil should make everybody suffer [a]nd first of all the person who commits it," and then he adds, when she asks why he wants to conquer Worms: "because that is doing evil." Next, Catherine inquires: "But why do Evil?" and he replies: "Because the Good has already been done . . . [by] God the Father. I, I invent."[40] Clearly, he views himself not just as God's counterpart but as his superior; if God always acts in expected ways, Goetz is the more unpredictable and creative one!

Next, Goetz proclaims that, after he has destroyed Worms, he will sneak away. When Catherine wants to know what will become of her, Goetz states that he does not care: "becoming a whore . . . appears the best solution to him."[41] She is willing to do anything to be able to stay with him but Goetz replies: "What does it matter to me that I am loved? If you love me, you will have all the enjoyment. Go away, you slut. I don't want you to profit from me." Goetz can only make others suffer and he views other people's enjoyment as their benefitting from him and depriving him. In this case Catherine's willingness "to give" herself to him throws a curious light on the notion of "the gift." Rather than seeing it as an act of generosity, he views

---

39. Sartre, *The Devil*, 34–35.
40. Ibid., 46.
41. Ibid., 48.

it as her depriving him of something precious and he casts her aside. Now Catherine takes her revenge and yells out: "You asked for it, Goetz! You asked for it." This is supposed to be her signal for Hermann to sneak up to Goetz and stab him to death but at the last moment she betrays Hermann and warns him: "Watch out."[42] As punishment, Goetz will have Hermann "broached like the big cask of wine that he is" and as for Catherine he'll "make a present of [her] to the soldiers [. . . and a]fterwards, if she is still alive, [h]e'll choose a nice one-eyed, pock-marked rascal, and the priest of Worms can marry [her] to him."[43] Clearly then, Goetz's evil impulses lead him to do whatever goes most contrary to the innermost desires of those around him because he can only "enjoy" suffering if others suffer by his doing.

Next, a discussion about the topic of evil ensues between Goetz, Nasti, and Heinrich and it results in Catherine and Goetz throwing dice in order to see if Goetz will continue to do evil or will now choose doing good as his sole motive. Nasti has never wavered in his belief that God is on the side of the poor and he is not afraid of Goetz because "God speaks to him directly." He has entered Goetz's camp because "God commanded [him] to speak to [Goetz] in order that he open [his] eyes."[44] Goetz counters him as follows:

> Supposing I had seen God, too? . . . It would be sunlight against sunlight . . . I hold you all in my hands, all of you: this whore who wanted to kill me; the envoy of the Archbishop, and you the king of the ragamuffins. God's finger has revealed the conspiracy, the guilty are unmasked; better still, it was one of God's ministers who brought the keys of the city with His compliments.[45]

Again Goetz's omnipotent position allows him a totally free hand but Nasti points out that he ignores one important element and reveals the actual consequences of his behavior: "Men of God destroy or construct. You conserve." And he explains: "You bring about disorder. And disorder is the best servant of established power . . . You serve the rulers, Goetz, and you will serve the rulers whatever you do. All muddleheaded destruction weakens the weak, enriches the rich, increases the power of the powerful."[46] And Nasti concludes that Goetz, as he is, will continue "to be . . . a useless uproar." Goetz's reaction reveals the crux of his motivation: "it is God I am deafening, and . . . He is the only enemy worthy of my talents." Goetz actually

42. Ibid., 49.
43. Ibid., 49–50.
44. Ibid., 51.
45. Ibid., 52–53.
46. Ibid., 53; translation amended.

views God as if He were human and, if it is conventional to say that someone will put the fear of God into a person, Goetz reverses that and claims that "God . . . is afraid" because He knows that Goetz will "dare." After all "in a few moments, [he] will march in His fear and His anger [and t]he city will blaze." And he concludes: "the soul of the Lord is a hall of mirrors, the fire will be reflected in a thousand mirrors. Then, I shall know that I am an unalloyed monster."[47] In a variation upon *No Exit*, where the characters had already made a hell for others in their past existence, Goetz will do his evil deeds in the immediate future by creating a hell for Nasti, who wants to save the poor, Catherine, who loves Goetz, and Heinrich, who wanted to save Worms's priests. Nasti will be tortured and hanged but before that Heinrich, his archenemy, will be forced to spend the night with him and give him his last rites. Heinrich will also be forced to "conduct the forced marriage" of Catherine and Hermann.

Now a dispute breaks out between the two enemies and Heinrich blames Nasti for having betrayed the city and holds him responsible for having "murdered the bishop." However, Nasti remains steadfast: "God commanded [him]." But Heinrich is having none of it: "then God commanded me to betray the poor because the poor wanted to murder the monks!" Goetz puts an end to the quarrel by seemingly consoling Nasti: "Come now, brother, the last word has not been said; I decided I would take Worms, but if God is on your side, something may happen to prevent it."[48] Of course, no miracle occurs, as Catherine points out, but the remark does prepare us for Goetz's sudden conversion. Next, Goetz elaborates on the hellish fate he has in store for the three. Heinrich and Nasti "will spend the night together like a pair of lovers." And he admonishes Heinrich: "Be sure to hold his hand tenderly while they are tearing his flesh with red-hot pincers." This is precisely the treatment Garcin expected to receive in hell but, instead, he will be tortured psychologically by the omnipresent gaze of Inès and his still living colleagues.[49] Next Goetz turns to Frantz: "If he agrees to confess, stop the torture immediately; as soon as he has been absolved, string him up." In turn, Catherine, who had wanted to be his exclusive sexual property, will be gang raped: "Frantz, you will assemble the stable boys, and introduce them to Madam. Let them do what they like with her, short of killing her." The horrified Catherine begs him "not to do that" and even admits that she had not believed that he would actually abuse her in that manner and next Goetz confesses that he had not "believe[d] in it [him]self" and adds in a

47. Ibid., 55.
48. Ibid., 58.
49. Sartre, *Théâtre*, 92.

revelatory manner: "One only believes in evil afterwards."[50] If, in the case of *No Exit*, the characters' past behavior becomes their eternal present and future, from Goetz's point of view his present deeds will first have to become past deeds before they can be viewed as evil and while his acts possess a future and a past, they do not as yet have a present. During Goetz's continuing peroration on his relationship to God, he views his defiance of God and his future evil projects as proof of his own uniqueness: "Hatred and weakness, violence, death and displeasure, all that proceeds from man alone; it is my only empire, and I am alone within it: what happens within me is attributable to me alone." And in language that is reminiscent of Molière's *Don Juan* and Mozart's *Don Giovanni*, he proclaims: "On the Day of Judgement, silence, shut lips; I shall let myself be damned without uttering a word." And he concludes: "Sometimes, I imagine Hell as an empty desert waiting for me alone." This remark immediately creates an opening for Heinrich who reminds him of Garcin's discovery when he saw all those eyes look at him and he realized that "Hell was [all those] other people."[51] Heinrich bursts out laughing and tells Goetz: "Hell is overflowing with people, you fool."[52] Goetz is not yet persuaded: "My wickedness is unlike their wickedness; they do evil as a luxury, or out of interest: I do Evil for Evil's sake." But Heinrich is not impressed by this pseudo "Art-for-Art-sake" argument in favour of doing evil; he is convinced that "no one can do Good" and that all of us depend entirely on God's "mercy."[53] Heinrich's insistence that doing "Good is impossible" provides Goetz with a new challenge. If doing evil is commonplace, he will take up that challenge and prove that he can equal God "and wager that he can be a saint." And Heinrich "will be the judge . . . in a year and a day from now."[54] Nasti dismisses Goetz's wager out of hand: "If you want to do Good, you need only make up your mind." But Goetz wants to challenge God and "drive [Him] into a corner. This time it is yes, or no. If He lets me win, the city burns, and His responsibility is established. Come now, play; if God is with you, you should not fear."[55] Catherine accepts to bet with him and it appears that Goetz has thrown the losing dice. He immediately proclaims: "I submit to the will of God. Farewell, Catherine."[56] However, Catherine announces that Goetz "cheated! I saw it! He cheated in

50. Sartre, *The Devil*, 59.
51. Sartre, *Théâtre*, 128.
52. Sartre, *The Devil*, 61.
53. Ibid., 63.
54. Ibid., 64.
55. Ibid., 64.
56. Ibid., 65.

order to lose."[57] Goetz has turned Pascal's admonition that we must wager on the existence of God into a game of "loser takes all" and it allows Goetz to remain the "master of his own fate." In addition, Goetz will be as fully committed to his saintliness as he was to his evil doing because his single mindedness will again prove his superiority and uniqueness.

However, Goetz's saintly behavior turns out not to be of much help to him or others and, in fact, this loser indeed comes up empty handed. Giving away the lands of Heidenstamm earns him the wrath of the nobility and neither Karl nor Nasti appreciate his "kindness."[58] Unlike Nasti who "want[s] to postpone the kingdom of God; Goetz has grandiose plans: he "want[s] to establish... it now, at least in a single corner of the world—here. Firstly: I give my lands to the peasants. Secondly: on this very land, I shall organize the first truly Christian community: all equal." He asks Nasti to "help" him because he "know[s] how to speak to the poor" and he already has a name for his "Utopia: [he wi]ll call it the City of the Sun."[59] Unlike the idealistic Goetz, Nasti is a pragmatist: "In seven years we shall be ready to begin the holy war."[60] Goetz is not convinced; he wants to create a paradise immediately even if it only occupies a small territory and he retorts: "Seven years! And then in seven years will come seven years of war, and then seven years of repentance because we shall have to build our ruins up again."[61] Goetz sees Nasti's dream as ever receding in the future; just as had so many revolutionaries who waited and waited for the propitious moment that never came. Just as in the scenario *L'Engrenage* which deals with the impossible situation that is created when a small country attempts a revolution while it is surrounded by powerful states, Goetz's attempt to create an instant paradise cannot withstand the assaults of the much more powerful barons.[62] The dialogue between Goetz and Nasti reminds one also of the one between the protagonists of *Dirty Hands* in which the purist Hugo's arguments stand in sharp contrast to those of the realistic Hoederer. When Goetz asks Nasti: "Could you kill me?" The latter answers: "Yes, if you stand in my way."[63] Now Brother Tetzel enters to sell indulgences to the peasants; Goetz readily kisses a leper to prove his limitless love but the peasants follow Tetzel into the church when Tetzel holds out for the "Holy Church [who] is

57. Ibid., 66.
58. Ibid., 68.
59. Ibid., 70–71.
60. Ibid., 72.
61. Ibid., 74.
62. Sartre, *L'Engrenage*.
63. Ibid., 75.

our universal mother: through her monks and her priests she dispenses the same maternal love to all her children."[64]

When Heinrich appears accompanied by the Devil, he announces that Catherine, abandoned by Goetz, is dying. Heinrich also announces that he "no longer belongs to the Church" and that he has "been forbidden to celebrate the offices and administer the holy sacraments." In order to exculpate the Church, he has lied and claimed to have "been paid to betray the city."[65] Heinrich explains that Catherine is "dying of . . . shame. Her body revolts her because of all the men's hands that have laid upon it. Her heart disgusts her even more because your image has remained within it. You are her mortal sickness." Goetz replies that "[a]ll that happened last year, priest, and I no longer acknowledge the sins of a year ago." But Heinrich retorts: "Then there are two men named Goetz." And Goetz agrees: "Two, yes. A living Goetz who lives by Good, and a dead Goetz who lived by Evil." However, Heinrich does not relent: "When you deflowered her you gave her far more than you possessed yourself: you gave her love . . . [T]hen, one fine day, you . . . drove her away. For this, she is dying." And he concludes: "But save one soul—save only one? How could a man like Goetz stoop to that? He had much more important projects."[66] Clearly, Goetz's past continues to haunt him and he drags his misdeeds along with him like a ball and chain. And once again we have a case of one character morphing into another. Goetz has already identified with Heinrich, now he appears to have invaded Catherine's psyche and, later on, Hilda will accuse him of having been 'victimized' by his love and, in fact, they do finally become one.

When Nasti appears on the scene, Heinrich informs him of the fact that in "Schulheim [r]evolt is brewing" and that he can "contain" it but, [i]n exchange, he want[s] Nasti to forgive [him]."[67] Then Heinrich lays out his plan; he wants Nasti's men to create a scandal and "at Righi, next Sunday, . . . carry off the priest in the middle of the mass . . . Drag him into the forest and return with their swords stained with blood. All the priests in the region will secretly leave their villages . . ." Bereft of their priests, the peasants will be gripped with "fear" and that "will stifle the revolt."[68] Nasti is willing to go along with Heinrich's plan but when they arrive in the church, he does not want Heinrich "to rejoice" because "[i]t's the first time I've brought [the peasantry] to their knees to prevent them from defending themselves . . .

64. Ibid., 81.
65. Ibid., 85.
66. Ibid., 86–87.
67. Ibid., 87–88.
68. Ibid., 89.

[and] I have compounded with superstition and formed an alliance with the Devil."[69] Like Hoederer, Nasti the strategist is willing to go to any length in order to win his cause.

The introduction of Hilda brings about another change of tone. She does not wish to provoke God into showing her that He exists because she is entirely on the side of mankind. When she hears of Catherine's agony, she proclaims: "if You do condemn her, I shall refuse to enter heaven . . . I am on the side of humanity, and I will not desert my fellow beings."[70] When she encounters Goetz, she insists that she knows not only Catherine but him too because of Catherine's love for him. Goetz inquires if: "She was talking about the other Goetz?" But Hilda replies: "There is only one."[71] Once again, Goetz's willful attempt to cast off his previous evil self has failed; he drags his past with him because it persists in the minds of the others. Hilda goes even farther; because of her total identification with Catherine, she now also loves Goetz but she stresses: "In dreams . . . It was in dreams. Her dream: she drew me into it. I had to suffer with her suffering . . . but it proved a snare; for I had to love you with her love." But unlike Catherine, she is not totally obsessed by him. When "I see you in the light, . . . I am free! By day-light, you are no more than yourself."[72] Her comments are significant because they reveal the particular psychosis that Catherine and Heinrich are suffering from. It is, as Hilda explains, as if both were possessed while she, on the other hand, can distinguish between dreams and reality.

When Catherine is brought in, Goetz wants to atone for his past misdeeds. He turns to God and begs Him to save her; but predictably God remains silent. Since God does not grant his wish, Goetz is once again forced to indulge in trickery. He exclaims: "Are You deaf? Good heavens, how stupid I am! God helps those who help themselves."[73] Goetz stabs himself; calls back the crowd and, showing them his stigmata, proclaims: "The Christ has bled . . . See, in His infinite mercy, he has allowed me to bear His stigmata."[74] This act of fakery rids Catherine of her fears and she dies in peace.

But now Goetz's attempt to be good is challenged even more strenuously. Karl comes to "the City of the Sun" where happiness reigns, to warn them that "armed men are everywhere [and t]he peasants and barons are

---

69. Ibid., 90.
70. Ibid., 93–94; translation amended.
71. Ibid., 96.
72. Ibid., 98.
73. Ibid., 102; translation amended.
74. Ibid., 102.

going to fight."⁷⁵ The peasants refuse to fight but Karl explains: "If you will not fight out of fraternity, then let it at least be in your own interest: happiness is something to defend." And he concludes by blaming Goetz: "Ah! You [the peasants] are not the ones to blame, the criminal is the false prophet who has filled your eyes with that deranged look of placidity."⁷⁶ When the peasants want to kill him Hilda intervenes; however, she does agree with Karl: "he speaks the truth . . . your City of the Sun is built on the misery of others; and for the barons to allow it, their peasants must resign themselves to slavery."⁷⁷ Hilda cannot stand the superficial happiness that now surrounds her and wants to leave but Goetz implores her to stay because: "[he] ha[s] made the gestures of love but love has not followed"; and he concludes: "I should have loved them with your heart. [Y]ou are warmth, you are light and you are not myself . . . I do not understand why we are two entities, and I should like, while remaining myself, to become you."⁷⁸ In this case, it is Goetz who wishes to blend into another character and be one with her.

Now Nasti enters and announces that "the revolt has broken out" and that only Goetz "can still prevent the worst. There remains one hope . . . If we can win one pitched battle, only one, the barons will sue for peace." This means that Goetz will have to become a "butcher" again and "waste lives." To persuade him, Nasti uses an argument similar to Hoederer in *Dirty Hands* when he decided to ally himself with the Prince: "You will sacrifice twenty thousand men to save a hundred thousand."⁷⁹ In the hope that Hilda will make up his mind, Goetz asks her to "help" him decide. Hilda "forbid[s him] to shed blood." Goetz wants the two to "make the decision together" and, as well, to "endure the consequences together." As a way out, Goetz proposes a compromise to Nasti; to dissuade the peasants, he will tell them "the truth" and Nasti agrees to his proposal.⁸⁰

When confronted by the peasants, Goetz takes on a "Hercules" and quickly demonstrates in a simulated fencing match (Goetz employs a stick!) that the peasants lack the military skills to take on the barons. He also pretends to be able to speak directly to God and in a pseudo-vision he reveals that "God is against this revolt, and [is] show[ing him] those who are marked for death."⁸¹ Now Karl shows up; he too makes himself bleed

75. Ibid., 105, 106.
76. Ibid., 108.
77. Ibid., 109.
78. Ibid., 112.
79. Ibid., 112–114.
80. Ibid., 115.
81. Ibid., 118.

but even though Goetz has no problem revealing that Karl is even a greater fake and that the blood flows from "bladders filled with blood concealed in his sleeves," Karl also conjures up other tricks and denounces Goetz while pointing to a beggar: "There's one who has understood. The lands are yours; he who pretends to give them to you is deceiving you, for he is giving away what is not his." And he concludes: "your love comes from the Devil, it corrupts whatever it touches."[82] Goetz is shocked when Nasti agrees with Karl and abandons him to himself. In fact, they both agree that Goetz's so-called generosity has turned into a destructive weapon because it is not sufficient to receive property for free; one must earn the right to it and even fight for it. Goetz denounces the peasants as "curs" and begs God's help: "Give me the good use of my misfortunes! Lord, I believe, I must believe that." Again he pleads: "O Lord, take me in the nets of Your night and raise me up above them." When morning comes, he proclaims: "The dawn is breaking. I have come through Your night. Blessed art You for Your gift: I shall be able to see clearly." In desperation Goetz has rejected the peasants because they have preferred Karl to him and now, as a solitary figure, he believes to be able to see the truth but, ironically, what he "sees" "[is] *Altweiler in ruins*" and "*Hilda is sitting on a pile of stone and rubble, her head in her hands.*"[83]

Goetz now withdraws from humanity to live in solitude and in a move reminiscent of John the Baptist, he proclaims that "[he] shall have eyes for nothing but the earth and the stones."[84] But just before a year and a day have passed, the emaciated Goetz gives in to Hilda, accepts a drink from her and declares it to be "[a]nother defeat" of his vow of asceticism and, satiated, wants to sleep with her.[85] Because Hilda "love[s] him," she does not reject him.[86] Since she is completely human, she will love both his body and his soul because, as she says: "for you do not love at all, if you do not love everything."[87] But she does agree to whip him because he "ha[s] ruined [their] love." At that moment, Heinrich shows up to hold Goetz to account. Initially, Goetz expresses "joy" at "seeing him again," but Heinrich is also the bearer of some very bad tidings: "The peasants are looking to kill [him] . . . Last Thursday, . . . the barons cut Nasti's army to ribbons. Twenty-five thousand dead; it was a complete rout. In three months the revolt will be

82. Ibid., 122.
83. Ibid., 124–125. Translation amended.
84. Ibid., 126.
85. Ibid., 131.
86. Ibid., 132.
87. Ibid., 133.

stamped out."[88] Clearly, no further proof is needed that Goetz's attempt to create an instant paradise on earth had no realistic chance of succeeding. Goetz and Heinrich then engage in a debate over the moral value of Goetz's behavior. Goetz agrees that even though his

> appetite for betrayal [had] not yet [been] assuaged [when] before the ramparts of Worms, [he] thought up a way to betray Evil... Only Evil, doesn't let itself be betrayed quite so easily; it wasn't Good that jumped out of the dice box, it was worse Evil.[89]

Next, he again asks Heinrich if "Good is possible for men?" and Heinrich's answer is still the same: "no." And he adds: "Man is nothing." He also remarks that he had always seen through Goetz's motives:

> Don't pretend to be surprised; you have always known it, you knew it the night you threw the dice. If you didn't, why did you cheat?... You cheated, Catherine saw you; you raised your voice to cover the silence of God. The orders you pretend to receive, you send to yourself.

Goetz concurs fully with Heinrich's damning remarks:

> I alone, priest; you are right... God does not see me, God does not hear, God does not know me... Silence is God. Absence is God. God is the loneliness of man. There was no one but myself; I alone decided on Evil, and I alone invented Good. It was I who cheated, I who worked miracles. I, who accused myself today, I alone who can absolve myself; I, man. If God exists, man is nothing; if man exists... Where are you going?[90]

Heinrich will not allow Goetz to conclude but Goetz will not let him flee and tells him: "I am going to tell you a colossal joke: God doesn't exist." Heinrich cannot accept Goetz's conclusion, he "would rather be judged by an Infinite Being than judged by [his] equals." However, for Goetz this is a new beginning and from now on he wants to be a man amongst men: "Farewell monsters, farewell saints. Farewell pride. There is nothing left but mankind... [because I am beginning a new] life."[91]

In the fight that follows, Goetz kills Heinrich and proclaims: "The comedy of Good has ended with a murder. So much the better. I cannot go back on my tracks." Goetz's stubborn quest to test God into demonstrating

88. Ibid., 134.
89. Ibid., 138–139.
90. Ibid., 140–141.
91. Ibid., 141–142.

His existence has ended. For a year and a day he dared Him to show Himself but the experiment has come to naught and therefore he can tell Hilda: "God is dead; [*takes her in his arms*]" and state: "We have no witness now, I alone can see your hair and your brow. How real you have become since He no longer exists."[92]

The final scene opens with a discussion between Karl and Nasti. Karl has a "witch rub . . . the peasants with a wooden hand" to make them "invulnerable . . ." Nasti denounces him as a "[p]rophet of error" and he, in turn, calls Nasti "a false prophet."[93] But Nasti disagrees: "[He] didn't want to fight this war . . . ; [he is] not a false prophet but a man the Lord has betrayed."[94] The peasants bring him Goetz who is now willing to fight because he "want[s] to be a man among men" and "serve under [Nasti's] orders as a simple soldier." But Nasti insists: "You shall command the army." However, Goetz still has not overcome all his scruples: "I am resigned to kill, I shall let myself be killed if I must; but I shall never send another man to his death."[95] This is a variation upon the conviction expressed by Camus that if one is willing to kill, one must offer oneself up to be killed and limit violence to its strictest minimum.[96] Goetz too wants to circumscribe the violent act strictly to the person committing it; however, Hilda reminds Goetz that he cannot be like other men because he is "[n]either better nor worse, [but] different." When the witch returns, Nasti, out of despair, permits her to rub him also. As he explains to Goetz: "I despise only myself. Do you know of a stranger comedy? I who hate lies, lie to my brothers to give them the courage to be killed in a war I detest." Goetz now recognizes that Nasti is as "lonely as [he is]" and therefore he can view him as a soul mate and accept to "take command of the army."[97] When a captain challenges his authority, he kills him and explains to Nasti: "I told you I would be hangman and butcher."

Goetz now defines his new role:

> I shall make them hate me, because I know no other way of loving them. I shall give them orders, since I have no other way of obeying. I shall remain alone with this empty sky above my head, since I have no other way of being among men. There is a war to fight, and I shall fight it.[98]

92. Ibid., 143.
93. Ibid., 144.
94. Ibid., 145.
95. Ibid., 145–146.
96. Camus, *Théâtre*, 1829.
97. Sartre, *The Devil*, 147–148.
98. Ibid., 149.

Goetz will now be both subservient to Nasti, since he is obeying his orders, as well as a leader, and as a result a new triad composed of Goetz, Hilda and Nasti is formed. This triad will no longer be typified by relations of omnipotence and abject dependency but will find its basis in relations of cooperative interdependence and equality. How different this conclusion is from *No Exit* where the three characters will pursue each other interminably in a vicious circle of desire, hatred and mutual dependency. But notice as well how similar this play's conclusion is to that of *Kean*.[99] Kean finally abandons the Prince, who always wanted to emulate him, as well as Elena, who continued to confuse role playing with love, and he leaves for New York with Anna, his spouse and manager, and Solomon, his trusty assistant and prompter.[100] Then again, *The Condemned of Altona* (1959) ends on a much gloomier note. Von Gerlach and his son Frantz commit suicide in a Porsche, a symbol of Germany's *Wirtschaftswunder*, and Leni, the sister with whom Frantz had had an incestuous relationship assumes his place upstairs while his brother Werner and spouse Johanna will continue to run the family shipyard as figure heads of a post-capitalist enterprise.[101] *The Devil and the Good Lord*'s conclusion also evokes the comments Sartre made about himself as a classic intellectual to Pierre Verstraeten in 1972. He now saw the need for him "to get off [his] horse [. . . and] come toward the people like one of the people, and not . . . on horseback."[102] Similarly, Goetz is not going to be an omnipotent general who will make all decisions by himself but use his superior talents to serve Nasti's and the peasants' cause. Finally, rather than acting as a self-serving tyrant who makes life a hell for other people, or, for that matter, becoming an ineffectual do-gooder who ends up doing great harm rather than good, Goetz finally agrees to become both servant and master and employ his military skills to further a popular cause. The play also illustrates how Sartre uses the background of the German Peasant War to allow Goetz to slowly gain insight into what should be his actual role in society. It first shows him attempting to rival and even outdo the devil by inventing more and more gruesome and diabolic treatments for his fellows and, next, he tries to create an earthly paradise within a world where power struggles, violence and treachery are the order of the day. Ultimately, however, Goetz works his way through these impasses and arrives at a new insight into what he can do for others by simply letting them make use of his natural talents.

99. Sartre, *Theatre*, 668.
100. Ibid., 668–670.
101. Ibid., 993.
102. Aronson and van den Hoven, *Sartre Alive*, 96.

I would also like to stress that there is little sense in analyzing these characters as if they were, like Jean Genet, real people; instead they should be seen as exemplary of certain attitudes which can be compared and contrasted. Doing such, allows one to see that certain attitudes lead to dead ends and others to relationships that recognize one and another's basic humanity and lead to more fruitful and cooperative undertakings.

Bibliography

Aronson, Ronald, and Adrian van den Hoven, eds. *Sartre Alive*. Detroit: Wayne State University Press, 1991.
Baudelaire, Charles. *Les Fleurs du mal*. Paris: Classiques Garnier, 1961.
Camus, Albert. *Théâtre, récits, et nouvelles*. Paris: Gallimard, 1962.
Ireland, John. *Sartre: Un Art déloyal*. Paris: Place, 1994.
Noudelmann, François and Gilles Phillippe, eds. *Dictionnaire Sartre*. Paris: Champion, 2004.
Pascal, Blaise. *Pensées*. Paris: Bordas, 1966.
Sartre, Jean-Paul. *Being and Nothingness*. Translated by Hazel Barnes. New York: Philosophical Library, 1956.
———. *The Devil & The Good Lord and Two Other Plays*. New York: Knopf, 1960.
———. *L'Engrenage*. Geneva: Nagel, 1948.
———. *Sartre on Theater*. Translated by Frank Jellinek. New York: Pantheon, 1976.
———. *Théâtre complet*. Paris: Gallimard, 2005.
———. *The Writings of Jean-Paul Sartre. A Bibliographical Life*. Vol., 1. Translated by Richard McCleary. Evanston, IL: Northwestern University Press, 1974.
———. *We Have Only This Life to Live: The Essays of Jean-Paul Sartre, 1939–1975*. Edited by Ronald Aronson and Adrian van den Hoven. New York: NYRB, 2013.
Shakespeare, William. *Twelfth Night, or What You Will*. In *William Shakespeare, The Complete Works*. General Editors, Stanley Wells and Gary Taylor, 691–714. Oxford: Clarendon, 1986.
Sprintzen, David. *Camus. A Critical Examination*. Philadelphia: Temple University Press, 1988.
Wolfman, Yaffa. "What Did Goethe's *Faust* Contribute to Sartre's *The Devil and the Good Lord*?" *Sartre Studies International* 10 (2004) 182–94.

PART THREE

Beyond French Existentialism

11

Kierkegaard on the Positive Role of Reason in Leading to Christian Faith

—Thomas Anderson

It is well known that Søren Kierkegaard stresses the limitations or boundaries of human reason. Some have classified him as an epistemological skeptic, namely, as someone who severely restricts the natural ability of human understanding to grasp the truth about any reality other than one's own self.[1] Although I believe this is exaggerated, it is true that the Dane insists on the limits or boundaries of human reason and understanding when it comes to Christian faith. Indeed, one of the main purposes of his entire authorship was to confront those philosophers and theologians of his day who, in his view, turned Christianity into a set of doctrines to be understood and who claimed that they could rationally comprehend Christian faith and, thus, that human reason and philosophy were superior to it.[2]

Like countless Christian writers before him, Kierkegaard insists that Christian faith goes beyond the natural powers of human reason. To become a Christian we must will to believe in Christ and this involves venturing further than all human calculations and objective knowledge can take us. Even more, Kierkegaard often asserts that Christian faith is not only beyond the boundaries of human reason and knowledge but *against* them. The Christian believes what is opposed to natural human reason, what to it

---

1. Anderson, "Kierkegaard's Skepticism."

2. Kierkegaard's criticism of the philosophers and theologians of his day is found throughout his works. See for example Kierkegaard, *Fear and Trembling* and *Postscript*.

is "absurd," in particular that a particular historical human being, Jesus of Nazareth, was the infinite eternal God.

There has been a great deal of discussion among Kierkegaard scholars about whether he himself did consider the object of Christian faith, the God-man, to be absurd in the sense of logically self-contradictory.[3] Many have correctly pointed out that for the most part it is one or other of Kierkegaard's pseudonymous authors who claim that the Incarnation is rationally or logically absurd. Kierkegaard himself in writings under his own name usually uses less strong language, most often stating that the God-man is an "offense" or "scandal" to human understanding. Nevertheless, he does delight in stressing how contrary, how opposed, belief in Christ and in Christianity in general is to natural human understanding, or as he often puts it, to the "natural man."[4]

However, it is not the opposition between faith and reason in Kierkegaard that is my topic here, since that has been extensively studied. Rather, I want to consider the *positive* role natural human reason can perform for faith according to Kierkegaard—a topic much less discussed. This is not to suggest that humans can reason their way into faith, for Kierkegaard accepts the traditional Christian position that faith is a Divine gift which human power cannot attain on its own. Nevertheless, he also thinks that the natural powers of human understanding can greatly assist one in coming to the place, the boundary, beyond which faith resides. Human reason can aid us in recognizing the deep need we have for faith and even, I dare say, the "reasonableness" of transcending the limitations of human reason and believing. (To put this in traditional terms, there is a sense in which for Kierkegaard natural human reason provides the "propaedeutics" for Christian faith.) Yet Christian faith always remains, in some sense, in opposition to human understanding for him.

In order to present the positive role human reason can play in leading a human being to venture beyond its boundaries, I will review Kierkegaard's account of the three stages of human existence, for they are, or are meant to be, the paths which lead to Christian faith. Note that these forms of life are not just a road he personally may have traveled but the route which, he believes, every human being must take to reach Christian faith.

First, what Kierkegaard calls the esthetic stage.[5] All human being are born totally self-centered and naturally seek a life of personal plea-

---

3. Evans, *Kierkegaard's Fragments*; Westphal, *Becoming*; Pojman, *Logic*; Fabro, "Faith and Reason."

4. See for example Kierkegaard, *Practice*, 111, 119, 212–213 and *Works*, 201–204.

5. The esthetic life is described in detail in Kierkegaard, *Either/Or*. "The Balance Between the Esthetic and the Ethical in the Development of Personality" in Part II

sure as their ultimate goal, Kierkegaard believes. Those who follow their spontaneous inclinations and center their lives on obtaining the things of this world, including other people, for their personal enjoyment, he calls esthetes. For them, nothing, not things, not human beings, not God, have intrinsic worth or inherent value. They are important only insofar as they promise enjoyment; when they cease to satisfy they are discarded. As Kierkegaard describes them, esthetes want nothing to limit their pursuit of self-gratification and so accept no moral code or responsibility to others and make no long-term commitments that might get in the way of future pleasures. That is to say that there is nothing that esthetes believe they *have to seek*, nothing they *must* do or be. As Kierkegaard describes them, esthetes come in many forms. They range from crude hedonists mainly interested in pleasure of the body, to cultured, talented, individuals able to appreciate qualitatively diverse pleasures, especially the pleasures of love. But in the esthetic lifestyle all love is fundamentally self-centered, Kierkegaard claims.[6] Love is simply mutual egoism, mutual self-love; each esthete loving the other in order to gain the pleasure of being loved. And, as we said, they will make no lasting commitment to love since that could hinder their attaining future pleasures.

Now if a person lives an esthetic life for some time, Kierkegaard believes that he or she will eventually come to a state of despair, for various reasons. For one thing, the esthetes' lives are not under their control. Whether they are able to attain much enjoyment depends on factors outside their power. No one can guarantee that they will possess sufficient money, health, friends, talent, energy or God's favor to attain the many pleasures of this world. They will if they are lucky, but that means that the esthetic life is fundamentally dependent on luck or fate. This in turn means, Kierkegaard states, that strictly speaking the esthete is not a self, for a self is someone who freely, consciously, takes charge of his or her life and accepts the responsibility to direct and shape it.[7] Esthetes are effectively slaves to the whims of fate, and more basically, to their own natural self-centered appetites for pleasure.

Another reason for their despair is that esthetes focus on the transitory and perishable. All moments of pleasure, however intense, eventually vanish and so esthetes can come to realize that their search for enjoyment will be unceasingly frustrated since they are chasing essentially perishable objects. Finally, since esthetes believe there is nothing they *must* seek, no obligations

---

contains an especially good presentation of the esthetic.

6. Kierkegaard, *Works*, 122–129, 236–238, 169; *Practice*, 111.

7. Kierkegaard, *Either/Or, II*, 158–168, 177–180.

or commitments which they *must* fulfill, that means, Kierkegaard says, that there is for them nothing that is *intrinsically worth doing*. This realization that nothing in their lives possesses in itself any permanent value also brings the esthete to despair.

Now what should esthetes do in their despair? Surprisingly, Kierkegaard advises them to "choose despair," which involves using the power of human reason to move beyond despair.[8] By choosing despair Kierkegaard means that esthetes should face their despair and use it as an impetus to attain a deeper understanding of themselves. Since one reason for their despair is the fact that esthetes are enslaved to fate and to their natural appetites for pleasure, they should realize that this means that there is a dimension of their being which seeks to be in control of their lives and master of their destiny, which is to say that they want to be selves. This means they should become conscious of their freedom, their innate ability to choose to take responsibility for their lives and for the kind of person they come to be.

In addition, since despair results from the esthete centering his or her life on transitory things which lack inherent value, the individual should also recognize that he or she wants to be an "eternally valid self," that is, a self which endures through time and possesses imperishable value.[9] Every human being seeks a life intrinsically worth living, a life with lasting meaning and value, Kierkegaard believes. He also thinks that if we look deeply within ourselves we will find not only a drive to become an eternally valid self, but a *task* or *obligation* to be the best human selves we can be. When Kierkegaard counsels esthetes to choose despair, then, he asks them to willingly accept the fact that they need and want more than a life enslaved to pleasure and centered on the transitory. He asks them to accept their freedom and their obligation to make themselves into the ideal persons they should be. Those who do so, who choose their own selves as their absolute end by freely committing their lives to becoming the virtuous persons they should be, thereby move to the ethical stage of existence.[10]

Ethical individuals fully accept their responsibility to become selves possessing permanent meaning and value. Since the moral order is eternal—for moral virtues such as justice, courage, and honesty are always inherently good—by incorporating them into one's life one becomes a self-possessing imperishable value. Kierkegaard describes ethical individuals as theists. Eternal moral values, along with one's obligation to become a self,

---

8. Ibid., 211, 208–213.

9. Ibid., 189–190, 206, 211.

10. The ethical is set forth in detail in *Either/Or, II* especially in "The Balance Between the Esthetic and the Ethical in the Development of the Personality."

are not merely subjective human creations able to be uncreated at will but are grounded in an objective eternal realm rooted in the eternal God. In fact, since ethical individuals consider moral perfection to be the ultimate goal of their lives, they in effect take the moral order to be supreme, i.e. divine. God functions for them as the ultimate basis of the objectivity of moral values and obligation, and nothing else, Kierkegaard says.[11]

Now Kierkegaard has high praise for those who accept their obligation to become completely virtuous selves. He agrees that they have truly found something intrinsically worth living and dying for. From a religious perspective, however, he criticizes the ethical person for considering morality or the moral order equivalent to God. Of course if the moral order is supreme, there can be no exceptions to it. Accordingly, he uses the Biblical story of Abraham, the father of faith, who is asked by God to violate morality by killing his only son, to show that an individual's personal relation in faith to God is more than, and higher than, their relation to morality. God, not moral values or obligations, is (or should be) the absolute goal of one's life.[12]

Along the same line, Kierkegaard criticizes the ethical for taking one's own virtue and moral perfection as its ultimate goal. The primary reason ethical individuals behave justly, honestly, faithfully, etc. toward other human beings is because such behavior is necessary for them to become the virtuous selves they are obliged to be. Others simply furnish the occasion for the ethical person to develop the social virtues. In a sense, then, ethical individuals are not unlike esthetes, basically focused on themselves.[13] This is one reason they too will end in despair, Kierkegaard believes. They are simply too self-centered, too self-assured, too self-confident. Let me explain.

Ethical persons vividly experience their moral obligation to become perfectly virtuous selves. They know they are obliged to live every moment in accordance with moral values. However, they will eventually become aware how far short they fall. Since they accept Kant's dictum, "If I must, I can," they believe they are themselves capable of achieving moral perfection. Accordingly, because they continually fail to live up to that ideal, they feel completely responsible for their failures and so completely guilty. They may sorrow over their guilt, repent of their moral failure, and resolve to be better. Still, they continue to be to some degree selfish, prideful, unjust, unkind, etc. The lasting meaning and value an ethical life promised appears

---

11. Kierkegaard, *Fear and Trembling*, 54–55.

12. This is the major point of *Fear and Trembling*.

13. In "The Esthetic Validity of Marriage" in *Either/Or, II*, the ethical man sees marriage to be of value because it enables *him* to develop certain virtues. He hardly mentions his wife at all! (I thank Teresa Reed for pointing this out to me.)

continually out of reach. Instead of an eternally valuable self, their repeated failures to attain moral perfection have resulted in their "moral bankruptcy," Kierkegaard says, which brings unmitigated guilt.[14] Eventually, they despair of achieving moral excellence.

Yet here again Kierkegaard gives human understanding a crucial role to play. We noted earlier that from their experience of an esthetic life, individuals should come to the realization that transitory objects of this world cannot give their lives the eternal meaning they seek. Now, from their experience of the ethical life, they should realize in addition that their own efforts to take charge of their lives and make themselves eternally valuable, virtuous selves by achieving moral perfection are also failures. In other words, Kierkegaard hopes that by living on the esthetic and ethical stages, they come to understand that neither from the world nor from their own efforts can they attain the meaningful life they so desire. Let them, then, he says, *give up* trying to achieve a permanently meaningful existence by themselves. Let them become "dead to every merely earthly hope, to every human confidence in their own powers or in human assistance," Kierkegaard writes, and become "fully convinced that [they themselves are] capable of nothing, nothing at all."[15] Let us humbly admit that if permanent value is going to come to our existence, it will come neither from ourselves nor from anything in this world, but only from something or someone which transcends both.

Paradoxically, it is here, where he stresses the need for us to admit our total inability to attain eternal value by our own powers, that Kierkegaard's confidence in the natural powers of human understanding seems to be at its peak. For he believes that human beings, after despairing of the ethical life, can move beyond its boundaries and by their own powers attain a great deal of knowledge of God and of their relation to God this side of Divine Revelation. As we said above, ethical individuals who in guilt and despair admit their total helplessness can come to realize that they will become an eternally valuable self only by the assistance of a being beyond both themselves and this perishable world. Such individuals, like despairing esthetes, can see the need, Kierkegaard says, to totally "renounce" or "resign themselves" from everything in this world by ceasing to make such things their ultimate end.[16] Likewise, as despairing ethical individuals they can understand that they need to move beyond the ethical stage and renounce *themselves* totally,

---

14. The limitations of the ethical are mentioned in various places besides *Fear and Trembling*. See Kierkegaard, *Either/Or, II*, final section "Ultimatum," 266–268; *Postscript* 266–68; and *Journals and Papers*, I, #998.

15. Kierkegaard, *Self-Examination*, 77; *Eighteen Discourses*, 307.

16. Kierkegaard, *Postscript*, Part II, Chapter IV, A, Section 1.

which means to restrain their spontaneous tendency to place absolute value on finite things and their natural desire to achieve self-worth by their own efforts. Such "self-denial," "dying to self," or "self-annihilation is the essential and proper form for the relationship with God," Kierkegaard asserts and he further claims that through self-renunciation God's reality will become manifest: "someone who is conscious that he is capable of nothing at all has every day and every moment the desired and irrefragable opportunity to experience that God lives."[17] His reasoning seems to be that those who truly recognize they can do absolutely nothing themselves, and yet do act, must experience the assistance of a creative power who is the source of all they are and do. That source is God. He states, "The person who himself is capable of nothing at all cannot undertake the least thing without God's help, consequently without becoming conscious that there is a God," he writes, a God "who is capable of all things."[18] Needless to say, such a person lives on the religious stage. Note, however, we have not yet come to Christianity whose basic tenets must be revealed. We are at a prior and preparatory region of the religious that Kierkegaard designates as Religion A and that he says is within the realm of "universal human nature," that is, within the power of every human being—and, in fact, was present in paganism.[19] (Let me simply note here that Kierkegaard was very impressed by the extent of Plato's and Aristotle's knowledge of God. He is also very influenced by the German Idealists of his time, especially Hegel, who maintain that the finite mind or spirit can come to realize that it is part of Absolute Spirit or Absolute Will, i.e. God).

Although the person in Religion A is said to "experience that God lives," I should point out that such experience cannot be so overwhelmingly clear that he or she is rationally convinced that God is. Kierkegaard insists that on this level it is only by faith that one asserts the Divine reality, intuitive or demonstrative certitude are unattainable.[20] Yet such faith is totally within

17. Kierkegaard, *Postscript*, 461; and *Eighteen Discourses*, 322.

18. Kierkegaard, *Eighteen Discourses*, 310, 322. A similar statement is found in *Works*, 362: "it is self-denial that discovers that God is."

19. Kierkegaard, *Eighteen Discourses*, I, 559. Kierkegaard's most extensive treatment of Religion A is in *Postscript*, I, 385–541 and 555–561. The religion described in *Eighteen Discourses*, I, 256 is also apparently Religion A (see in this regard, *Postscript* 256, 273). Arnold Come, *Kierkegaard as Humanist*, chapters 6 and 7, claims that most of the content of Kierkegaard's *Works* and *Sickness* also fall under Religion A. Actually, for Kierkegaard any religion other than strict Christianity would be on the stage of Religion A (*Postscript*, 557). However, he describes only one form.

20. Kierkegaard, *Postscript*, 204, 210, 422–429; *Eighteen Discourses*, 25–26, 36. Kierkegaard often uses the term faith in a very broad sense. Any knowledge that goes beyond immediate sensation and cognition is uncertain and, therefore, must be *believed*

human power, he states, and he describes it as the result of a deepening self-knowledge which he calls by the Platonic term recollection.[21] Although he does not spell out the movement in detail, he suggests that the individual, who by recollection probes deeply into his or her self, can come to believe that he or she essentially participates in the eternal God. In Religion A God is understood to be the eternal, all knowing, omnipresent, infinite ground or creator of everything and thereby to be within everything.[22] Or, better, every creature is believed to be within the Creator who sustains it in existence, and human beings by the exercise of their own powers can affirm this.

Clearly Religion A understands God to be much more than eternal moral duty and human fulfillment to involve more then the embodiment of moral virtues and becoming an eternally valid self. One's eternal value, or, to use a properly religious term, one's eternal salvation, comes only through a relationship to the infinite God. This is why Kierkegaard insists that each person should establish an "absolute relation to the absolute [God]" which means that one should totally renounce all finite goods, that is, refuse to make them the ultimate goal of life. One should make eternal salvation, eternal happiness, with God his or her absolute or supreme end.[23]

However, therein lies a problem. Although individuals in Religion A, according to Kierkegaard, know a great deal about God and the self and clearly recognize their obligations to totally renounce the finite and establish an absolute relation to God, the fact of experience is that, even with God's help, they do not do so. No matter how much we want to, we never die to the finite once and for all. We cannot completely eradicate our inborn inclination to take finite goods as ultimate and to make eternal salvation/ God just one of a number of goods we choose, Kierkegaard says. At best we can occasionally attain the desired God relationship. However, an occasional relationship is not the absolute one that our total dependence on God requires and so, once again, we find ourselves to be guilty.[24] Furthermore, the quality of this guilt is much deeper and severe than that of the

---

to be true. See Kierkegaard, *Fragments*, 81–85.

21. Kierkegaard, *Eighteen Discourses*, Discourse 1, "The Expectancy of Faith," stresses that such faith is within the power of every human being. See also Kierkegaard, *Postscript*, 204–213, 555–561, 582; *Journals and Papers*, II, #2274, III, #3606; *Eighteen Discourses*, 309, 312–319. For a good discussion of this point see Pojman, *Logic*, chapter 3 and Evans, *Kierkegaard's Fragments*, chapter 8.

22. Kierkegaard, *Postscript*, 560–561. It is worth noting that Kierkegaard considered pantheism "the only consistent position outside Christianity" (*Postscript* 226).

23. Ibid. An entire section is devoted to infinite resignation or renunciation of all finite things: Part II, Section II, Chapter IV, Division 2, A (Pathos).

24. Kierkegaard, *Postscript*, 404–405, 431–432, 460–461, 525–528.

ethical individual since the guilt in Religion A is in relation to an infinitely benevolent God from whom one receives everything, not simply in reference to impersonal moral duty. Kierkegaard designates it as "total," apparently meaning that it is not due to particular evil acts but is thoroughly part of the human self and so is not removable by particular acts of repentance.[25] Yet, as we noted, Religion A does believe in an all powerful God and so the guilty may obscurely suspect and hope that it might be possible for such a God to remove their guilt.[26] What is certain is that like the ethical individual and the esthete described earlier, this religious person has also reached the end of the road, the boundary of Religion A. Because of their guilt they realize that they are only minimally and negatively related to their eternal salvation in God, although they are more aware than ever of their need and of their desire for that goal. Because of their total guilt, which they cannot remove, they understand even more fully than did the ethical person their utter impotence to attain eternal meaning and value.

This is as far as human understanding can go; this is its boundary. Yet individuals who come this far have, through their own powers, attained a great deal of knowledge of their nature and of God, knowledge that is absolutely necessary, Kierkegaard states, if one is to come eventually to the place where they are faced with the choice to believe in Christ or not.[27] To review, persons who have come this far are aware of their freedom and the deep eternal dimension of themselves which seeks eternal meaning/salvation. They are aware of their unconditional obligation to become eternally valuable selves by ultimately gaining eternal salvation in God. They believe in their utter dependency on, and thus their obligation to choose, God as their absolute end as well as their total guilt because of their failure to do so. In despair they understand that they are not able to remove this guilt which estranges them from God and eternal salvation, and, therefore, that they need forgiveness. Perhaps most important, they believe in an infinite God for whom all things are possible.

Such a God is able to break through the limitations of human power. When individuals have come to the boundary, the utmost extremity, of despair over their guilt and powerlessness and feel their absolute need of God, Kierkegaard believes that God *will* reveal the full depth of their misery

25. Ibid., 529–538. Kierkegaard seems to have original sin in mind here. Fortunately, a discussion of his complex and possibly inconsistent views on hereditary sin is beyond the scope of this paper.

26. Ibid., 536, 541; *Sickness*, 38–41,71.

27. Kierkegaard states that a person must go through the ethical stage and Religion A in order to reach Christianity and that one never totally leaves either of these stages behind: *Postscript*, 249, 388, 556–567; *Stages*, 477.

and its remedy. (I say "God *will* reveal" because Kierkegaard apparently believes that, if we acknowledge our total need for him, God will see to it that that need will be fulfilled.)[28] For one thing, God will reveal that humans are in even worse shape than Religion A knew for they are fundamentally and intrinsically sinful and so completely severed from God. It is their sin which renders them powerless and selfishly focused on themselves and the things of this world. But God will also reveal the remedy. The opposite of sin, Kierkegaard states, is not virtue but faith, faith in God's overpowering love incarnated in Jesus whose death has atoned for human sin.[29] If we do believe, our sins will be removed, our nature will be recreated (reborn) and, with God's help, we will be able eventually to become eternally valuable selves by attaining eternal salvation.[30]

Of course, all these truths are beyond human understanding. That the infinite eternal God became a particular temporal human being who suffered and died, that humans are completely cut off from God by their sin and yet that God still loves them so much that he sent his son to die for them and thereby atone for their sin, that one who has been born can be reborn by faith, such things "did not arise in any human heart," Kierkegaard writes quoting Scripture.[31] Humanly speaking, these things that Christianity teaches are unimaginable and inconceivable and so each person remains free to believe in this revelation or to reject it as ridiculous and nonsensical. Yet even though Christian truths are incomprehensible and offensive to human reason, and although Kierkegaard sometimes seems to describe Christian faith as a sheer act of the will unaided by human understanding,[32] the fact remains that knowledge of the self and of God gained by human reason is necessary, as we have seen, to bring people to the place where the choice to accept Christ or not is a meaningful one. Such knowledge can even give them an impetus to believe since it makes them keenly aware of their despair and of their profound need for a Divine Savior.

---

28. Kierkegaard, *Christian Discourses*, 244–245; *Self-Examination*, 13–14, 69, 83; *Upbuilding Discourses*, 77, 173, 227. Also see Kierkegaard, *Practice*, 67; *Works*, 180; *Eighteen Discourses*, 87–88, 97, 250.

29. Kierkegaard, *Postscript*, 207–208, 582–584; *Sickness*, 80–83, 95–96, 100, 105–106, 131.

30. Kierkegaard, *Postscript*, 576, 583–584; *Fragments*, 14–22; *Practice*, 159–160. In Kierkegaard, *Christian Discourses*, especially Parts 1 and 4, he emphasizes the comfort, peace, and joy that will come to the Christian because his/her sins are forgiven.

31. Kierkegaard, *Fragments*,109. Also see Kierkegaard, *Sickness*, 83–87, 116, 121–122, 125; *Postscript*, 224, 578–581; *Practice*, No. II; *Works*, 25.

32. Kierkegaard, *Postscript*, 209–213, 564–566, 579–581; *Fragments*, 83, 93; *Fear and Trembling*, 65-67. Also see texts of previous note.

If, by passing through the stages that we have described, human beings bump up against their limitations and discover in despair their abject powerlessness and radical sinfulness, it will not be all that difficult, Kierkegaard feels, for them (with God's help) to accept the Divine Physician. He writes,

> The difficulty is not when feeling absolutely one's wretchedness to grasp the consolation of Christianity, to grasp . . . this matchless exaggeration that God let himself be crucified for my sake in order to save me and to show how he loves me.
>
> No, the difficulty is to become wretched in this way, to want to risk discovering one's wretchedness.
>
> To be made well with the aid of Christianity is not the difficulty; the difficulty is in becoming [aware of one's] sick[ness].
>
> If you are sick in this way, Christianity comes with matchless ease, just as it is incomparably easy for the starving person to be interested in food. Especially the food the preparation of which heaven and earth were set in motion so that it might be delicious and tasty—if one is totally famished.[33]

Furthermore, while human reason cannot demonstrate or understand the truths of Christianity, especially the central truth, that God became a man, human imagination can be of some assistance.

To illustrate, I will close with a story that Kierkegaard proposes as an analogy:[34] A great king falls in love with a humble maiden and desires a loving union with her. How can the king express his love and truly receive hers? How can he overcome the tremendous distance between them without offending or overwhelming her? He dare not appear before her in all his majesty and glory for then he would overpower her and she would be unable to freely respond in love for him. Nor should he elevate her to his level for that would imply that he does not love her as she really is. Only if the king lowers himself to the level of the maiden and becomes her equal can a genuine loving union between them be realized. (I trust the application of this story is obvious.)

I conclude, then, that no matter how much Kierkegaard emphasizes the difference, even at time the opposition, between Christian faith and the natural powers of human understanding, the latter play for him an indispensible role in assisting us to move through life's stages to the place, the boundary, where we must choose to believe or not in Christ as Love

---

33. Kierkegaard, *Journals and Papers*, II, #1137. Kierkegaard repeats throughout his religious works that consciousness of sin is the *only* path to Christian faith. See, for example, Kierkegaard, *Practice*, 67–68, 155–157; *Works*, 287–297; *Christian Discourses*, 258–267.

34. Kierkegaard, *Fragments*, 26–32.

incarnate who offers us eternal salvation. For, again, to even take such an offer seriously, we must become acutely aware of our absolute need for a Redeemer—and it is human reason that can bring us to that awareness.

Bibliography

Anderson, Thomas. "The Extent of Kierkegaard's Skepticism." *Man and World* 27 (1994) 271–89.

Come, Arnold B. *Kierkegaard as Humanist*. Montreal: McGill-Queen's University Press, 1995.

Evans, C. Stephen. *Kierkegaard's Fragments and Postscript*. Atlantic Highlands, NJ: Humanities Press, 1983.

Fabro, Cornelio. "Faith and Reason in Kierkegaard's Dialectic." In *A Kierkegaard Critique*, edited by Howard A. Johnson and Niels Thulstrup, 156–206. New York: Harpers, 1962.

Kierkegaard, Søren. *Christian Discourses*. Translated by Howard V. Hong and Edna H. Hong. Princeton: Princeton University Press, 1997.

———. *Concluding Unscientific Postscript, I*. Translated by Howard V. Hong and Edna H. Hong. Princeton: Princeton University Press, 1992.

———. *Eighteen Upbuilding Discourses*. Translated by Howard V. Hong and Edna H. Hong. Princeton: Princeton University Press, 1990.

———. *Either/Or, I and II*. Translated by Howard V. Hong and Edna H. Hong. Princeton: Princeton University Press, 1987.

———. *Fear and Trembling*. Translated by Howard V. Hong and Edna H. Hong. Princeton: Princeton University Press, 1983.

———. *For Self-Examination*. Translated by Howard V. Hong and Edna H. Hong. Princeton: Princeton University Press, 1990.

———. *Philosophical Fragments*. Translated by Howard V. Hong and Edna H. Hong. Princeton: Princeton University Press, 1985.

———. *Practice in Christianity*. Translated by Howard V. Hong and Edna H. Hong. Princeton: Princeton University Press, 1991.

———. *Søren Kierkegaard's Journals and Papers*, 7 vols. Translated by Howard V. Hong and Edna H. Hong. Bloomington: Indiana University Press, 1970–1978.

———. *Sickness unto Death*. Translated by Howard V. Hong and Edna H. Hong. Princeton: Princeton University Press, 1980.

———. *Stages on Life's Way*. Translated by Howard V. Hong and Edna H. Hong. Princeton: Princeton University Press, 1988.

———. *Upbuilding Discourses in Various Spirits*. Translated by Howard V. Hong and Edna H. Hong. Princeton: Princeton University Press, 1993.

———. *Works of Love*, Translated by Howard V. Hong and Edna H. Hong. Princeton: Princeton University Press, 1995.

Pojman, Louis. *The Logic of Subjectivity*. Tuscaloosa: University of Alabama Press, 1984.

Westphal, Merold. *Becoming a Self*. West Lafayette, IN: Purdue University Press, 1996.

12

Farewell to Postmodernism?

—William McBride

Thomas Busch has been a strong force in the effort, which has been more successful than not, to prevent philosophy in America from succumbing to the dominance of a monolithic spirit, according to which only certain ways of thinking and speaking about a very limited number of questions are to be regarded as seriously, genuinely philosophical. Like a number of others who have collaborated in this effort, he has found in some of the philosophers of Twentieth Century Continental Europe, in his case especially French thinkers, many of the resources needed to undertake it. He has been a "professional" philosopher, as measured from the outset of his graduate studies in 1960, for nearly half the life-span, up to the present, of professional philosophy in America, as measured by the date of the first meeting of the American Philosophical Association, just past the turn of the last century; this has given him the opportunity to make a sustained contribution to its evolution, and he has indeed done so.

Some years ago, I wrote a brief review of Professor Busch's book, *The Power of Consciousness and the Force of Circumstances in Sartre's Philosophy*. In retrospect, it is not a brilliant review, even if it does convey some of the essential content of the work. What struck me anew about this review when I recently re-read it, however, was its reference in two places, near the beginning and at the very end, to the anti-universalistic tendency of postmodernism, "a term that," as I say, "is not evoked *eo nomine* in this study."[1] I suggested that some points made by Busch about the development of Sar-

---

1. McBride, "Review of Busch," 475.

tre's own thought over time might, if correct, situate Sartre as an historical link in the direction of postmodernism within contemporary philosophy, although Busch himself did not seem to have been very much influenced by postmodernism's critique of "universalistic, conceptual thinking."

How was I to know that, only two years later, Professor Busch would be the co-editor of a volume with the word "postmodernism" in its title? *Merleau-Ponty, Hermeneutics, and Postmodernism* is a useful, attractive anthology. I prefer, however, to focus here on a question that I find interesting although extremely difficult, in my opinion, to conceptualize, and that may be illuminated by some references in Busch's later monograph, *Circulating Being: From Embodiment to Incorporation*: What is, or was, postmodernism, and is it now *passé*?

As many will remember, "the postmodern condition," if not the ideology of postmodernism, was depicted in a small book with that title written by Jean-François Lyotard.[2] This effort had more than a few ironic features. It was commissioned by a governmental agency (of the Province of Québec), a route to publication in philosophy that few others in the millennial history of our discipline have managed to follow. Its sub-title, *Rapport sur le savoir*, was as pretentious as any in that same history, even while heralding something far shorter than most of its rivals in this respect. (Think *Summa Theologiae, Capital, Appearance and Reality, Being and Nothingness*, etc.) Its author is said later to have dismissed it as an inferior piece of work, for which he had been ill equipped; indeed, a recent university press catalogue, in announcing a forthcoming study of Lyotard's philosophy, baldly asserts that his "wide-ranging and highly original contributions to thought were overshadowed by his brief, unfortunate association with 'postmodernism.'"[3] (Note the scare quotes around the word "postmodernism.") And, best of all, as many commentators have noted, the book undertakes to define—that is, to offer a metanarrative concerning—a phenomenon that, it contends, consists above all in the rejection of metanarratives. (Oh, yes, postmodernism was also said by Lyotard to have a good deal to do with information technology, a hobby, unlike postmodernism, that Lyotard never lived to regret.)

If there is a single discipline to which the term "postmodernism" is thought—by some, at least—to be especially congenial, it is neither philosophy nor literature, but rather architecture. No less reliable a source than the *Lafayette, Indiana, Business Digest* of March 19, 1990, made that point in an article entitled "Post-Modernism Next Architectural Trend" that I cited at the conclusion of my essay, "Sartre and His Successors: Existential Marxism

2. Lyotard, *Postmodern Condition*.
3. Woodward, "Philosophy 2014–15," 6.

and Postmodernism at Our *Fin de Siècle*," adding that I planned to make increased use of my word processor henceforth.[4] (How late '90s is *that*?) But my faith in the architectural creation story about postmodernism, to which I had seen reference even in some literature not published in my hometown, was somewhat shaken when I later read the entries on "*postmoderne*" and "*postmodernisme*" in the 2004 edition of the dictionary, *Le Petit Larousse Illustré*, which informs readers that it all has to do with eclecticism, of which the single concrete example given is "*danse postmoderne*." This is characterized, the reader is told, by a minimalist and conceptual approach to choreography "which was developed in New York at the end of the 1960s and in the course of the 1970s" and of which the principal representatives are Simone Forti, Steve Paxton, Trisha Brown, and Lucinda Childs.[5] (Names that are so familiar on the New York scene!) In any case, one gleans from these two dictionary entries, "postmodern" means above all eclectic, whereas "modern" means formal or rigorous. So there! As is said in German, "*Alles klar*."

In fact, it is my distinct impression, albeit an anecdotally based one, that the label "postmodernist" was never extremely popular among French philosophers as a means of self-identification. (Neither, if truth be told, was "poststructuralist," although the latter probably had a little more cachet.) Ironically, if my memory serves me well, I first heard the expression "postmodernism" used in a conversation that I had with none other than Richard Rorty, editor of *The Linguistic Turn*, who had just returned to the United States from a sabbatical leave in Europe, a trip that had contributed to his growing interest in Continental European philosophy. I say "ironically" because in later years I recall having had more than one conversation with European philosophers who told me that they regarded Rorty as the quintessential postmodernist. Rorty did in fact take the idea of postmodernism seriously for a certain period of his career, to the point of publishing a short essay in the *Journal of Philosophy* entitled "Postmodernist Bourgeois Liberalism,"[6] which at the time he considered an ironic self-description of his own position, and in another essay drawing an extended contrast between Lyotard's philosophy and that of Jürgen Habermas, a consistent critic of postmodernism, in an early issue of the Yugoslav journal *Praxis International*.[7] (Dear reader, do you remember Yugoslavia?) The fact that in that article he concluded his effort to "split the difference" between Lyotard and Habermas by invoking the thought of John Dewey anticipated Rorty's ever-

---

4. McBride, "Sartre and His Successors," 91.
5. *Le Petit Larousse Illustré*, 810. Author's translation.
6. Rorty, "Postmodernist Bourgeois Liberalism."
7. Rorty, "Habermas and Lyotard on Post-Modernity."

increasing sense of affiliation with pragmatism in his later years. He eventually became rather dismissive of postmodernism (dismissiveness, I think it must be said, was one of Rorty's most characteristic stances toward many thinkers and things), but the postmodernist label still haunts his memory.

I shall return later to the matter of haunting. For the moment, however, I would like to devote a little more attention to the case of Rorty, regarded, *nolens volens*, as incarnation of the postmodern spirit. He was nearing the end of his life, as it turned out, when my same 2004 *Larousse* dictionary, which has the admirable feature of including a very large separate section devoted to place names and people, had the following to say specifically about him: "Opposing his relativism to the pretentions of science and of philosophy, he defends a type of liberal utopia."[8] (In support of this characterization, the compilers of the dictionary parenthetically cite Rorty's best-known work, *Philosophy and the Mirror of Nature*.) Now, the simple fact is that Rorty, however much he changed certain positions and especially his fundamental approaches to philosophy over his relatively long career, always denied the charge of relativism that was leveled against him, insisting that to reject the view that there is any one absolute system of thought, one absolutely true theory, is not the same as asserting that there is no such thing as truth. As Thomas Busch well puts it in describing Rorty's real position: "Ironists such as Nietzsche, Sartre, Derrida, and Foucault are heroes for Rorty for showing up the contingent nature of purportedly necessarily grounded narratives about life and for being examples of those who would creatively renarrate life."[9] But then, as Busch points out a few pages later, there was an aspect to Rorty's thinking that seemed to contravene the latter's claim to dislike "final vocabularies," to wit, his affinity for John Stuart Mill's liberalism, which he regarded as, at least in certain respects, "pretty much the last word."[10] Or consider, I would add, the elements of flag-waving in one of Rorty's strangest publications, *Achieving Our Country* (published in 1998), in which, while of course offering serious criticisms of some recent American policy, Rorty exalted the tradition of the "pre-Sixties reformist left" as opposed to what he called the "cultural left" of more recent times.[11] It is remarks such as these, scattered throughout his later writings, that lend some credence to the *Larousse* description of him as the defender of a type of "liberal utopia" (a notion to which Rorty himself made reference). But the same can certainly *not* be said, however far one tries to stretch one's imagi-

---

8. *Le Petit Larousse Illustré*, 1659. Author's translation.
9. Busch, *Circulating Being*, 15.
10. Ibid., 19.
11. Rorty, *Achieving*.

nation, of any of the four Rortyan "heroes" named by Busch—Nietzsche, Sartre, Derrida, or Foucault. Indeed, Rorty could also be very sarcastic, at times, concerning Nietzsche in particular.[12]

In short, the effort better to define "postmodernism" as a philosophical notion, "*de le préciser*," as the useful French expression would have it, through the work of the later Rorty as one-time bearer of that label appears to lead to an impasse—probably even more of an impasse than does reliance on Lyotard. Through whose work, then, might we try to gain alternative access to this definitional Holy Grail? In *Circulating Being*, there is only one indexed reference to the word "postmodernism," and that occurs in Professor Busch's fine essay on Gabriel Marcel, whom he depicts (rightly, I believe, although I should add that he is much more familiar with Marcel than I am), contrary to some other commentators, as being anti-essentialist and hence, in at least this one important respect, as anticipating a major postmodern tendency.[13] But this fact hardly makes Marcel into a full-blown postmodernist *avant la lettre*, nor was that Busch's intention.

There is one name on Busch's list of four Rortyan "heroes" that is perhaps most frequently identified with postmodernism as a Continental European philosophical phenomenon, and that is Jacques Derrida. Derrida, like Rorty, enjoyed a relatively long career and certainly evolved in both his style of writing and thinking and the objects of his thought over time. He could be exceedingly playful with language—more intensely so, I think, than Rorty ever could—and hence outraged readers too heavily imbued with the spirit of seriousness. He became an advocate above all of the practice of "deconstruction," an idea for which, as he acknowledged, he was greatly indebted to Heidegger. What are to be deconstructed above all, one might think, are familiar metanarratives—very much in keeping with Lyotard's core characterization of the postmodern condition. So far, well and good in the consideration of Derrida as quintessential postmodernist, at least after his very early works.

However, in his later years Derrida made increasing forays into the political realm, about which he had had very little to say in his previous writings. (This was also the case, incidentally, with Rorty, who at one point appeared not to believe that sociopolitical theory was serious philosophy, and who to the end of his life remained rather unenthusiastic about it, but

---

12. In his essay, "The Priority of Democracy," Rorty notoriously characterizes both Nietzsche and Ignatius Loyola together as "mad," not because Loyola (much less Nietzsche!) was not an Augustinian, but rather because that is the way "we heirs of the Enlightenment think of enemies of liberal democracy" (Rorty, "The Priority of Democracy," 187).

13. Busch, *Circulating Being*, 40.

who ended up trying to come to grips with it, as in his Tanner Lectures on pragmatism and feminism.[14]) More than one philosopher otherwise attracted to postmodernist tendencies felt uneasy about the common complaint that it was not possible to square such tendencies with any clear political commitment; this was especially true, it seems to me, of feminist philosophers at a certain period. (Drucilla Cornell was one such.) Derrida, at any rate, eventually turned serious attention to the great political issues of what were to be the last years of his own life—the European Union, terrorism, and the ongoing realities of dominance and subordination in today's world. It is with respect to this last and broadest question, what I am calling the ongoing realities of dominance and subordination, that he wrote what may well be his most important later work, *Specters of Marx*. It was with this book in mind that I said earlier in this paper that I would be returning to the question of haunting.

I would like to explore a few of the features and peculiarities of *Specters of Marx* and its context by way of justifying my proposal to bid farewell to postmodernism.[15] This book is, as is true of most of Derrida's later work, strange in several ways. It began, Derrida tells us, as a lecture that he was invited to give at a university in California that was holding a conference in April 1993 on the future of Marxism, with a sub-text raising the question as to whether Marxism was about to disappear. To the conference organizers he proposed the title, "Specters of Marx," not remembering at first—or so he later claimed (let us not pretend that there is a subconscious)—that the same word, "specter" (*Gespenst* in German, "ghost" in more colloquial, modern English), is the first word in Marx's *Manifesto of the Communist Party*. ("*Ein Gespenst geht um in Europa—das Gespenst des Kommunismus.*") While Derrida went on to find and analyze many more references to specters in various texts by Marx, the book that had its origin in this lecture actually devotes more attention to Shakespeare's play, *Hamlet, Prince of Denmark*, in which the appearance of the ghost of Hamlet's father demanding that Hamlet take revenge on his murderer is the principal stimulus of all that happens thereafter. Derrida makes a great deal, in particular, of one line in the play in which Hamlet says that "the world is out of joint." Derrida takes this to be true of our own time, as well, and he gives as the sub-title of his book the following somewhat puzzling word sequence: "The State of Debt, the Work of Mourning, and the New International." I said earlier that Derrida's style tended to be very playful; in *Specters of Marx* he is still very playful with words, but his message is most serious. Of course he is not asking his readers to adhere to the literal doctrines of Marx—I have said that, in fact, Marx plays a somewhat less central role in the book than does Shakespeare (who

---

14. Rorty, "Feminism and Pragmatism."
15. Derrida, *Specters*.

was, of course, one of Marx's favorite writers)—but he does insist that we today are haunted by many of Marx's central concerns, the objects of Marx's critique, and that we should be. While this message does not amount to a metanarrative in the strict sense—a coherent body of philosophical doctrine—it is equally far, or even further, from being a message of relativism, according to which several different possible interpretations of both reality and moral obligation may be regarded as indifferently true or false. If, as I have heard it asserted often enough in many settings, the latter attitude is taken to be the spirit of "postmodernism," then nothing could be further from postmodernism than *Specters of Marx* is.

The world, in Europe and far beyond, continues to be haunted in various ways by the specter of Communism with which the *Manifesto* begins. We are all haunted as well, as Derrida insisted, by the specter of Marx himself. And yet more specters hang over us now, as philosophers trying to understand and interpret our world—among them, certainly in my own case, the specters of Richard Rorty and of Jacques Derrida. Both of them, as is well known, offended many of their fellow-philosophers by taking new paths that put into question dominant conventional ways of doing philosophy. (A notorious example of this, illustrative of the spirit of intolerance among certain philosophers to which I alluded at the outset of this essay as having encountered strong and successful resistance from Thomas Busch throughout his career, was the late Ruth Barcan Marcus' effort, in highly insulting language, to get Derrida's election to the Directorship of the *Collège International de Philosophie* rescinded by the French government; her letter was passed on to Derrida by the Minister to whom it had been addressed, and Derrida proceeded to cite it in one of his books.[16]) Although I occasionally met and spoke with Derrida—for the first time in 1968 when his fame was just beginning to spread beyond France—I saw Rorty on many more occasions, mostly at philosophy conferences. I had the honor of publishing an article, on "Rights and the Marxian Tradition," in the same issue of *Praxis International* as that in which Rorty's essay on Habermas and Lyotard, which I mentioned earlier, appeared. I also wrote an essay, entitled "The Contingency of Style," for the *Library of Living Philosophers* volume on Rorty.[17] He died in June 2007, having devoted many of his working hours during the final months of his life to writing responses to the various criticisms that make up the bulk of that volume (as is usual for the *Library of Living Philosophers* series). He did not much like some of my criticisms, which was no surprise. But I miss him greatly, as I miss two other philosophers, both friends of mine, to whom, along with Rorty, I paid formal tribute at the

---

16. Derrida, *Limited Inc*, 158–59.
17. McBride, "The Contingency of Style."

UNESCO World Philosophy Day gathering in Istanbul in November of that year: Alan Gewirth and Iris Young. For that matter, I miss Ruth Marcus, too.

And in these somber times I miss the spirit of a philosophical movement, the postmodernist movement, that may perhaps best be characterized as having been very serious about not taking itself too seriously. It haunts me, to some extent it no doubt haunts all of us, probably including the very astute, sensitive critic that Thomas Busch has always been and continues to be. But in my opinion at least, while we witnesses to and participants in the parade of philosophies of the late Twentieth and early Twenty-first Centuries—*la foire sur la place* so to speak—survive, postmodernism itself is past.

Bibliography

Busch, Thomas. *Circulating Being: From Embodiment to Incorporation: Essays in Late Existentialism*. New York: Fordham University Press, 1999.

Derrida, Jacques. *Limited Inc*. Evanston, IL: Northwestern University Press, 1988.

———. *Specters of Marx: The State of the Debt, The Work of Mourning, and the New International*. Translated by Peggy Kamuf. Introduction by Bernd Magnus and Stephen Cullenberg. New York: Routledge, 1994.

Lyotard, Jean-Francois. *The Postmodern Condition: A Report on Knowledge*. Translated by Geoff Bennington and Brian Massumi. Minneapolis: University of Minnesota Press, 1984.

McBride, William. "The Contingency of Style." In *The Philosophy of Richard Rorty*, edited by Randall E. Auxier and Lewis Edwin, 509–20. The Library of Living Philosophers 32. Chicago: Open Court, 2009.

———. "Review of Thomas W. Busch 'The Power of Consciousness and the Force of Circumstances in Sartre's Philosophy.'" *Review of Politics* 52 (1990) 475–77.

———. "Sartre and His Successors: Existential Marxism and Postmodernism at our Fin de Siècle." *Praxis International* 11 (1991) 78–92.

Rorty, Richard. *Achieving Our Country: Leftist Thoughts in Twentieth Century America*. Cambridge: Harvard University Press, 1998.

———. "Feminism and Pragmatism." http://tannerlectures.utah.edu/_documents/a-to-z/r/rorty92.pdf

———."Habermas and Lyotard on Post-Modernity." *Praxis International* 4 (1984) 32–44.

———. "Postmodernist Bourgeois Liberalism." *Journal of Philosophy* 80 (1983) 583–89.

———. "The Priority of Democracy to Philosophy." In *Objectivity, Relativism and Truth, Philosophical Papers I*, 175–196. Cambridge: Cambridge University Press, 1991.

Woodward, Ashley. "Edinburgh University Press: Philosophy 2014–15." https://edinburghuniversitypress.com/media/wysiwyg/images/Catalogues/Philosophy_2015_LowRes.pdf]

13

Edith Stein's Experiential Critique of Heidegger

—Robert Wood

Edith Stein did her dissertation *On the Problem of Empathy* under Husserl, for which he gave her high praise. Later she was Husserl's assistant who put in order the master's piecemeal reflections that appeared as the second part of *Ideas*. She also had a hand in organizing the reflections which would eventuate in *Phenomenology of Internal Time-Consciousness* and which appeared under Heidegger's editorship without acknowledgement of her spadework.

Her major work is *Finite and Eternal Being*, written by 1936, but first published in 1950.[1] It follows her attempt, presented in the *Jahrbuch für Philosophie und Phänomenologische Forschung* Festschrift for Husserl, to integrate phenomenology and the philosophy of Thomas Aquinas.[2] In the book she refers to Heidegger seventeen times. The German edition has two appendices. First is a sixty-four page appendix entitled "Martin Heidegger's Existential Philosophy" which takes up the issues in the notes and in which she gives a lengthy exposition followed by an evaluation.[3] Seventeen pages are dedicated to, as far as I can tell, an accurate exposition of *Being and Time*. Her own critique is twenty-two pages long, within which she also moves into an exposition and critique of three of Heidegger's works from

1. Stein, *Finite and Eternal Being*; German edition, *Endliches und ewiges Sein*.
2. Stein, "Husserl and Aquinas," 1–64.
3. Stein, "Heidegger's Existential Philosophy," 55–98.

1929: *Kant and the Problem of Metaphysics, On the Essence of Ground*, and *What is Metaphysics?*

I will treat the second appendix ("Die Seelenburg") in the second part of this paper and relate it back to the first, as I think she intends the reader to do. So, on to part one: exposition and critique of Heidegger's Existence-philosophy.

1.

Here are her opening remarks:

> It is not possible, in a few pages to give a picture of the richness and power of the often truly enlightening investigations that are contained in Heidegger's great torso, *Sein und Zeit*. Perhaps no other book in the last ten years has influenced philosophic thought today as has this work.[4]

She follows with her exposition and then an assessment.[5] As we will see, much of her assessment has to do with how one situates Dasein. This essay will focus upon her treatment of *Being and Time*. I will not attempt to summarize her summary of that work but will highlight the areas upon which most of her critique centers.

Exposition

As the title indicates, Heidegger's aim is ontological, to consider Being in terms of time, in fact in terms of the inner temporality of Dasein's life. Heidegger launches into a consideration of Dasein because its distinction among other beings is that it involves an understanding of Being as a whole and of its own being as a matter of concern. Later he hyphenates it as Da-Sein, the place where being as a whole lights up.

For Heidegger, Dasein is fundamentally Being-in-the-World. He begins his clarification of Being-in-the-World with a distinction between the *Zuhanden* and the *Vorhanden*, which are contrasted with Dasein. Dwelling in a cultural world, Dasein is for the most part preoccupied with the *Zuhanden*, things "ready-to-hand," ready to take up and use, such as with pots and dishes, pens and paper, computers, clothing, doors, furniture, cars, hammers and nails, and the like. They present themselves for what they are

---

4. Ibid., 57.
5. Ibid., 57–70.

in terms of a functional pre-understanding that they fulfill a purpose within a functional context: the hammer goes with nails in the context of building. Dasein dwells in that context. When a hammer breaks, it becomes *Vorhanden*, "present-at-hand" as a sensory object describable in terms of its empirical properties which now become focal, whereas before, in the building process, they were marginal. In art museums today there are items from an earlier period, for example, pre-Columbian stirrup vases, that are present-at-hand as aesthetic objects, but stripped of their original meaning, apart from the world within which they served a function, probably religious. Heidegger goes on to link the *Vorhanden* with the understanding of beings in the tradition: they are descriptively there, present-at-hand. Heidegger then goes into a description of how Dasein inhabits that functional world.

Stein goes on to say that the description of the modes of dwelling in terms of the distinction between *Eigentlichkeit* and *Uneigentlichkeit*, usually translated as "authenticity" and "inauthenticity," is masterly. These overall orientations are involved in different co-implicated relations to time. Dasein, Heidegger says, is a "thrown project," thrown into a world already articulated from the past, being in the world with others, and aimed at the future in life-projects. Corresponding to these three temporal orientations are *Befindlichkeit, Verfallen, and Verstehen*, or disposition, fallenness, and understanding, respectively. The future has priority, for it is in the light of understanding our projects that we take over our past and live in the present. These three modes are abstract factors that are concretely modulated for the most part in "inauthentic" ways: ambiguous as to what is disclosed and what is merely passed on from *the past*, oriented toward *the future* by roaming curiosity, and living in *the present* through everyday chatter, saying what "they say," and operating in the way expected of the anonymous "one." Underlying everyday existence is a basic unsettledness, an *Angst* that is to be distinguished from fear, for fear has a definite object. *Angst* concerns one's life as a whole and exhibits *Sorge* or care for one's being as the disposition underlying one's life-course.

Heidegger traces the path to authenticity: running ahead to the end of one's Being-in-the-World, to one's death, one is in position to view one's life as a whole. In a moment of vision, death becomes a presence and not simply a thought. Heidegger speaks here of being "in passionate anxious *freedom toward death*."[6] From this arises the question of the meaning of one's life, and from this could arise what Heidegger describes as the *call of conscience*. The proper response is *resoluteness* that discloses one's life project and from which one can enter the present in the mode of appropriation, taking over

6. Heidegger, *Being and Time*, 245.

one's past in an "authentic" way, choosing one's "hero" to follow. The call is understood as a call from within oneself to be resolute and authentic, truly one's own. But whatever one chooses, one is guilty for not having chosen alternate possibilities. Thus far the exposition of Heidegger; now we begin her critique.

Critique

Parallel with describing the hammer, one can also abstract from the functioning of a biological organism to describe its sensory presentation as an immediately verifiable set of mechanisms.[7] Stein claims that Heidegger misunderstands the tradition and leaves out essentiality and substantiality.[8] Thus she notes with some surprise that the notions of body and soul are barely mentioned, yet they underpin the existential exposition. This shows the split, she says, between *Wesen* and *Dasein*. *Dasein* is the Who or the Self, but the *Wesen* of its bearer is body and soul. So, one of the major contrasts to Dasein lies in the matrix of body and soul. In this way, the analysis of Dasein is, she says, incomplete.[9]

Stein objects to the claim about guilt: that being guilty means not being able to realize all one's possibilities. Heidegger does not distinguish between finitude and the guilty denial of obligations which involves real inauthenticity.[10]

She also says that much is strange about the discussion of death. "If it is the ultimate meaning of Dasein to be "being toward death," then the meaning of Dasein should be clarified by the meaning of death. How is this possible, however, if nothing else can be said of death than that it is the end? Is this not a completely fruitless circularity?"[11]

Stein observes that, in his treatment of Being-towards-death, Heidegger puts aside the most obvious and significant question, Is there anything after death? And if so, what difference does that make in how we live our lives? Stein asks: Does the possibility of an afterlife really remain open for Heidegger? And isn't that decisive for the meaning of being human?[12]

---

7. Would Aristotle's description of organisms or Merleau-Ponty's presentation of the perceptual field also be *Vorhanden*? We might also ask: what is the status of Heidegger's own descriptions of the existential features of Dasein: are they also *Vorhanden*?
8. Stein, "Heidegger's Existential Philosophy," 82.
9. Ibid., 70.
10. Ibid., 73.
11. Ibid., 75.
12. Ibid., 75.

This is linked to his ignoring the question of the nature of soul and body as the essential mode within which Dasein carries on its existence. Death occurs because of the ensouled body which carries Dasein.

Probably recalling her own work during World War I in a field hospital for contagious diseases, she notes that some of those who are dying are irradiated from within and their corpses appear like that of a victor showing "a majestic calmness and deep peace." She says that one who does not believe in the afterlife would meet the likelihood of its existence in attending such deaths.[13]

She goes on to describe various relations to death. "One dies" means nothing until one has watched others die, watched them laid out, watched them lowered into the ground. Childhood oblivion to death disappears. One's healthy and natural life-feeling is shaken by near-death experiences, serious illness, the loss of one's powers. Concern stops, living in the world with others stops, but care for one's own being remains. Even so, death is not ordinarily a living presence but rather a thought of something far off. And so Heidegger's meditative focus on "the moment of vision" has much to recommend it.

Stein wonders why Heidegger considers the call as coming from oneself, from a higher or deeper self and not as being guided, given a vocation by God. She thinks that is because "the fundamental attitude that issues from and dominates the whole work, that the *solus ipse* . . . that from which all answers concerning being are to be expected, [is] the ultimate origin beyond which there is nothing further." Against that she claims that the *solus ipse* is not ultimately fundamental and not the ultimate light.[14]

In Stein's terms, Heidegger is describing as inauthentic what extrovert and irresponsible existence involves and he describes as authentic major aspects of what is involved, but only from a limited point of view. She thinks that all this, while true, is not sufficiently concretized by taking into consideration the specificity of the psychosomatic being. What remains of man, she asks, when body and soul are not discussed? We cannot especially understand *Befindlichkeit* or present disposition concretely without attention to the underlying psychosomatic ground.[15] And what is the relation, she asks, between the two forms of inauthentic and authentic existence as forms of the self? Following Scheler, for Stein the person or the I is bearer of the

---

13. Ibid., 78.

14. Ibid., 74.

15. Ibid., 70. Merleau-Ponty, for one, carried out analyses that factor in these grounding features in *Phenomenology of Perception*.

modes of existence. She complains that, along with "soul," Heidegger evades "spirit," "person," "I."[16] (We will come back to her notion of the "I" later.)

One of Stein's most perceptive comments is the observation that the term "one" is not only negative and is not universally applied in the same way. Human beings live in different interpersonal spheres, each one of which has standard expectations for what it takes to function in that sphere, as one who, like Werner von Braun, would work on advanced rocketry is required to have a degree in aeronautical engineering.[17] Furthermore, in speaking about the orientations toward time, one inevitably refers to "one" in whom they are instantiated.

She goes on to note that Heidegger does not seem to have any significant positive observations regarding the development of traditions and the nourishing role of institutions, such as the family, the school, the Church.[18] Though there is a kind of sclerosis into which institutions and practices fall, there is also their essential function of preserving the treasure of inherited wisdom. Heidegger ignores induction into the latter; and Stein thinks he does so because, once more, he has no adequate notion of the human essence as psychosomatic, with its stages of maturation.[19] Stein says of the individual human being, "Its ownmost being is in need of the preparation provided by being-with-others in order to be, in its own terms, guiding and fruitful for others." Here she refers to the role of community leadership and spiritual guidance.[20]

Further, she thinks that Heidegger's description of everyday being is ambiguous, close to viewing community life as deteriorated and viewing authenticity as loneliness.[21] Stein sees the call of conscience as the call to play a positive role in one's community. "The person is called to be a member as to be an individual."[22] There are authentic and inauthentic modes of participation in community life as well as authentic and inauthentic ways of being a self. "Deterioration does not consist in communal life as such nor in letting oneself be guided," but in ignoring the call of conscience to take one's place in the community.[23] True inauthenticity lies in failure to heed

16. Ibid., 71.
17. Ibid., 72.
18. Ibid., 73.
19. Ibid., 73–74.
20. Ibid., 73.
21. Ibid., 74, 81.
22. Ibid., 73.
23. Ibid.

that call. Heidegger does not distinguish between rising through a process of development and rising out of a degenerate state.

Stein wonders also why Heidegger uses the term *Verfallen* for the general description of dwelling in the present, especially since he insists that it is not a falling away from a previous higher state. Of course, she will supply at this point the theological notion of original sin which effects the mal-orientation of human life generally: ego-centric, extrovert, and appetite-driven.[24]

Though the future has a priority in terms of life-projects, Stein thinks Heidegger over-valuates the future and is silent on the sense of fulfillment in any present.[25] She claims that Heidegger leaves no room for moments of joy, happiness, or love.[26] She further claims that "All moments represent a fullness which should be brought out . . . The temporal touches something which is not temporal but which reaches into its temporality." "The moment" is when the eternal enters into time.[27]

In Stein's view, the care structure and *Angst* are not the last words for Dasein. In order for the eternal to enter into one's life, what she calls "the disfiguring tension of care for its own existence" must be transcended by embracing "abandonment and the relaxation of the self-forgetting gift of self to eternal being," so that "even its temporal being is already filed with the eternal." "A being that has reached full possession of its own being is no longer concerned for it." "Care and temporality must be surpassed as far as possible in order to reach the fulfillment of the meaning of being." That fulfillment lies in the "transition from the dispersal of temporal being to the gathering in authentic, simple, eternity filled being."[28]

In her treatment of Heidegger's *What Is Metaphysics?* Stein notes a further dimension that Heidegger sees in *Angst* and that goes beyond the individual Dasein: in *Angst* "is revealed the primary overtness of that which is as such. It is and is not nothing." Setting things over against nothingness involves going beyond beings in their totality.[29] In Stein's own thought, nothingness and being as plenitude are set over against the mixture of being and non-being that belongs to finite beings. Following, without acknowledging it, the analyses of Parmenides, in the mixture of being and non-being involved in the overarching characteristics of the world of plurality

24. Ibid., 74.
25. Ibid., 76.
26. Ibid., 80.
27. Ibid., 79.
28. Ibid., 80.
29. Stein, *Finite and Eternal Being*, n. 36, 556–558.

and temporality within which we live, we are able to abstract out the notion of nothingness as absolute non-being and the notion of being as pure, immutable, unchanging being. She says that the awareness of the nothingness underlying our own being makes possible "the breakthrough from this our finite, non-existing being to infinite, pure, eternal being."[30] Being and nothingness belong together, but not because being is essentially finite. All finite being falls between the most authentic Being of eternal plenitude and nothingness. "The manifestation of nothingness in our own being indicates the breakthrough from this our finite, non-existing being to infinite, pure, eternal being."[31] Temporality is the way in which finitude takes part in the eternal.

Most basically, Stein charges that Heidegger works with a preconceived idea of being. "Everything is designed from the outset to demonstrate the temporality of being. This is why the horizon of the eternal is everywhere rigidly barred out" and why there is no essence for Dasein. For Heidegger eternal truths are "residues of Christian theology . . . which have not been radically extruded."[32]

In what she calls "the obvious anti-Christian feeling of BT," Stein sees "an anti-Christian resentment" indicative of a struggle with his own inherited Christian substance. She complains that medieval philosophy is not taken seriously. In particular, in locating Aquinas' notion of truth in the judgment of correspondence, he misses the deeper meaning of truth as the self-revelation and self-explication of being that Aquinas derived from Hilary of Poitiers and which moves in the direction Heidegger himself indicated as the ground of correspondence.[33]

And if one takes off the brackets of death as the end of Dasein, eternal bliss is what the human being is ultimately about. She approvingly cites Nietzsche: "Woe to the one who says: end! For all desire seeks eternity, seeks deep, seeks deep eternity," though she has a completely different idea of eternity than Nietzsche.[34]

Of course here is where she stands completely opposed to Heidegger. He cites Plato's conception of time as "a moving image of eternity" only to reject it. Stein claims: "There is no more distortion of the eternal than in Heidegger's remark, "If God's eternity can be constructed philosophically then it must be understood only as a more primordial and "infinite"

---

30. Stein, "Heidegger's Existential Philosophy," 93.
31. Stein, "Heidegger's Existential Philosophy," 81; *Finite and Eternal Being*, 480.
32. Stein, "Heidegger's Existential Philosophy," 90.
33. Ibid., 83.
34. Ibid., 79. Nietzsche, *Zarathustra*, 253–255.

temporality."³⁵ After all, Stein's book, which contains the appendix on Heidegger, is called *Finite and Eternal Being*. It provides an entirely different way of understanding finitude than Heidegger, who understands it in terms of inner temporality. Since she accepts the understanding of the finite to involve a contrast with infinity, one would expect she would have entitled her work *Finite and* Infinite *Being*. She chose "eternal," I think, as contrast to set her approach off from Heidegger's focusing on temporality as the index of human finitude.

She says, "*The understanding of being of finite spirit is as such always already a breakthrough from the finite to the eternal.*"³⁶ Hegel makes what seems to be a similar claim: "The awareness of the finite as finite indicates being beyond the finite."³⁷ By reason of our relation to the Eternal, she claims that Heidegger' understanding of temporality must be completely revised. The three temporal ecstasies are ways of participating in the eternal. The past is durability in the flux; the present, openness to fulfillment through the incursion of the eternal; the future, openness to eternal fulfillment in the afterlife.³⁸

Stein further questions whether going through Dasein's openness to Being is the only way to question being itself. One can ask the question of being without asking how it is achieved. From Heidegger's basic contention that, because Dasein has understanding of its own and other beings, it should follow that reference to itself is not the only way to the meaning of being. Each thing has a meaning expressed through outer appearance. The thing speaks to us of its own meaning and can do so because we are open to being, but we don't have to go through our own understanding of being to arrive at that meaning.³⁹

Overall, Stein makes the basic claim that Heidegger's analysis "reveals something of the basic constitution of the human being, and sketches a certain way of being human with great clarity." But what he describes is *unredeemed being*.⁴⁰ The experience of *Angst*, she says, "brings people face to face with nothingness." It "accompanies the unredeemed human being throughout life and in many disguises." But Heidegger's anxiety-stricken freedom toward death is not the fundamental authentic disposition. It is

35. Ibid., 80.
36. Ibid., 86.
37. Hegel, *Philosophy of Mind*, 386z, 24.
38. Stein, "Heidegger's Existential Philosophy," 80.
39. Ibid., 87.
40. Ibid., 81.

like a child who fears that her mother might drop her. We are rather carried by a sense that we are held in being over against nothingness.⁴¹

Because of the operation of the notion of being, "the self-present ego by nature shrinks back from nothingness and desires not only an endless continuation of its own being but a full possession of being as such: it desires a being capable of embracing the totality of the ego's contents in one changeless present . . . The ego thus arrives at the *idea of Plenitude*" of Being."⁴²

In the second appendix, "Die Seelenburg," Stein focuses on the notion of the "ego" which is present in the illumination of the outer and the inner world, the latter of which is the object of the second appendix. She complained that it was absent in Heidegger. The ego, she says, is grounded in the center-point where it returns to find itself at home. The ego is the movable part of the soul; it usually settles in its place when the light of consciousness illumines a specific area, whether in the interior of the soul or in the outer world. Despite its mobility, the ego is at home in the center-point of the soul to which it is continually recalled. It is that center point which is basic to the analysis she will make in the second appendix. It is the point where the final decision by the human being must be freely made. The center-point of the soul is the place in which the voice of conscience as God's voice lets itself be heard; it is the place of the free personal decision to follow or not.⁴³

In summary, she claims that Heidegger's exposition is incomplete insofar as he understands being without essence and Dasein without body and soul; it is deceptive insofar as it isolates Dasein from the totality of ontological relations by excluding the dimension of the Eternal and the afterlife connected with it. The analysis often halts in front of references which present themselves in a direct and imperious manner. She discusses thrownness, death, call, and ground. Thrownness requires the question of origin and reveals itself as creaturely. What Heidegger presents is "thrownness" without a "throwing"; what he needs is "one that throws and the thrown." What is required is "an Unthrown Thrower."⁴⁴

Death raises the question of the afterlife. Call is the call from something deeper than the self and is a call to play a role in the community. Of course, God is the ultimate Ground as the Source of the call. Heidegger' analysis, for all its insight, still describes *unredeemed being*, human being closed to the Eternal.⁴⁵

Thus far the first appendix.

41. Stein, *Finite and Eternal Being*, 57.
42. Ibid., 56.
43. Stein, "Die Seelenberg," 524–525.
44. Stein, "Heidegger's Existential Philosophy," 74, 71.
45. Ibid., 81.

2.

Exposition

Now for the second part of this paper, presenting the second of Stein's appendices that she juxtaposes to her treatment of Heidegger by providing an entirely different sense of human existence. "Die Seelenburg" is a much shorter, twenty-four page summary and comment upon Teresa of Avila's *Interior Castle* written in 1577.[46]

Teresa played a leading role in Stein's own life whose conversion began while reading the saint's autobiography that she chanced upon in the library of her friend, philosopher Hedwig Conrad-Martius. Stein, though a sophisticated intellectual, was so astonished by what was disclosed in that work that she decided then and there to move from agnosticism to Catholicism, having previously given up her original Jewishness. She was so impressed that she had the intent of immediately following in the footsteps of the founder of the Discalced Carmelite sisters. To make sure her convert's zeal was lasting, Church authorities made her wait ten years before they allowed her entry into the order. When she finally entered, she took the name of Teresa Benedicta of the Cross. Upon entry, she thought she would have to give up philosophy, but her superiors ordered her to complete the book *Finite and Eternal Being*. That was done in 1936. Because of their Jewish origin, she and her birth sister were killed by the Nazis at Auschwitz in 1944. She was subsequently canonized as a saint by John Paul II.

The juxtaposition of Heidegger and Teresa of Avila is meant to highlight the differences. When she criticizes Heidegger for too much emphasis on the future, a one-sided treatment of Being-toward-death, the rule of anxiety throughout life, and for understanding the call of conscience as coming from oneself, she has Teresa and her own experiences in mind. Not downplaying the future itself, Stein focused rather on those moments of fulfillment where the Eternal invades the present of the dedicated religious. Being-toward-death is Being-toward-eternal-life. The rule of anxiety is undercut by the sense of security, resting in the arms of the Eternal Father—though never without trials. Finally, Stein herself has experienced the call coming from without on the occasion of reading Teresa's work.

Now that all sounds like the sort of pious things we expect a dedicated religious to say. But in Teresa's *Interior Castle*, we have a kind of phenomenology of the interior life, a hierarchy of states or "rooms" farther from or closer to the center of the soul. There are seven rooms to this castle. Outside the walls are where "the worldly" dwell. The *first* inner room is the one

---

46. Stein, "Die Seelenburg," 501–525.

where most religious people live and where the divine light is present but dim.[47] The *second* is where one begins to experience various situations in which one is called to move in a certain direction, as in Stein's own reading of Teresa's autobiography. But it also includes various gentle nudgings that together point in a certain direction for action.[48] The *third* room is where one works at the re-ordering of one's life in accordance with the call.[49] Note that these rooms are located more and more deeply in the person's interior, reaching toward the center point.

There is a *fourth* room which involves the transformation of one's interior itself and of which not all have the experience: that of *the prayer of quiet*. Though it is prepared for through meditation, the prayer of quiet is a pure gift. It comes from the innermost part of one's soul where God is said to dwell. In it intellectual activity is suspended during prayer and a higher light shines, the light of love.[50]

The *fifth* room is that of the *prayer of union* in which God Himself enters into the center of the soul in such a way that one cannot doubt that it is God. Coming out of the experience, one is prompted to the kind of acts that lead to what Meister Eckhart describes as *Gelassenheit*, an inner tranquility derived from self-abandonment and involving a detachment arrived at through acts of prayer and penance. The latter was called the practice of "mortification," literally, the death to one's self-will and to one's attachment to bodily enjoyments through fasting and even more severe methods. But, more important, since all this might simply be a mode of heightened self-enjoyment, all along one is moved toward a deeper love of one's neighbors and their relation to God.[51]

But that is still preamble to the *sixth* room, that of *spiritual betrothal* or engagement. Things at this level are not all sweetness and light. The soul is tested, passing through difficult inner storms which God's gift alone can overcome.[52] The culmination is *the nuptial relation*, which takes place in the *seventh*, the most interior room of the castle where the King dwells and into which few people are privileged to enter. There is now complete detachment from all things and from oneself and complete attachment to the Spouse. There is in that center the deepest union of the faculties that is addressed in what Teresa speaks of as "locutions" in which many insights are compressed

---

47. Ibid., 503.
48. Ibid.
49. Ibid., 504.
50. Ibid., 504–507.
51. Ibid., 507–510.
52. Ibid., 510–516.

into a single locution. She had an experiential understanding of grace, sacraments, humility, love, and even something of the Persons of the Trinity. Though many of the "visions" are of visual presences, some of them, for example of the Trinity, are, she says, not matters of imagination but of what she calls "intellect"—probably for lack of a less misleading term.[53]

Teresa also had states of ecstasy where, like St. Paul, she was not sure she was in the body or out of it, where she was given things to see that involve distinctive modes of understanding appearing in tandem with deeper self-understanding.

In one of her imagistic visions, she reports on being pierced in the heart with a golden spear carried by a small angel that, like a lightning bolt, burned away all that stood in the way of her union. Bernini gives expression to this in his sculptural piece, "The Ecstasy of St. Teresa." But once again, the purpose is not some private experience; it is to enable one to draw others to the ways to God. In spite of the raptures and visions, when she sets about her tasks she has full command of her own natural powers as she founded and ran the first reformed Carmelite house and as she went on to found many more.

What Teresa shows overall is how the Lord Himself calls the soul back from being lost in the outer world and draws it to Himself until He can join her to Himself in her interior center. Through such inwardness, the soul is led to the continual practice of good works while living in the constant awareness of the presence of God.

Response

In Stein's response, she relates Teresa's descriptions to her own text. She points out that, like Heidegger, Teresa had not made clear the nature of the soul and its relation to the body. Nor did she indicate other ways to God than interior prayer, especially through relation to others. Nontheless, both Teresa and Stein, like Augustine, view the interior life as a vast inwardness, more sublime than the mountains or the sea.[54] But it is our fallenness to be stuck in outwardness and to have to come back into ourselves to overcome it. Heidegger's view of the fallenness of the everday involves for Stein, as I said, a fall from primordial innocence, what the religious tradition termed "original sin."

Stein sees the human vocation to understand and work in the world while cultivating an interior life. That is especially pertinent because Stein

53. Ibid., 516–519.
54. Augustine, *Confessions*, vol. II, Bk X, viii, 99–100.

herself was ordered to "engage the world" through writing. Rapture is not the end; working with others is. The deeper the inwardness, the clearer the picture of the world within which one works. "World" here refers to the inter-human world, as in Heidegger, but also the world that is creation itself. The call involves appreciating creation as theophany while finding one's place in that inter-human world which sustains a tradition of wisdom as well as a tradition of fall.

As Stein reports it, modern psychology—and, I would add, Heidegger himself, though opening up the depth-dimension—has ignored the depth presented by Teresa. Modern psychology has therefore degraded the view of the human being, against which Heidegger recalls us to the authenticity of *Gelassenheit*.[55]

In contrast to Heidegger's thought, this whole exposition centers upon how the fullest authenticity is realized, the greatest self-possession, the strictest resoluteness by answering the call that comes from God, both from without and from deep within. One is called to action as counterpoint to being drawn increasingly more deeply in to the center point of the soul and into the living Presence of God as the Eternal Who enters time. If one is drawn fully into the center, Teresa tells us, awareness of the divine presence remains beneath all of one's activities.

Stein also grounds her treatment of Heidegger's Being-toward-death in how Teresa describes her own life: "The more she fixes herself in her center point, so much the more freely can she ascend beyond herself and loosen herself from being implicated in matter (*Stoffverhaftung*): until the cutting of the bond between soul and earthly body—as occurs in death, but also in a certain way already in ecstasy—and the transformation of the "living soul" into a "life-dispensing Spirit.""[56] A treatment of Being-toward-death that subtracts from the possibility of an afterlife never glimpses the experiential dimension within which the great saint moves. But such sensibility raises the question of the essentiality of the body for human existence.

3. The Late Heidegger

Stein knew nothing of Heidegger's move during those ten years after *Being and Time* in the direction of what he called *das besinnliche Nachdenken*, usually translated as "meditiative thinking," in contrast to *das rechnendes Denken* that represents and orders representations and is operative not only in mathematics, science and technology, but also in the systematic

---

55. Heidegger, "Memorial Address."
56. Stein, *Endliches und Ewiges Sein*, 525. Author's translation.

philosophy and theology found in Stein's own book. In his memorial address entitled *Gelassenheit*, meaning "abandonment" or "releasment" in Meister Eckhart but "letting-be" in Heidegger, he introduced the notion of meditative thinking to his audience which consisted largely of Messkirch villagers and farmers. There is a thinking that masters and thinking that learns to "let be." The latter is the province of everyman, villagers and farmers as well as philosophers and theologians.[57] Stein also didn't know of Heidegger's calling for a sigetic or method of silence that would play counterpoint to logic as the method of calculative thinking.[58] It is the practice of internal silence where one can come to learn *Gelassenheit*. Heidegger's later thought moves in proximity to the mystical.[59]

Even when reading *Being and Time*, I am reminded of the Ignatian Exercises during the thirty-day retreat which is aimed at discernment of one's call. They begin with meditation on death, approaching it as a living presence. That introduces mediation on the Four Last Things: Judgment, Heaven, Hell, and Purgatory, from which Heidegger abstracts. One then moves into several weeks of meditation on the life of Christ. The exercises culminate in discerning one's call and making one's choice to pursue the call. Being-toward-death, the call of conscience, and resoluteness in taking over one's own life parallel such exercises; but Heidegger has abstracted from the centrality to one's choices in life of what takes place after death, from meditation on the Life of Christ, and from choosing to follow one's vocation as a call from God, whether in the religious life or in the world, to take one's place in the existing order of human relations.

Conclusion

In one of the footnotes to the body of *Finite and Eternal Being*, Stein cites Hedwig Conrad-Martius, her godmother, friend, and fellow philosopher, on Heidegger's work:

> It is as if a door which had remained locked for ages and of which people had come to believe that it could never be opened, was— after long, careful and tenacious preparation—suddenly blown open with tremendous force and then immediately slammed shut, bolted, and so strongly barricaded that there seems to be no possibility of ever opening it again . . . Heidegger elaborated his conception of the human self with an inimitable philosophic

---

57. Heidegger, "Memorial Address," 54–56.
58. Heidegger, *Contributions*, 54.
59. See Caputo, *The Mystical Element*.

energy and keen insight and therewith had in his hands the clue to an ontology which—by banishing all the specters of subjectivism, relativism, and idealism of the now ending era of philosophic thought—might have brought about a return to a genuine cosmology and the idea of a divinely informed universe ... [Instead] the I is thrown back upon itself.[60]

Those of us who appreciated the tradition of religious spirituality welcomed Heidegger's thoughts on Being-toward-death, authenticity, call, resoluteness, and later on *Gelassenheit*, sigetic, and meditative thinking. It was like a breath of fresh air from the stuffy classroom of Thomistic formulae or the spiritual deserts of Positivism. But when you set it in contrast with the phenomenology of the interior life provided by Teresa of Avila, one sees that Heidegger only negotiates the hills of the Schwarzwald while she rises to the height of Mt. Everest. Those of us who cannot climb—or be lifted—to such heights can at least try to live by our best lights, listen for those gentle nudges that begin to point in a certain direction, and, if possible, pray. In following those nudges, we might enter into an authenticity and resoluteness that might lead where Heidegger never chose to trod.

Bibliography

Augustine. *Confessions*. Translated by William Watts. Cambridge: Harvard University Press, 1979.

Caputo, John D. *The Mystical Element in Heidegger's Thought*. 2nd ed. New York: Fordham University Press, 1986.

Heidegger, Martin. *Being and Time: A Translation of Sein und Zeit*. Translated by Joan Stambaugh. SUNY Series in Contemporary Continental Philosophy. Albany: SUNY Press, 1996.

———. *Contributions to Philosophy (From Enowning)*. Translated by Parvis Emad and Kenneth Maly. Studies in Continental Thought. Bloomington: Indiana University Press, 1999.

———. "Memorial Address." In *Discourse on Thinking*, 43–57. Translated by John M. Anderson and E. Hans Freund. New York: Harper & Row, 1966.

Hegel, G. W. F. *Hegel's Philosophy of Mind*. Translated by William Wallace and A. V. Miller. Oxford: Clarendon, 1971.

Merleau-Ponty, Maurice. *Phenomenology of Perception*. Translated by Donald Landes. London: Routledge, 2012.

Nietzsche, Friedrich. *Thus Spake Zarathustra*. In *The Portable Nietzsche*, 103–439. Translated by Walter Kaufmann. New York: Viking, 1954.

Stein, Edith. "*Die Seelenburg*." In *Endliches und ewiges Sein: Versuch eines Aufstiegs zum Sinn des Seins*, 501–25. Freiburg: Herder, 2006.

---

60. Stein, "Heidegger's Existential Philosophy," 81.

———. *Endliches und ewiges Sein: Versuch eines Aufstiegs zum Sinn des Seins*. Freiburg: Herder, 2006.

———. *Finite and Eternal Being: An Attempt at an Ascent to Being*. Translated by Kurt F. Reinhardt. Washington, DC: ICS, 2002.

———. "Husserl and Aquinas: A Comparison." In *Knowledge and Faith*, 1–64. Translated by William Redmond. Washington, DC: ICS, 2000.

———. "Martin Heidegger's Existential Philosophy." Translated by Mette Leitich. *Maynooth Philosophical Papers* 4 (2007) 55–98.

14

Living Existentialism

An Interview with Thomas W. Busch

—Thomas Busch and Gregory Hoskins

*T*homas W. Busch is the author of two books, the editor and co-editor of two others, and he has published over forty peer-reviewed articles on figures and themes in continental philosophy. He wrote his dissertation on Merleau-Ponty at Marquette University, and the work of Jean-Paul Sartre is the subject of his first book, The Power of Consciousness and the Force of Circumstances in Sartre's Philosophy *(Indiana UP, 1990)*. His second book, Circulating Being: From Embodiment to Incorporation (Essays on Late Existentialism) *(Fordham UP, 1999) is a collection of chapters on key elements of the work of Albert Camus, Gabriel Marcel, Jean-Paul Sartre, and Maurice Merleau-Ponty that seeks to show that the assertion of individualism and the rejection of essences that characterized their early works gave way in their later works to an emphasis on communicative rationality and the exemplarity of art as a form of communication.* According to Busch,

> What is far less established and publicized is how their works, particularly their late works, move beyond, without denying, [the centrality of] embodiment [and individual lived experience] to what I call "incorporation," the transcendence of individual experience in the discursive circulation of Being, a circulation which, while admitting individual differences, calls discussants together ethically and politically.[1]

1. Busch, *Circulating Being*, x.

Busch has taught at Villanova University (Villanova, PA) for over fifty years. He served as chair of the department in the early 1980's and helped found the Doctoral Program in Philosophy in 1994. He was awarded the Faculty Research Award for Distinguished Scholarship in 1991, and he was awarded the Faculty Teaching Mentor Award in 2008. Gregory Hoskins is a former student of Busch's who currently works in Villanova's first-year seminar program, the Augustine and Culture Seminar Program. The following interview took place during June and July 2016.

Hoskins: What drew you to philosophy? Why did you decide to go to Marquette to pursue a graduate degree? Who were your mentors early on?

Busch: My first encounter with philosophy took place when I was a student in a Catholic seminary. Philosophy attracted my attention because of the questions it asked. The courses I took centered on ancient and medieval philosophers and I got the impression from some of my professors that philosophy stopped at the end of the thirteenth century. My advisor, Fr. Robert Lechner, who had just founded and was editing *Philosophy Today*, recommended Marquette University to me, when I decided to leave the seminary and pursue graduate study in philosophy. This was a pivotal time in the history of Catholic universities in the United States. They were taking up the recommendation of the Second Vatican Council to open windows to the wider intellectual world, with the result that departments of theology and philosophy were expanding their courses well beyond the traditional offerings based on Thomism. Marquette established a strong program in the history of philosophy, which included courses in continental philosophy. During my time a visiting professor from Louvain offered courses in Husserl and Merleau-Ponty and Professor Kenneth Schmitz offered a range of courses in phenomenology and existentialism. I recall reading Kierkegaard for one of Schmitz's courses and knew I was hooked.

Hoskins: What were some of the specific questions that drew you in? So many of the existentialists' concerns are also central to theological reflection—wrestling with how to meaningfully live one's life, with how to understand and establish significant relations with others, with friends and strangers, with family and various communities, and perhaps with a wholly (divine) Other, and so on. Why not take up those questions from a theological starting point?

Busch: Perhaps because the questions that interested me were now so existential: the meaning of life, of history, values. I had not studied theology and assumed that it was basically Thomistic—formal and systematic—and so I was not tempted in that direction. I think at the time I was at Marquette that lay students were just entering the doctoral program in theology.

Hoskins: When you were in graduate school, you had the opportunity to meet Gabriel Marcel. Can you tell us about that encounter? What is it in Marcel's work that drew you to it? It seems that Marcel is read less often than some of the others, than Sartre, say, or Merleau-Ponty. Do you think there is a future for Marcel studies?

Busch: I did personally meet Gabriel Marcel when he came to lecture in Milwaukee while I was a student at Marquette. One of our new professors was European and had known Marcel previously, even attending the famous discussion sessions Marcel held in his apartment for anyone interested. This professor introduced me to Marcel after he delivered his lecture and Marcel invited me to attend a seminar he was presenting the next day. Needless to say, I was very keyed up for this event. I was a bit let down however when Marcel spoke most of the time about his interest in psychic phenomena, particularly appearances of the dead to the living. I knew of his interest in that regard, but he had never featured it in his philosophical writings.

I attended several meetings of the Marcel Society, even presented papers. The Society continues and has an online journal. I occasionally encounter a student who asks for an independent study on him and invariably the student becomes an enthusiast. I consider that his essays such as "Existence and Objectivity" and "On the Ontological Mystery" are existentialist classics. Marcel did not come out of Husserl's phenomenology (even as he employs the term in some of his works. But existentialist movements in Russia and Spain did not come out of the phenomenological method either). I rather see him in the tradition of "hearing" instead of "seeing," the biblical tradition of Buber and Levinas. I recall that Ricoeur, in differentiating Marcel from Heidegger, said that "Heidegger's metaphors are Greek, your own are biblical."[2] I agree. I cannot predict whether his work will become more relevant or less so as our culture becomes less a "face to face" one.

Hoskins: You mentioned that Marcel was not by training a phenomenologist, or at least that he was not a follower of Husserl. Yet Marcel seems to share the same "phenomenological desire," so to speak, the desire to get back to the things themselves. What are the sources, the inspirations, of Marcel's work?

---

2. Marcel, *Conversations*, 243.

Busch: Marcel developed his existential philosophy in rejecting his initial commitments to idealism based upon his personal experience of working for the Red Cross during the First World War, what he called "the shock administered by the war." In his *Metaphysical Journal*, one can see him working out of the abstract toward the concrete: "Looking back on it now, I see that I was trying to establish a concrete and dramatic type of relationship in place of the abstract relationships of inherence or of exteriority between which traditional philosophies claimed to make me choose."[3] His concrete philosophy dissolves traditional dualisms, emphasizes the crossing of boundaries, the porousness of being. Marcel is very much a philosopher of communication and relationships and that is why I wonder whether his work will become more relevant or less so as our culture becomes less a "face to face" one.

Hoskins: Many, but not all, of your publications, articles and books, engage with what we might call the first-generation of *French* existential thinkers: Marcel, Sartre, Beauvoir, Merleau-Ponty, Camus, and maybe Ricoeur just makes it in under the wire. Of course, there is a dominant *German* existential tradition, obviously with Heidegger the major figure. Why this apparent preference for the *French* thinkers and tradition?

Busch: Of the phenomenologists and existentialists that I read, it was the French who attracted me the most and I am not sure that I can fully explain why (was it not William James who said that temperament plays a role in our philosophical preferences?). Certainly the emphasis upon embodiment, sexuality, work, communication, cultural and historical situatedness, in general the concrete, was central for me. And of the French, even though I gave much attention to Sartre, it was Merleau-Ponty who stood out for me. He seemed the best at putting together the themes I mentioned above in the most convincing way, and as well as dialoguing with the sciences on the way. In that regard, I thought that his attention to developmental psychology was extremely significant, because existential subjectivity was most often portrayed as adult, hanging around cafes, haunted by anxiety, etc. Merleau-Ponty pointed out that this subjectivity had a childhood, a particularly vulnerable time span, where it was exposed to institutional conditioning, a time very marked by passivity. This aspect of the facticity of subjectivity had to be appreciated in understanding freedom and self-understanding

---

3. Marcel, "Autobiography," 126.

for Merleau-Ponty. Childhood and the development of subjectivity were, as well, major concerns of Beauvoir, and then eventually of Sartre.

Hoskins: The story of continental philosophy in America is significantly a story about philosophy in American *Catholic* universities. Your friend and colleague Jack Caputo, in an address on the 50th meeting of *SPEP*, suggested that what Catholic philosophers found in continental philosophy was an attention to concrete existence and a critique of some of the alienating features of the Modern world (instrumental reason, technological fetishism, individualism, consumer capitalism, etc.).[4] Yet, many of the existentialists were rather staunch if not notorious atheists (Sartre and Camus; if we go back further, Nietzsche). Were there any conflicts or tensions for Catholic philosophers working with these thinkers? It is perhaps noteworthy that in your book length study of Sartre, *The Power of Consciousness and the Force of Circumstances in Sartre's Philosophy*, you do not per se address Sartre's atheism or the implications or significance of his atheism for the believing philosopher. Why is that?

Busch: I mentioned how the Second Vatican Council moved Catholic universities to open their curricula. In many cases continental philosophy found a hearing, and even a specialization, in Catholic universities. I mentioned Fr. Robert Lechner, my advisor in the seminary. He had received his doctorate in philosophy in Europe and become a proponent of continental philosophy. His journal, *Philosophy Today*, was one of the earliest sources in English for continental philosophy, at first dedicated to translations of, and then original articles on, continental philosophy. He was an extraordinary person, who remained an advisor to me throughout his life. Why did continental philosophy find a home in so many Catholic universities? One reason, I believe, is that existentialism defended the human person from various reductionisms—scientific, political, economic—an interest shared in Catholic teaching. Also, the existentialists raised questions of the meaning of life in an experiential way that resonated with religious questioning, as did not seem to be the case with the approaches to meaning at the time proposed in analytic philosophy. But there were nonetheless tensions. Senior members of the philosophy department at Marquette, committed Thomists, were very uneasy with student interest in continental philosophy and I was advised, in a friendly and fatherly way, to avoid this growing commitment of mine for my personal welfare. This occurred, as well, when I came to Villanova University directly from Marquette. Some of the Thomist

---

4. Caputo, "Continental Philosophy of Religion."

professors did not think that philosophers such as Sartre should be taught at a Catholic university. I think I told them—I should have told them—that Sartre was a powerful defender of freedom and responsibility and that their time would be better spent talking to the behaviorist professors in our psychology department.

Hoskins: You retired this year after more than 50 years of teaching. What was your aim, or were your aims, in teaching philosophy? Within recent years Philosophy departments, and the Humanities in general, have come under attack within and without the academy from so-called neo-liberal forces that insist in one way or another that a college education should only concern itself with developing marketable skill-sets and "real-life," applied, vocational, training. Do you think there is a future for Philosophy departments?

Busch: I have always been astonished that I was paid to teach, something I myself would have paid to do. While I delighted in teaching my French existentialists, just teaching philosophy was always personally fulfilling. The highest and most rewarding teaching experience was in our graduate program. To be able to work with such bright and committed students, to learn with and from them, to know many of them as friends, to see them in successful careers and to know I was a part of that is overwhelming.

I am totally committed to the importance of philosophy, both in personal and social development, in opening one's mind to new ideas, to reflect, to self-criticize, to offer reasons. But I sense the environment for philosophy in the future may not be conducive for it. I see widespread emphasis upon the professional colleges over the humanities. And there is a growing literature from neuroscience about how our brains are being modified by our technology, how for example, the constant concern with the latest and greatest information is degrading those parts of our brains that involve introspection and reflection. If that is true, it is not good news for philosophy.

Hoskins: What subjects or texts have you had the most success—or simply enjoyed—teaching? Many of the philosophers you regularly covered in class—Sartre, Camus, Beauvoir, especially—were of course also artists, writers of novels and plays. Did you assign works of literature in your classes? Did any text(s) stand out as particularly effective or appealing to students?

Busch: I do use novels and films in my classes. Students in my French Existentialism course were encouraged to explore the novels, plays and short stories of the philosophers for their research and writing. In other courses I stressed the relation of philosophy and film, using such films as *The Matrix, 2000 Space Odyssey, Her, Eternal Sunshine of the Spotless Mind*—and the students responded well, even enthusiastically. In many courses I used plays and novels by such authors as Pirandello, Huxley, Golding—texts where philosophical ideas stuck out and were able to provoke discussion. Of all my authors Camus was by far the most responsively received by undergraduate students. They seem drawn by his straightforward style, his decency and honesty. And his literature is a seamless reflection of his philosophy.

Hoskins: In your book-length study of Sartre's philosophy—*The Power of Consciousness and the Force of Circumstances in Sartre's Philosophy*—you argue that freedom is a "unifying thread" in Sartre's work but that the theme cannot be understood in any merely, or organically, evolutionary way, that is, as progressing smoothly from point A to point B: his thinking and conceptualization of freedom is marked by disruptions and breaks, and not merely by radical revision. What is Sartre's mature view of freedom?

Busch: I think it is true that the unifying concern of Sartre's philosophy is freedom, but that his understanding of freedom evolved. His reputation to this day for many people, even professional philosophers, is that of a defender of an "absolute" freedom and subjectivity. He himself noted how the evolution of his thought was neglected: "They all stop too soon. I think that a study of my philosophical thought should follow its evolution. But no, they don't do it. It's odd."[5] For example, in *Being and Nothingness*, in discussing temporality, he tells us that "I am my past" and "I am not my past." Both statements have to be held together in order to understand temporality. But he goes on to emphasize "I am not my past" to the point of marginalizing "I am my past." He uses hyperbolic expressions such as "there is an absolute distance" which severs past from present so that the present and past exist "without contact," "without connections." He goes as far as saying that the present is not "conditioned" by the past. His hyperbolic language expresses that the present is not a causal effect of past conditions, but has the effect of effacing the intelligible continuity between past and present. This changes after the Second World War when Sartre admits "that life taught me *la force des choses*—the power of circumstances." He goes on to admit that "*L'Etre et le Neant* traced an interior experience, without any coordination with the exterior experience of a petty-bourgeois individual."[6] From then on Sartre's

---

5. Sartre, "Interview with Sartre," 8.
6. Sartre, "Itinerary of a Thought," 35.

project was to understand freedom in terms of this coordination. His final expression of this is the unfinished work on Flaubert.

Hoskins: A distinctive feature of your graduate seminars—you regularly taught courses on Sartre, Merleau-Ponty, and on topics such as Body Politics, which might include texts by Camus—is an engagement with first-generation existentialist thinkers, almost always French, as well as an engagement with primarily American feminist philosophers. I recall, for instance, in our Body Politics course reading Judith Butler's *Gender Trouble* and essays by Susan Bordo, from *Unbearable Weight*, and the essay "Throwing Like a Girl" by Iris Marion Young. These philosophers for the most part are quite critical of the primary sources. What is your interest in feminist philosophy? Why did you primarily turn to these critics instead of others, say some of the structuralist or post-structuralist figures (Levi-Strauss; Foucault)?

Busch: I introduced feminist philosophy into my graduate and undergraduate courses for a number of reasons. Most importantly, I recall being very challenged by Judith Butler's article "Sexual Ideology and Phenomenological Description: a Feminist Critique of Merleau-Ponty's *Phenomenology of Perception*" and Iris Marion Young's "Throwing Like a Girl: a Phenomenology of Feminine Body Comportment, Motility and Spatiality." These articles made me see clearly how phenomenological descriptions belong to describers, who, in turn, are situated in social, cultural and historical realities. To understand phenomena it is impossible to bracket out these "influences" since they compose who we are. (I guess I learned the "power of circumstances" as well as Sartre.) Understanding is a matter of reaching beyond the perspective of our own lived experience to other lived experiences, with the result that philosophy must be dialogical. In my own academic career perhaps the most important event I witnessed was the women's movement in philosophy and how philosophy has been enriched by their incorporation in the dialogue.

Hoskins: In *Circulating Being* you gather your reflections on specific existentialists—there are essays on Camus, Marcel, Sartre, Merleau-Pointy, Judith Butler, and Ricoeur—under the heading of "incorporation." The subtitle of the work is "From Embodiment to Incorporation: Essays in Late Existentialism." What do you mean by "incorporation"?

Busch: I do contrast "embodiment" and "incorporation" when I discuss the development of existentialism. For me, embodiment represents the emergence of existentialism, of its critical thrust: anti-dualism, decentering the subject, its anti-essentialism, its emphasis upon the individual's lived experience, contingency. You know, the stuff that attracted a whole generation to philosophy, and that remains to a great extent its reputation. Incorporation represents for me the development of existentialism in terms of expression and communication, where life erupts from an inchoate lived experience into expressive and communicative forms, where life is represented and responded to, where individual perspective encounters other perspectives. That is what I mean by "circulating being," and that is what calls lives together. In communicative life others are encountered as subjects, in the role of the thou, if you will, and this revelation has an ethical dimension. Later existentialism is very much a communicative philosophy that is linked to ethics and politics. You can see this, for example, in Sartre's *What is Literature?*, in Merleau-Ponty's essays in *Signs*, in Camus' appeal for dialogue in *The Rebel*.

Hoskins: The element of communicative rationality in "Incorporation" sounds a lot like Habermas' work on the topic: how is incorporation unlike (or like) Habermas' communicative rationality?

Busch: What is distinctive about the existentialists' concern with communication and its ethical implications is their emphasis upon art and consequently upon the interpretative nature of communication, where differences are inevitable within the communicative community, what Ricoeur called the "conflict of interpretations," as opposed to Habermas' ideal communicative situation and consensus.

Hoskins: In *Circulating Being*, you make the claim that "existentialism's story is still being written," and that existentialism "remains capable of haunting today's scene as an important and relevant critic." What do you have in mind?

Busch: I see myself primarily as an historian of philosophy whose focus is on a small, and enormously interesting and important slice, of that history. I find my own philosophical commitments reflect very much the people we call French existentialists and think that they will be around to haunt and bother future philosophy in the form of testing, prodding and questioning in terms of embodiment, lived experience, perspectivity, interpretation, contingency. Existentialists were called pessimists and even nihilists, but to me their philosophy is hopeful. They rejected *stasis* for *poesis*. I could not state it better than Sartre who spoke of the ability one has to make something out of what has been made of oneself. Living existentialism is not a matter of coinciding with their original texts, but as Merleau-Ponty so beautifully put it "to give the past not a survival, which is the hypocritical form of forgetfulness, but a new life, which is the noble form of memory."[7] Living existentialism is confronting one's own historical situation with existential concerns. That is what they did. Any mention of my own work reminds me of my own indebtedness to my teachers, colleagues, scholars in my field of interest, my students—many of whom have graciously agreed to contribute to this volume. I can only say that I am most grateful.

Bibliography

Busch, Thomas. *Circulating Being: From Embodiment to Incorporation, Essays on Late Existentialism*. New York: Fordham University Press, 1999.

Caputo, John. "Continental Philosophy of Religion: Then, Now, and Tomorrow." Special Issue with the *Society for Phenomenology and Existential Philosophy*. *Journal of Speculative Philosophy* 26 (2012) 347–60.

Marcel, Gabriel. "An Essay on Autobiography." In *The Philosophy of Existentialism*. Translated by Manya Harari, 104–29. New York: Citadel, 1956.

———. "Conversations between Paul Ricoeur and Gabriel Marcel." In *Tragic Wisdom and Beyond*. Translated by Stephan Jolin and Peter McCormick, 217–56. Evanston: Northwestern University Press, 1973.

Merleau-Ponty, Maurice. "Indirect Language and the Voices of Silence." In *Signs*, 39–83. Translated by Richard McCleary. Evanston, IL: Northwestern University Press, 1964.

Sartre, Jean-Paul. "Interview with Sartre." In *The Philosophy of Jean-Paul Sartre*, edited by Phillip Schlipp, 2–54. LaSalle, IL: Open Court, 1981.

———. "The Itinerary of a Thought." Translated by John Matthews. In *Between Existentialism and Marxism*, 33–64. New York: Verso, 2008.

---

7. Merleau-Ponty, "Indirect Language," 59.

www.ingramcontent.com/pod-product-compliance
Lightning Source LLC
Chambersburg PA
CBHW051638230426
43669CB00013B/2355